The Sauchie

(And other Scottish ghostly tales)
By
Malcolm Robinson

ISBN: 9798650294658

CONTENTS

iii

This book is dedicated to my grandchildren,
Abby Conner, Sara Innes, and Daniel Innes.
I am so enormously proud of you all.

Other books by Malcolm Robinson

UFO Case Files of Scotland (Volume 1)

UFO Case Files of Scotland (Volume 2)

Paranormal Case Files of Great Britain (Volume 1)

Paranormal Case Files of Great Britain (Volume 2)

Paranormal Case Files of Great Britain (Volume 3)

The Monsters of Loch Ness (The History and the Mystery)

The Dechmont Woods UFO Incident

(All by Publish Nation www.publishnation.co.uk)

Book Cover photo by Mark A. Randall

Mark A. Randall Photography.

www.facebook.com/markarandallcreativeartist

DISCLAIMER

The author gratefully acknowledges the permission granted to reproduce the copyright material in this book. Every effort has been made to trace copyright holders and to obtain their permission for the use of copyright material.
The author apologises for any errors or omissions in the book and would be grateful if notified of any corrections that should be incorporated in future reprints or editions of this book.

ACKNOWLEDGMENTS

Writing any book, one must do research and often contact others to assist in the process and collecting information for this book has been no different. I would like to thank the following people who have kindly helped with information and assistance in the compiling of this work. My thanks firstly go to fellow seeker of the truth, and a wonderful author in his own right, Darren W. Ritson for the foreword for this book. I would also like to thank several people from the Sauchie Legends Facebook page, most of whom I have had to give pseudonyms, due to some of them not wishing their real names disclosed. A big thank you goes to one particular person from the Sauchie Legends Facebook page however, and that is Peter Anderson Macgregor Johnstone, who provided me with a wealth of knowledge and information about this case, and who himself, was a former classmate of Virginia Campbell, the young eleven year old girl who was at the epicentre of these troubling events. I would also like to thank Drummond Grieve from Australia for supplying me with some photographs of Sauchie School which Virginia attended, and was subject to a number of paranormal disturbances. A big thank you must also go to the following people who contributed to the piece in this book on what 'they' believe a poltergeist to be. They were Anthony North, Cindy Dolowy, Nick Kyle, Tricia Robertson, Jenny Randles, Phillip Kinsella, John Fraser, Vivian Powell, Ron Halliday, Brian Allan, and Steve Mera. A massive thank you goes to Mark A. Randall who designed the front and back cover for this book, Mark is a wonderful artist and it was a pleasure to work with him again. Thanks also to former Doctor, Sheila Logan, for providing a wonderful interview regarding her experiences and thoughts when she personally visited the Campbell home in Sauchie, and who heard the strange events for herself. Heartfelt thanks go to the chaps from One Tribe T.V. Tom Parry, Cameron Howells, Sonny Mackay, and Joe Hufford, who I worked with in February 2020 for a BBC segment for the 'BBC One Show' they managed to track down the long lost and forgotten BBC Radio Scotland programme 'Scope' on the Sauchie Poltergeist which featured interviews with, (amongst others) Doctor Nisbet, Doctor. Logan, the Reverend T.W. Lund and Reverend Ewan Murdo MacDonald, and of course, allowed us to hear for ourselves, the sounds of the Sauchie Poltergeist. Thanks, also go to some former residents of the same haunted house in Park Crescent after the Campbell family had moved out, they were, Nicola Bernard and Ellen McCleish. They provided me with their own accounts of the strange ghostly experiences in the same house that Virginia and her family had occupied back in 1960. I would also like to thank Juliette Gregson for allowing me to use the photograph that she took of me when I presented a lecture at the Outer Limits Conference in Pontefract in 2019. Thanks also go to Jason Gleaves for the use of his photograph in this book. Further thanks go to Garry McKenzie, for allowing me to use his photograph of the Sauchie Poltergeist house as it is today, and also his photograph of the houses which now occupy the site of the demolished Sauchie Primary School where the poltergeist also plied its trade.

Finally, I would like to thank you the reader, for buying this book. For like me, you have this deep held fascination for all things weird and wonderful. We all recognise that the world we live in, is a far more stranger place, than we can ever imagine, and the poltergeist, is but one of the world's most puzzling mysteries, and this one, the Sauchie Poltergeist, deserves its place in history.

ABOUT THE AUTHOR

Before a book begins, it is always good to let the reader know a little bit about the author. Well I have been interested in the strange world of UFOs and the paranormal for as long as I can remember. I recall when I worked for a company called United Glass based in Alloa Central Scotland, I worked alongside a chap called William Harrison from Clackmannan. I was 23 years old at this time and was just beginning to take an active interest in these fascinating subjects. Whilst at work, William used to regale me with tales of the paranormal and was highly knowledgeable on subjects such as UFOs, ghosts and the supernatural. Looking back, I can say that William helped fuel my passion for all things weird and wonderful and it is only now, through this book, that for the first time I am giving him credit. So, thanks William for all those wonderful conversations on the night shift your views and stories sure helped my paranormal journey. In 1979 when I still lived in Scotland, I formed my own research society entitled, Strange Phenomena Investigations, (SPI). Since forming this society, I have moved down to the lovely town of Hastings in East Sussex England. SPI Scotland is now in the hands of fellow researcher Alyson Dunlop who is doing a wonderful job. The aims of SPI are basically to collect, research, and publish, accounts relating to most aspects of strange phenomena, and to purposely endeavor to try and come up with some answers to account for what at present eludes us. Our research group does not hold or express any preconceived ideas as to the nature of the events of which we research, we tend to keep an open mind and hope that further study can shed some light and answers to these perplexing enigmas. I have written many articles which have appeared in many of the world's UFO and paranormal magazines, and I have assisted many of the U.K's National and Regional newspapers in connection with stories concerning ghosts, poltergeists and UFOs. I have also been interviewed by many of the U. K's major (and minor) radio stations regarding the above-mentioned subjects. Needless to say, I have travelled extensively throughout the U.K. on research projects, and I have lectured to various clubs and societies throughout Scotland and

England, I have also represented my country Scotland at International UFO conferences.

My television work on these wonderful subjects over the years, has seen me appearing on Scottish Television, BBC Reporting Scotland News, Scottish Television news (STV), American television's 'Sightings' programme. I have also worked for Japanese television, German television (Twice, ARD and PRO 7) Mexican television, Australian television, Italian television, and Australian television. And I have appeared twice on the Michael Aspel show, 'Strange but True?' I have also appeared on Grampian television, and completed documentaries for BBC Scotland, (Cracking Stories) and the BBC 2 programmes 'Strange Days' and 'The Right to Differ'. Both Lorraine Kelly and Eammon Holmes interviewed me live (twice) at the G.M.T.V. Television studios in London regarding a ghost case that our society had been working on. I have also appeared on the Disney Channel and London Weekend Television's 'Ultimate Questions'. Other television shows that I have worked on have been the Chris Moyles Channel 5 show, U.K. Horizons 'Paranormal Files'. I've also participated in a television show along with Melinda Messenger and Richard Arnold entitled, 'Loose Lips'. I have also assisted Mentorn Television for a programme regarding UFOs for the Discovery Channel, and in June 2015, I was interviewed live on the popular breakfast television show, 'This Morning' hosted by Amanda Holden and Philip Schofield. Sitting alongside me on the This Morning couch, was Sean Ryder, front man from the pop group the Happy Mondays, and a man deeply interested in the UFO enigma himself. I have also completed documentaries for the Paranormal and Unexplained channels for SKY Television. I've also appeared on Channel 5's Conspiracy programme aired in July 2015. In May 2019, I was also featured on the BBC One Show for a piece on Scotland's A70 UFO abduction. And in February 2020, I again assisted the BBC One Show on a further two short documentaries, one regarding the Dechmont Woods UFO Incident, and the other on the Sauchie Poltergeist. These are but some, of the many T.V. shows that I have participated in over the years.

As far as my public speaking on these wonderful subjects, I have been fortunate to speak to many clubs and societies both here in the United Kingdom, and abroad. I was the very first Scottish UFO researcher to speak in Laughlin Nevada USA in February 2009 at the 18th International UFO Conference. I was also the first Scotsman to speak on UFOs in France (Strasbourg) and I was also the first Scotsman to lecture on UFOs in Utrecht Holland in November 2009. I am also one of the few people on this planet to have gone down into the murky depths of Loch Ness in a submarine. So far I have written eight books on these perplexing mysteries, UFO Case Files of Scotland (Volumes 1 & 2) 'Paranormal Case Files of Great Britain (Volume 1, 2 and 3) 'The Monsters of Loch Ness' (The History and the Mystery) and the 'Dechmont Woods UFO Incident', (An ordinary day, an extraordinary event) and this one, 'The Sauchie Poltergeist' and other Scottish Ghostly Tales. My goal in life is to continue researching cases pertaining to the strange world of UFOs and the paranormal and to ensure that the public continue to have the full facts of these alluring mysteries. Do I have all the answers to the mysteries that I have been researching all my life? Indeed, I do not. I have my own theories ideas and beliefs yes, but concrete proof, well, let us just say, that this is still to be conclusively proved, not to me as such, but certainly the sceptical people of society. If people would only take a long hard look at these subjects, then I'm sure they would be very much surprised. Yes there is a lot of nonsense out there, but once you whittle that down, you are left with some astonishing cases, and it has been to 'those' cases, that has held my interest over these past 40 odd years. That said, I still believe I've much to learn. The world is full of mysteries dear reader and the book you are holding is but one. So, join with me as we look at Scotland's biggest ever poltergeist case, the Sauchie Poltergeist.

AUTHOR'S PREFACE

As a young man growing up in Central Scotland, I always held this deep fascination of all things weird and wonderful, and as I have stated in my previous books, I just knew that the world of UFOs and the Paranormal were for me. They were subjects that I just had to get involved with, and even although at that time in my life I honestly believed that there could not be any truth in these subjects. I still wanted to get out there and find out. All this nonsense of people seeing UFOs and witnessing ghostly apparitions surely was just wishful imagination, boy how wrong was I. And whilst yes, a lot of UFO reports and ghostly sightings can be put down to a combination of things, such as overactive imaginations and pareidolia. Pareidolia, for the uninitiated, is a type of apophenia, which is basically misinterpreting faces and images in normal visual circumstances. For instance, you may see what looks like the face of Jesus in the clouds, but that is all it is, just clouds. The human brain is hard wired to try and make sense out of 'nonsense'. Sadly, people will see and report things which have a natural explanation, that's human nature, the eye can easily be fooled and it is up to each and every paranormal researcher to sort out the wheat from the chaff. But one thing I soon learned whilst doing my research, was that there was no denying that 'something' was afoot with all these weird and bizarre reports, and in 1979 I set out on a one-man crusade to get to the truth. 41 years later I am still looking for answers to some of the mysteries that I have chased down over the years. I say 'some', because since 1979 my own personal research has clearly shown to me (after I have got rid of all the nonsense) that there is a 'Life after Death', in other words, that there is a continuity after physical material death and that we will all see those loved ones who have gone before us. As for UFOs, again, for me, the evidence that I have looked at, has convinced me, that we are dealing with some form of non-human intelligence as the testimony in my other books on UFO sightings have clearly shown. Yes, again, there is a lot of misidentifications, but in the main, there are some outstanding UFO cases, which at this point in time, (certainly for me) defy explanation.

Anyway, this book is all about one of the subjects that really fascinates me, and that is the poltergeist, which, as seasoned students of this subject will know, is way different than your normal ghost or spirit sighting. The destructive nature of this spirit (if it is such, and we will cover all the possibilities later in this book) shows that we are dealing with something different, and something of which clearly has an agenda. Now, growing up in the small village of Tullibody near Stirling in Central Scotland, I had heard tell of the Sauchie Poltergeist, and young and naive as I was, I felt that all these stories were simply rubbish, and for a while didn't pay too much attention to them, but there, at the back of my mind, there was this little niggle, *'but what if'? 'What if all these stories were true'? 'What could it mean'?* But as a teenager I had other things on my mind, I was more into football, following my beloved Hibernian Football Club all over Scotland and playing in a local pop band (which I would later give up devoting all my time to the paranormal, sorry chaps) When I set up my research group Strange Phenomena Investigations in 1979, I did it with a clear purpose, to get to the truth, my passion for the subject knew no bounds. Meeting like-minded people fuelled the fire of my passion and I have spoken at numerous UFO and Paranormal conferences and have made many television appearances. These T.V. and radio appearances were not done to further my career in a *'look at me'* scenario, they were done simply to try my very best to educate and inform the people of the United Kingdom and elsewhere, that if you look very closely at these subjects, then you will clearly see, that things are not always what they seem! I would like to think that my well-travelled lectures and television and radio spots have at the very least, opened up many enquiring minds to the possibility of not just poltergeists of which this book is aimed at, but at the many other UFO and paranormal mysteries which abound. The paranormal being a public interest subject, saw the television and radio people knocking on my door, and not the other way around. They wanted a talking head, and I was more than happy to be that, so long as they treated the subject matter fairly with an honest and enquiring approach. I am not an expert, I do not know it all, my views after all my research, are my own. Most people love a good mystery, I know I certainly do, and I hope that this book will whet your appetite to continue your study into the strange world of the poltergeist.

(Malcolm Robinson, Hastings, East Sussex, England, June 2020)

GUEST FOREWORD
BY DARREN W. RITSON

Darren W. Ritson is a prolific author who has had an interest in
the paranormal for most of his life, following some strange
experiences that he had as a child. He is a Civil Servant who
lives in North Tyneside England.

Malcolm Robinson is in my opinion, one of Scotland's most
dedicated and prolific paranormal investigators and authors; and
of all the paranormal researchers, ghost hunters and psychical
researchers I have ever known, Malcolm is the one I have
actually known the longest. I first became aware of Malcolm and
his research group *Strange Phenomena Investigations* (SPI) back
in 1993 in my early days of active paranormal investigation and
ghost hunting. By 1994 Malcolm and I were corresponding on a
regular basis using good old fashioned pen and paper.

Malcolm would often assist me by means of pointing me in
the right direction when I had queries in regards to carrying out
investigations into ghostly phenomena and alleged UFO
encounters. His advice in regards to certain steps that I should
take, were always given to me very promptly, and very
meticulously. Although my interests and passions in ghostly
matters went back further than the early 1990s, it was Malcolm
Robinson that essentially encouraged me to take the next step,
and delve into world of information and data gathering, and of
course getting some hands on practical experience in
interviewing witnesses as well as carrying out on-site
investigations. To be asked by Malcolm to provide a foreword
for this exciting new book is indeed a great honour for me and I
am more than happy to put my name to his work.

This book is about the poltergeist phenomenon and details a
number of cases old and new that have been recorded in
Scotland. Those that know anything about the poltergeist will
know that they are indeed a terrifying force to be reckoned with,
they enter your lives when you least expect it and cause upset,
mayhem and abject misery. They tear through your house like a

tornado destroying anything that gets in its path, leaving it looking like a bomb has went off costing you your time and your money and in some cases, your health, before it departs from your life leaving it as quickly as it entered it and there is *nothing* you can do about it. It takes a special sort of individual to research, study and speculate thoughts and theories regarding the poltergeist. It is very much a delicate and complicated process to which the paranormal researcher ultimately has to become a reporter, and a writer, but more importantly, a social worker, a guidance counsellor, and an all-round support for the victims one hundred percent of the time during the outbreak and all in a voluntary capacity too. If you document and share your findings publicly afterwards and *only* afterwards you will also certainly need a thick skin!

There is certainly more to this world than we can know at this present moment in time, and that I can say with total conviction after investigating a case in 2006 now famously known as The South Shields Poltergeist. I subsequently co-authored a lengthy book with Michael J. Hallowell, who I invited along to help investigate with me (*The South Shields Poltergeist, One Families Fight against an Invisible Intruder; Sutton Publishing 2008*), which documented the entire affair. With an introduction from the late Guy Lyon Playfair (1935-2018) of the Enfield Poltergeist fame. Our book presents the story of what happened after we visited the home of a terrified and troubled couple and experienced for ourselves the bizarre antics of this incomprehensible and unknown force. We saw things that most psychical researchers or ghost investigators could ever wish to see during this prolonged outbreak. What we experienced along with dozens of other bewildered onlookers throughout this intense investigation changed our way of thinking and forced us to realise that reality is certainly not what we thought it was. I never thought I would ever see paranormal phenomena displayed at this level but I did. Of course, don't just take my word for it, there are one or two seasoned researchers, educated people, extremely clever and scientific notables out there that can and will testify to the authenticity of the poltergeist phenomenon. There are even more in my opinion that are convinced of the reality of it but will *never* actually admit to it for fear of reprisals. I can say it happens because I have seen it first-hand. However, for every person that is ready to accept the reality of the phenomenon, there are probably dozens that do not; and some of them have no problems whatsoever letting you know about it.

I remember many years ago now, back in 2007, sitting in a flat in the Earl's Court area of London supping a nice cup of tea and enjoying an interesting conversation with Guy Lyon Playfair, debating the poltergeist phenomenon. During our exchange the topic of troll-like sceptics came up you know the ones that seem to avoid reasonable argument and discussion altogether and opt for all-out character assassination and often libellous slander. After receiving my fair share of *ad-hominem* attacks post South Shields, I asked Guy rather naively in retrospect, if after six months or so it would ever dwindle, to which Guy looked at me, and said to me, *"Darren, it's been thirty years since Enfield and I still get it today!"* At the time of writing these words, it's been thirteen years since Guy and I had this conversation at his home, and I still receive much unfounded accusation; so I guess he was right, it won't ever go away, so this is where the aforementioned 'thick skin' comes in handy! Anyway, I digress.

Scotland is a country that is rich in history, a place of aesthetic beauty with stunning rolling countryside that is festooned with countless stately homes, magnificent castles, and manor houses. It has fantastic historic and olde world pubs, inns and hotels, numerous battlefields, acres of ancient woodland and the highest and most exhilarating rugged mountain landscape the UK has to offer. I have visited Scotland as an active paranormal investigator on many occasions now to attempt to seek out its resident ghosts in places such as Culzean Castle, Greenan Castle, Hollyrood Palace, Mary Queen of Scots House, Jedburgh Castle Gaol, Inveraray Gaol, Greyfriars Cemetery, Mary Kings Close and the Edinburgh Vaults to name a few places, and I have to say, I wasn't disappointed. I was also once part of a team that investigated the alleged haunted ruins of Urquhart Castle on the shores of Loch Ness for Metro FM, a local radio station in my native North East England. I love everything about Scotland. I remember many years ago getting off a coach during a trip to Loch Ness while a bagpiper in full Scottish attire played away on his bagpipes man, it sent shivers down my spine and made my hairs stand on end; just marvellous quite simply, Scotland is a stunning place.

But please do not be fooled, as romantic as it all sounds, Scotland has a dark side; it is place of terrifying myth and a place of untold magic. It is steeped in folkloric tales with *Kelpies, Brownies, Glaistig, Trows, Red Caps* and the like haunting the ancient lands ready to jump out on and surprise the unwary and the incautious. The *Boobrie* and the *Bean-nighe* reside in Lochs, rivers and other such lonely waterways waiting to be chanced upon ready to foretell your impending doom; however, catch the *Bean-nighe* in a good mood, and she may just grant you three wishes instead; a spine chilling grey man inhabits the steep slopes of Ben Macdui Scotland's second highest peak after Ben Nevis, and let us not forget a very famous monster lurks, so they say, in the dark murky depths of Loch Ness and I haven't even begun to touch upon the countless ghosts and poltergeist infestations Scotland has to offer you, but I think it's only fair to leave that one to Malcolm. Believe me when I tell you, you are about to embark on a nail-biting page turning journey of true-life accounts that will chill you to the bone Malcolm, over to you.

Darren W. Ritson, 2020.

CHAPTER ONE

A BRIEF HISTORY OF POLTERGEISTS

"There is a suggestion that the Sauchie poltergeist may have been imported. Their journey has been represented as a flight from the things that were already happening to Virginia, but this is not exactly clear".

Narrator. Scope Programme on the Sauchie Poltergeist.
BBC Radio Scotland December 1960

EARLY POLTERGEIST CASES

The Oxford Interactive Encyclopaedia tells us that the word Poltergeist is a German word, and in effect is broken down into two words, *'poltern'* which means to make a noise and create a disturbance, and *Geist,* which means a ghost or a spirit believed to manifest itself by making noises and moving physical objects. History books are awash with tales of poltergeist activity and in my research, I found that the earliest record of poltergeist events, probably come from the first Latin writer, Titus Maccius Plautus (251-184 BC) who wrote about poltergeist effects in his book *Mosterllaria*. Another Titus, Titus Livius (59 BC-AD17) also wrote about poltergeist effects in his major work, *'History of Rome'*. As far as ghostly tales go, they too, go way back into antiquity. From the letters of Pliny, we learn that one Athenodorus, who was a stoic philosopher (74-7 BCE) travelled far and wide in the Greco-Roman world and rented a house which allegedly was haunted by a ghost! And whilst I could regale you the reader with numerous takes of ancient activity to show you how significant and alarming the poltergeist can be, it's really not the purpose of this book. And whilst admittedly I will in a moment, briefly

1

discuss a few classic poltergeists tales with you, these are given, just as a precursor, and an introduction to the fact that whatever you believe a poltergeist to be, the phenomenon is real, but what causes that phenomenon is clearly open to question, and question it we will at the close of this book.

MORE EARLY POLTERGEIST CASES.

Doing research for this book, I came across a wealth of information regarding early poltergeist cases. These all clearly showed that this was 'not' and never has been a modern phenomenon. In his book, *The Poltergeist,* (A Star book published by Wyndham Publications) author William G Roll tells us that in the year 858 near the town of Bingen which is near the river Rhine in Germany, the usual poltergeist effects rained down on a family, this comprised of the fall of stones, and loud knockings. I further learned through my research of this case, that author Colin Wilson, in his book, *'Poltergeist'* (A Study in Destructive Haunting) (New English Library 1981) that this case was first featured in a chronicle called *Annales Fuldenses.* The family concerned, lived in a farmhouse and not only were they subjected to the stone throwing poltergeist, but apparently the walls of the house also shook as well, which in anyone's language must have been disconcerting! Author Colin Wilson also states that it would appear that the farmer himself may well have been the focus of the poltergeist as it followed him around. This poltergeist did not just rain his menace down on the family home; however, it extended its devilment outside and burned the famer's crops! Not only that, this poltergeist had a voice! And went on to denounce the farmer of his various sins, which apparently included sleeping with the daughter of the foreman or overseer of the farm! Colin goes on to inform us that the Bishop of Mainz decided to send out to the farmhouse some priests who were armed with various Holy Relics. These priests also heard this poltergeist stating that the man had committed adultery (seems like a deeply knowledgeable poltergeist!) This case was also written up in another account entitled, *Golden Legend* which went on to say that when these priests sprinkled Holy water and sang hymns,

2

the poltergeist began to throw stones at them. William Roll also tells us that in the year 1184 at a home in Wales, a poltergeist was clearly in a destructive mood as it threw lumps of dirt and tore up family clothes. William further tells us that in the year 1682 at Great Island New Hampshire, a poltergeist was given the name of 'The Stone Throwing Devil' due no doubt to its alarming stone throwing. But even before the above early poltergeist cases, there is evidence that goes way back even further! Again, from my research, I found that authors John and Anne Spencer, in their book, *The Poltergeist Phenomenon,* Headline Books, 1996, state that sixteen hundred years ago, the philosopher Porphyry, was writing about poltergeist activity. Authors John and Anne Spencer tell us that contained within this work, were stories about a stone throwing poltergeist who threw stones against the Romans during the Second Punic Wars. John and Anne do state however, that these could have been meteorites, (which in itself) is even a more astounding relevance! They go on to say that perhaps we can take this account with a pinch of salt as the author was known more for his style than his accuracy. Nonetheless, who's to say that there might not be some grain of truth in his reports? I guess with all these ancient times accounts, we have to be very careful of what we read into them. For instance, is there an element of embellishment to make the tale even scarier? Has the initial tale grown arms and legs in the re-telling, akin to Chinese whispers where the initial story at the end, bears no semblance to the story at the start? As children, I'm sure that we have all heard (if not read) the works of the Brothers Grimm. Children's fantasy stories, but did you know that Jacob Grimm, studied philosophy and folklore and in his book, *Deutsche Mythologie* he recorded several poltergeist cases. John and Anne Spencer further record that there are many poltergeist cases which stem from before AD1000. We have reports from China (damaged clothing and written messages) and also from Turkey and other countries as well. There is no denying that the poltergeist effect has been with us for a very long time indeed and has touched the frightened minds of many a poor individual. Indeed, back in AD530, we learn from Cyprian's *'Life of St. Caesarius of Arles',* that Deacon

3

Helpidious who was the physician to King Theoderic, had many paranormal events occurring in his home. These consisted of noisy spirits, showers of stones which, we are told, were actually flying around 'inside' the family home! More stone throwing poltergeists made their presence known back in 1170 where St. Godric was hit by numerous stones. In 1549, the Cieza de Leon told that during his conversion to Christianity at the Cacique of Pirza in Popyan, he too was absolutely pummelled by numerous stones which appeared magically and instantly out of thin air! Writer, Mr Dennys wrote up in his book 'Folk Lore of China' which was published in 1876, told of a Chinese man who had to flee from his house from a poltergeist that threw crockery about and made his life completely hopeless. Between 1659 and 1660, a Monastery in Malbroun Malaysia, was also troubled by a constant invisible stone throwing poltergeist. Not only that, it also caused fires to break out in the monastery and tore bedding from beds. Things got so bad, that a regiment of soldiers had to be called in, but the phenomenon still occurred even although they were in attendance.

I won't labour the point of providing you the reader of the many historical cases that I came across in my research as this is not the purpose of the book, but I hope that the above few cases, illustrate the fact that this is not only a historical phenomenon, but a global phenomenon, and one in which is still being reported somewhere in the world today. I strongly suggest that you the reader continue your own research and further reading of this alarming subject by obtaining one, if not some, of the books that I mention at the end of this book. I cannot stress highly enough the work of Geoff Holder with his book, 'Poltergeist over Scotland', The History Press 2013, for this book alone, will show you how vicious and nasty and destructive the poltergeist can be.

This book of mine, will not only showcase probably Scotland's biggest ever poltergeist case, which had the added bonus of numerous witnesses, but will also include just a few more classic Scottish cases, again, the sole purpose of which is

4

to educate the reader to the facts of these mysterious events. And whilst I have already covered the Sauchie Poltergeist case in one of my previous books *'Paranormal Case Files of Great Britain (Volume 1)* Publish Nation 2010, available from Amazon and Lulu.com, I have always felt that a 'stand-alone' book on this famous case should be presented. In an ideal world, it would be great to provide a conclusive answer and to present to the reader some facts that were not available at the time, I'm afraid we have but a few facts to add to what has already been written, but it's fair to say that over the subsequent years since that case finished, I managed to gather a few further bits of information which paints a very convincing picture of a phenomenon that bears witness to quite a challenging event, an event that still lives long in the surviving minds of those witnesses who happened to cast they frightened eyes on these alarming events. We will come to those events in due course. But like any good book, one must gently lead the reader down through the corridors of poltergeist events, and as I do so, I would ask you to sit back, and open up your mind to the wonder that is the poltergeist. Before we get there however, let us first of all remind ourselves as to what it is that poltergeists can do!

The poltergeist is certainly far more different than your ordinary haunting, though having said that, I don't think any haunting is truly ordinary! Of course, the poltergeist is not just a fascination for paranormal researchers. The fascination that the public have for the poltergeist has created many major movies and television programmes. There is no denying, that whatever the poltergeist may be, and we will come to what a poltergeist could be, later in this book, the poltergeist is truly something 'powerful' and worthy of study by not only paranormal researchers the world over, but by scientific men and women as well.

POLTERGEIST EFFECTS

I would now like to inform my reader about the most common Poltergeist effects, these are usually percussive sounds, which can be a combination of thuds, crashes, bangs and raps. There is also the displacement of objects, the lifting and hurling of objects of which some of these objects can be quite small, whilst others can be quite large and weighty. Other aspects of poltergeist effects are the outbreaks of fire, and mysterious pools of water appearing on floors. Another major facet is the interference of electrical equipment either being switched on and off without anyone being near them. This can comprise of television sets, radios, and other electrical equipment from hair dryers to washing machines. There is also the flicking on and off of household lights. We also have mysterious musical sounds, sounds that are heard coming from various rooms in the house, and upon the individual approaching that room, they suddenly and mysteriously stop! What people should realise is that the poltergeist is more than a 'noisy and harmless spirit'; it's not, not by a long chalk. It can be very destructive and seems to take great pleasure in ripping and tearing people's clothes. Moreover, there are even cases in which the poltergeist has interfered with family pets and animals. Some witnesses claim that they have seen small animals which have been moved, or gently lifted into the air. Another facet of the poltergeist is the replication of the human voice, more so of family members, and you'll read about a case that I personally was involved with later on in this book, this also had the self-same replication of a family member's voice, yet they were not in the house at the time! Another big facet of the poltergeist is the re-arrangement of objects, which can be anything from wine glasses to kitchen utensils. These have also been found to have been placed is various patters or designs, arranged in a row or even a circle. Chairs have been found stacked upon each other. Smells too, are a common feature of the poltergeist effect. They can comprise of anything from a sweet-smelling perfume, to tobacco smoke. In the instance of tobacco smoke being discerned, sometimes it's the case that this smell has been noticed in the family home where no family members have smoked! However, in some cases, these smells can be more horrible and distasteful, people have smelt what they stated was putrid decaying flesh but probably (for me) out of all the various poltergeist effects, is the scratching on the bodies of family members by an unseen presence. One particular case in point would be the English South Shields poltergeist case researched by my good friend Darren Ritson and his colleague Mike Hallowell. (History Press 2009) The poltergeist also likes to throw stones, which is another big facet of its repertoire.

DREADFUL POLTERGEIST ATTACKS

You will see as we go through this book that the poltergeists do more than throwing stones, it has been known to throw children as well, as this next case will illustrate. Admittedly this case goes way back in time and I guess with all ancient poltergeists' cases we must take it with a pinch of salt. Stories can grow arms and legs as the years roll by, but then again!

This case was featured in P.G. Maxwell Stuart's book, *A History of Violent Phenomena,* Amberley Publishing 2011. And it details a case in which a poltergeist was hell bent of killing a child! The story comes from Alcuim in his Life of St Willibrord who described a near fatal incident from the year C.738. Apparently, this particular household were subjected to some horrendous poltergeist effects, so much so, that each member of the household was terrified by all these paranormal events. The poltergeist would carry off food, clothing, and certain household items and then with a vengeance, throw them onto the fire. More disturbingly however, it reached a new level of terror when it apparently picked up a young child which was sleeping in its parents' bed and proceeded to throw him on the fire. The child's screams drew the attention of his parents who thankfully rescued him from the fire. Needless to say, the parents quickly got in touch with their local ministers who tried to move the nasty poltergeist away, all sadly, to no avail. The family soon moved out the house taking some of the furniture with them, which, turned out to be, a blessing, as no sooner had they done this, then their house burned down. P.G. Maxwell Stuart's book is jammed packed with malicious poltergeist attacks from way back in the day, to present time, all of which, go to show that the poltergeist is much more than an annoying stone throwing entity (if indeed an entity it is!)

PRESENT DAY POLTERGEIST CASES

Coming into modern times, we again have a plethora of poltergeist cases, way too many to mention in this study, but it would be remiss of me not to at least mention just a few of the more modern day classic poltergeist outbreaks, and which for me, are truly indicative of what the poltergeist can do. I won't go into any of the following cases in any great detail, as these have been covered extensively elsewhere. What I will do though, is to give you the more interesting bits of which for me, and others, are indicative of poltergeist phenomenon.

THE ROCHDALE POLTERGEIST
Location: Rochdale, Greater Manchester, England, U.K.
Date: 1995

This is but one, of just a few English poltergeist cases, that I personally found to be highly relevant in presenting to you how serious the poltergeist phenomenon really is. Again, I am only providing the minimum of facts about the following cases more can be found on the internet. But here are the salient points of this fascinating case, a case researched by one of my colleagues, Steve Mera, along with his colleagues, Peter Hough, Alicia Leigh, Victoria and Val.

It all started when Steve Mera from the Manchester Anomalous Phenomena Investigation Team read an article in the Manchester Evening News, entitled, *'Spooky Spills Scare Family From Home'*. This was your typical journalistic headline to entice the reader to read more, everyone loves a good ghost story, and this sure was one. This case had it all, from pools of water which would suddenly appear, which incidentally, lasted for over a year to a whole lot more. The family lived in one of those prefabricated bungalows in the town of Rochdale which is a town about 10 miles northeast of the city of Manchester in England. These prefabricated houses were erected across numerous towns after the Second World

8

War as temporary accommodation. Manchester had suffered quite badly in the blitz during the war and many properties of this prefabricated nature were erected. One of the most disturbing elements that the family had to endure whilst staying in this property, was the continuous outpouring of water from the ceilings of their home, needless to say, this saturated everything, from carpets to furniture to bed covers. It got so bad that the family, (Jim and Vera Gardner and the daughter Jean and granddaughter Alison) had to call in some housing inspectors to try and get to the root cause of the problem. After a thorough inspection of the property, the workmen could find no rational explanation to account for the problem. The family soon knew that they were dealing with something untoward and in all likely hood, this was supernatural in origin, and on that thought, they decided to seek out the services of a local vicar who conducted a service and blessing in their home in hopes of alleviating if not getting rid of, this destructive unseen presence in their home. Sadly, all this was to no avail, and if anything, things got worse.

My thanks to my colleague Steve Mera for allowing me to use the following paragraphs from this impressive case from his report, it starts when Steve read the initial newspaper report in the Manchester Evening Times. Steve stated.

"Vera had stated to the local media on more than one occasion that she thought she might have a poltergeist or that it may be some kind of supernatural happening. She also mentioned that it might have been her first husband's spirit that was displeased that she had remarried. The incidents apparently took place anywhere, anytime, without rhyme, without warning, and without reason. Vera and Jim were having problems sleeping due to wondering where 'it' will strike again".

Vera was quoted as saying.

"Sometimes the water breaks out in the form of huge droplets covering large areas of the ceilings and will disappear

as quickly as it comes" Vera said. *"At other times the family say it gushes like heavy rain".*

Jim stated that the water came pouring through the kitchen ceiling when council workmen were there. It was as if it was raining inside and an umbrella often came in handy. The local vicar said.

"I went to support the family. I hoped that by praying with them in each room, a solution might be found. There appears to be no rational explanation for what is happening, and they are clearly very distressed at the situation".

A spokesman from the council admitted.

"The cause is a mystery to us. We have carried out extensive checks, but we have not found anything that could be responsible".

Steve Mera continues.

"Well, you can imagine what was going through my mind after reading the newspaper article. I decided to act fast and contacted the family. They were more than welcome for me to interview them. I sensed anticipation in Mr. Gardner's voice. I arranged to visit the family and took along two investigators, one of whom was author Peter Hough. As we pulled up outside the family home, I remember thinking how hot it must be inside the prefabricated bungalow. Its walls were made of a non-corrosive light metallic structure which must inevitably cause temperatures to rocket inside. These prefabs were only designed as temporary accommodation in the 1940s; however, the council had obviously seen fit to continue leasing them. I grabbed my briefcase and headed up the path. I was met by a small friendly but obviously distraught Mrs. Gardner. We were immediately shown to the living room where after a minute of chit chat we headed into the interview. We were astonished at the amount of reported paranormal incidents".

10

Mr. Gardner explained.

"It started about ten months ago when we noticed a damp patch on the wall in the back bedroom, which started to leak. We got the council in and they searched all through the loft but could not find anything leaking. We left it to see how it went and at first it stopped. Then we had what we thought was condensation on the ceiling. It started at one place, and then it shot right across the ceiling from corner to corner and even seemed to curve around the ceiling light. It would happen in the bedroom and then stop, only to start in the kitchen. I rang the council again, and two men went in our loft while an electrician dismantled the ceiling lights whilst I was sat underneath an umbrella in the kitchen, that's how bad it was. The whole kitchen was wet through as if it were raining. The council men had no idea what was causing it and in the heat of desperation they decided to fit a fan in the kitchen window. Some good that did! It finally stopped in the kitchen and started in Jean's front bedroom. It stayed there for four to five months. It happened every day and was causing a lot of upset in the home. When we decided to move Jean's bedroom to another room, it followed as if it knew. The council workmen came again and brought some detectors. They were looking for condensation. Of course, all prefabs will have some condensation, especially during the hot weather, but this was ridiculous".

"Then all of a sudden it stopped for about a week. We thought the ordeal was over. We moved the furniture back and lay the carpets again, and within ten minutes it was back with a vengeance. We daren't put the stuff back down. Apart from the water, I was sitting here one night when the handle on the hall door turned and the door opened on its own. I was expecting someone to be there but we all knew there was no-one as we were all sat in the living room watching T.V. Last Friday night we had decided to send Jean and her daughter to stay at a friend's house as they were finding it difficult to sleep at night. Myself and Vera were the only ones in the house. We lay in bed and could both clearly hear someone coughing from the corner of the room. Even though a little scared I did thoroughly check

11

the house and found nothing unusual. We have also smelt tobacco smoke in our bedroom and the smell of liquorice as if it was a flavoured cigarette paper. Last night the hairdryer flew off the drawers and hit my grad-daughters friend on the back of the head. It seems to be more concentrated around Jean and her daughter when they're here. The council first said it was a mystery, then said it was condensation, and when they accused us of throwing buckets of water on the ceiling, it was the last straw. We turned to the newspapers in hope of getting it sorted out. The family has lived here for 13 years and we didn't really want to move out but what else can we do? The council official suggested we shouldn't cook, shower or bathe due to our condensation problem. How are we to live under such circumstances? Alison was found crying yesterday. She said she had felt a cold presence over her whilst laying on her bed and now it's started banging things around at night and keeps us awake. We have even seen things fly off the wall for no reason and things that go missing and turn up in the oddest of places some days later when you're not looking for it."

Steve Mera in his report continues.

"Mr. Gardner's conversation was cut short by the crying out of Jean. We rushed out just in time to see a streak of water shoot across the ceiling as if intelligently controlled. I couldn't believe my eyes. For years I had wished to witness a paranormal incident and had never been lucky enough. Could this be evidence of truly remarkable phenomena? We quickly rushed for the cameras and took several photographs. Some of the water dripping from the ceiling was put into a sealed container for analysis and a secondary container was filled with tap water from the bathroom as a comparison. It lasted for about 15 minutes and quickly vanished, leaving nothing to show of its manifestation not even a water mark stain. From there we were called to the kitchen where another remarkable incident was taking place. Mr. Gardner was stood in the centre of the kitchen and it was raining. It sounds too remarkable to be true, but I assure you it was. Water was falling from the ceiling and had gathered in a large quantity on the floor meanwhile one of *my associates had seen water simply appear on a door in front of her eyes. We were totally caught off guard, not expecting anything to take place during the interview. After an hour or so things started to calm down and we reviewed what we had seen. Whilst the water was on the ceiling Peter Hough climbed up to the loft door and directly above the water in the loft was perfectly dry, in fact it was dusty. There was no sign of where the water was coming from. No hidden hoses, no buckets around, no squirty guns, nothing like that. No wonder the council workmen had no idea to what the cause was, we were just as stumped. We asked Mr. and Mrs. Gardner if we could conduct a vigil. Mr. Gardner said, "Will you want us to stay at friends the night". This was a fine opportunity to truly illuminate any form of hoaxing etc. We agreed and the vigil was set. We asked the family to keep a record of events so to show us next time we visit. As we pulled away the car was full of heated debate and excitement".*

Steve and his team went back to the house several times, and although the phenomenon was consistent in its appearances, they unfortunately could not get rid of the presence that was disturbing the family. Steve also speaks about the apport that appeared in the middle of the lounge carpet, when the team picked it up, they found that it was warm to the touch. Interestingly, the family said, this bronze statue ornament was usually next to the television on the stand but when Steve and his team checked through all their video footage, they could clearly see the T.V. and the stand, but the bronze ornament was 'not' there! (see photograph in photographic section)

Needless to say, with all this going on, it got too much for the family and they moved out. The next family to move in were Asian, and as far as we know, they haven't (as yet) reported any paranormal disturbances, sadly for the Gardner's however they were just two months into their new home when it all kicked off once more, but thankfully after a short period of time, stopped completely and has never come back.

13

THE PONTEFRACT POLTERGEIST
Location: Pontefract, East Yorkshire, England, U.K.
Date: 1966

Like the afore mentioned case (The Rochdale Poltergeist) there has been so much written about this case that it would fill volumes of books. As I never researched this case myself, I can only submit in general, what other people have written about this case whereby hopefully this will give you a flavour of what went on. This case occurred to Jean and Joe Pritchard along with their son Philip (15) and daughter Diane (12) back in 1966. They lived in a 3-bed roomed semi detached council house built in the 1950's numbered 30 East Drive which was situated on the Chequerfields Estate in East Yorkshire England. Probably the very first thing of a supernatural effect to occur in the family home was when in August 1966, both Joe and Jean took a short holiday. The Bank Holiday weather had been extremely warm and so they took themselves off for a short break. Back in the family home were Philip and his grandmother, both of whom were to witness the beginnings of strange events that were due to go on for a considerable amount of time. They were both shocked and startled to observe what has been described as a fine layer of chalky dust fall from mid air and settle on every surface. The most peculiar thing about this was that it did not fall from the ceiling as such, but from shoulder height. They then decided to call upon Philip's auntie to help and clear up this chalky mess, and upon coming to the family home, the auntie observed a puddle of water on the floor of which each time she mopped it up, it would come back again, right in front of her eyes!

A CATALOGUE OF PARANORMAL EVENTS

Like our previous case above, pools of water would suddenly appear in the family home, lights would switch themselves on and off whilst no one was near them. But things got steadily worse, and a destructive element soon began which consisted of furniture being overturned and family photographs being slashed. Heavy breathing was heard throughout the

14

house accompanied with horrible smells of which the family could not account for. The movement and levitation of household objects was also a big facet of the strange phenomenon that was occurring throughout the house. However, there was one marked difference from the Rochdale case, and that was a hooded Monk like figure which was observed in the family home. On one occasion Joe and Jean woke up from their sleep to be stunned by looking at a shadowy figure dressed in what looked like a Monk's robes and from then on, the term the Ghostly Monk stuck, and that apparently, was what was behind these mysterious goings on. And just like the Scottish Sauchie case which you will read about later in this book, the strange phenomena in the Pritchard Household, was not only seen by family members, but also by the police, a local M.P. and a Vicar. The Vicar it would seem failed to exorcise this Monk, and the paranormal happenings still occurred. Indeed, it's been stated that during these exorcisms, Holy water would suddenly appear dripping out of the walls, and the vicar would have his face slapped and be pushed by an unseen entity. Probably the most amazing thing to occur during the exorcism was when a pair of ghostly hands suddenly appeared floating in mid air and proceeded to conduct the hymns that were being sung to try and expel him. English paranormal researcher Tom Cuniff, one of the many paranormal researchers who researched this case, stated to the Sun newspaper that the town's gallows had been situated directly across from the Pritchard home and that a Cluniac monk was hung for the rape and murder of a young girl. He further stated that it was his opinion that it was the black monk himself who was haunting the property. Not only that, the Monk's body was then discarded down a well that sits under the lounge of 30 East Drive. As I have repeatedly stated, the poltergeist is far more different than your conventional ghost sighting. The poltergeist is destructive and 'can' cause personal harm. For instance on one occasion, it's been reported that the poltergeist/Black Monk, call it what you will, poured a full jug of milk over the head of one of the Pritchard's relatives', someone who had stated that he didn't believe in what was going on, that incident certainly changed him, not only that, it left Dianne with numerous scrapes and

15

bruises across her body, but more disconcerting, was the occasion when her hair was grabbed by the poltergeist and she was dragged backwards up a flight of stairs. It was also noticed that around Dianne's throat, appeared finger marks.

Needless to say, after a period of time, all this was too much for the family and they left the property. The house eventually ended up in the hands of Bill Bungay, a film producer who made a movie entitled *'When The Lights Went Out',* which is said to be based loosely on the events at 30 East Drive. Bill took the unusual (if not profitable) decision of not living in the actual house itself, rather, he got next door neighbour Carole to look after it whilst he allowed many paranormal teams to inhabit the house for one night to test the water so to speak, and see if they could detect any ghostly phenomenon. Well they did, as has Carole the caretaker of the property who states that after a period of calm when the Pritchard's left and Bungay bought the house, the paranormal events started up again. There are set stipulations on any paranormal team who are visiting the house. They must adhere to a number of conditions of which the following are but a few. All visitors first of all have to sign a waiver which means that Bill Bungay is not liable for anything that happens to anyone in that house. No alcohol must be brought in, which, as any paranormal researcher will tell you, is a no no anyway! Ouija Boards are strictly forbidden, but I dare say, that as there were no security cameras in the property, that aspect, cannot be guaranteed. And, as I dare say, Bill wants to ensure that nothing happens to the Black Monk of Pontefract. He does now allow any paranormal teams to conduct any kind of exorcism, as that might lose him his cash cow! It's been stated that when research teams visit the house, they may not be dealing strictly with the Black Monk, some people have said that there are the spirits of a young boy and some kind of elemental spirit within the property. And, would you believe, paranormal researchers have been told that when they enter the house of a night, they have been asked to ensure that the kettle remains unplugged but filled up, apparently if this is not done, the poltergeist will be none too pleased and may get up to its nasty tricks. Really! I would assume that to ensure you have a good night in this haunted house, you 'would' plug the kettle in and pour out the water contents, then stand back and await the poltergeist's wrath! One of the things that the poltergeist was known for (which, incidentally, was given the name of Fred!) was moving marbles around the property, hence bringing marbles to the property by paranormal teams was always a good thing to do. Apparently not only will the poltergeist move the marbles around, but it will drop them down 'through' various ceilings to the unsuspecting person below. If that wasn't bad enough to the frightened individual, the marbles would follow the research team home, and would appear in their own property! Neighbours have also reported ghostly figures roaming around their gardens at night and have themselves, experienced a few paranormal events in their own homes, thankfully not to the extent of 30 East Drive. So, quite a dramatic house, and I have hardly scratched the surface regarding the many events attributed here. It's still going on folks, and the house even has its own paranormal web site! The house is also advertised on the holiday site, 'Trip Advisor'!

THE ENFIELD POLTERGEIST
Location: 284 Green Street, Brimsdown, Enfield, London, England.
Date: Between 1977 and 1979

Many people would say that the following case must come to the top of the bunch when it comes to poltergeist events. There is no denying that of all the poltergeist cases in this book, this one is the most well known, indeed a mini drama series based on the Enfield case, featured award winning actors and actresses, Timothy Spall, Matthew MacFadyen, Juliet Stevenson, Eleanor Worthington-Cox and Rosie Cavaliero which was aired on the SKY Living channel in 2015 where they re-created the disturbing events of 1977. The main thrust of the bizarre events in the Enfield case, centred around two sisters, Margaret (13) and Janet (11) Our story starts in August 1977 where single parent Peggy Hodgson claimed that her house was haunted and desperately sought help from the authorities to somehow stop the bizarre events that were happening in her

17

home. The events consisted of furniture moving of their own volition, loud noises being heard coming from the walls that no one could account for, toys being thrown throughout the house, and chairs moving or being found overturned. On one occasion, Peggy Hodgson took her daughter Janet up to bed and tucked her in. A few minutes later as Peggy was downstairs, she was startled to hear some loud scraping noises coming from the bed room that Janet shared with her brother Johnny. Needless to say, Peggy bounded up the stairs to see what the source of all this commotion was. No sooner had she got to the bedroom door, than upon opening it, she was gob smacked to see a large heavy wooden dresser, slide across the room whilst her two children looked on in disbelief. Peggy decided to push the dresser back to where it came from, and as she did so, she clearly heard the sound of knocking coming from the walls which reverberated throughout the council house. Knowing that something strange was happening, she quickly grabbed all her children and ran out the house where she informed one of her neighbours to these alarming events.

POLICE INVOLVEMENT

Some of the early authoritative figures to visit the house were two police officers, who on the 31st of August 1977 witnessed a chair in the kitchen start to wobble then slide across the floor unaided by any human agency. The police woman who accompanied her male police colleague, stated in her report and I quote,

"Many objects materialised out of thin air, spoons were bent and fires broke out spontaneously in the family's home. The family had to endure practically every known phenomenon in a poltergeist case there were four distinct taps on the wall and then silence. About two minutes later I heard more tapping from a different wall. The other police constable checked the other walls, attic and pipes, but could find nothing to explain the knocking"

18

The phenomenon eventually reached the ears of paranormal researchers Maurice Gross and Guy Lyon Playfair, both of whom were members of the Society of Psychical Research. They both were quick on the scene and were themselves, witness to many weird and wonderful poltergeist events. But were they paranormal? Well we will come back to this shortly. For the moment though, there is no denying that these two seasoned researchers were either in the right place at the right time to see probably the most genuine paranormal effects ever, or they both were duped by two young girls. Both men were witness to the following events.

1) Weird whistling and barking sounds which appeared to come from Janet's direction.
2) Small fires break out in a drawer.
3) The bending of cutlery.

Since the outbreak of the poltergeist events which started in 1977, there were over 30 people who were witness to the events in the house, these comprised of local neighbours, Journalists, and psychic researchers. Needless to say, a number of newspapers picked up on these incredible events, namely the Daily Mail and the Daily Mirror. Photographer Graham Morris, who went on to take some astonishing photographs of both girls being apparently thrown out of their bed, stated the following to the BBC.

"I got hit by a Lego brick one of the kids' toys just above my eye which left a mark there for a few days. Everyone that was stood there just saw these things with amazement and couldn't believe what was happening. I wouldn't believe it if I hadn't been there. You had to see it to believe it."

In a BBC Radio 4 Special on the Enfield case recorded on the 8th of April 2018 Photographer Graham Morris had this to say.

"I stood in the gloom in the kitchen and one by one they brought the children into the adults' arms and the last one to

come in was Janet. Suddenly things just took off and started flying around the room. Everyone wanted to see it. They came in as sceptics and left believing they had seen something."

Paranormal researcher Maurice Gross had this to say in an earlier BBC report.

"The voice was just part of it, the girl levitated going from horizontal to vertical in a sixth of a second and furniture was thrown around the room. The house was swarming with journalists, but after four days, they were baffled and frightened and called my team for help".

Both Maurice and his colleague Guy Lyon Playfair went on to catalogue numerous paranormal events, one of which simply seemed to defy explanation, and that was the levitation of Janet from her bed. During the course of the investigation Maurice Gross asked the poltergeist to do something and stated.

"Are you having a game with me"?

No sooner had he said this, than a cardboard box which was full of cushions lying on the floor positioned close to the fireplace, immediately rose up into the air and proceeded to fly over a bed travelling for around eight feet. It then hit Maurice squarely on the forehead, whether Maurice was amused or stunned we simply don't know. I guess by way of another illustration of how the poltergeist can act on people's suggestions is this. In their book *'The Poltergeist Phenomena' (Headline Books 1996)* Authors John and Anne Spencer, give a few stories of ghosts that have harmed people. Take for instance what happened to American paranormal researcher William Roll. He was attending a haunted house at the Felix Fuld Housing project in New Jersey USA where he calmly stated to the occupants of the haunted house that at least their ghost didn't hit people, at which point a small bottle which had been standing on the edge of a table by a sofa, flew off the table and hit him squarely on the head. I guess of all the many weird events in the family home, probably one of the strangest was that of a voice of which appeared to be coming through the voice box of young Janet allegedly from a deceased man all captured on audio tape.

THE VOICE

Probably the most astonishing facet of this case was what appeared to be the sound of a gruff man's voice coming from Janet. Was she simply making this all up, or was there really a disembodied dead man using Janet's vocal chords to come through? This puzzling aspect of the case came three months into the investigation. Both Guy Lyon Playfair and Maurice Gross, soon discovered through their investigations, that a 72 year old man by the name of Bill Wilkins had died in his favourite arm chair in this house, and it would seem that the spirit of Bill Wilkins was in effect, latching on to Janet to try and convey some message from the 'other side'. For at this time, Janet was going into numerous trances and would be found babbling away incoherently. Thankfully Richard Gross (Maurice Gross's son) managed to capture the sound of the voice that was emanating from Janet which in point of fact, started out initially as a series of barking and whistling sounds which eventually turned into the voice of an old man. The following is but a brief part of what this voice said.

"Just before I died, I went blind, and then I had a haemorrhage and I fell asleep and I died in the chair in the corner downstairs".

Both investigators discovered (to the best of their ability) that Janet did 'not' know that Bill Wilkins had died in the house, the voice was also in the habit of giving out foul language and moreover, said that he was still sleeping in Janet's bed! One of the things that the investigators did to see if Janet was making up this gruff voice up herself, was to firstly ask Janet to hold water in her mouth without swallowing it, upon which cello tape was applied on Janet's mouth. Incredibly, the voice was still heard! The voice was also partial to singing

21

nursery rhymes, and also stated that it had lived in this house previously.

History on this case also tells us that in the early part of January 1978, Janet's sister Margaret also began to speak out in a rough voice, but this voice apparently did not have the same intensity as Janet's. A microphone was placed at the back of Janet's neck which managed to capture these sounds which in itself caused a lot of controversy from various people who were not in the house themselves, and only heard the voice on audio tape. One person, who did visit the house, was Ventriloquist Ray Alan. After observing Janet and the strange voice that was coming through her vocal chords, it was his opinion that these were nothing more than just vocal tricks. More on this aspect of the case and the scepticism of others can be found on the internet. Newspaper reporters also managed to record this gruff voice coming from Janet which was quick to tell the reporters to *'shut up'*

In an article in the British Sun Newspaper of 12th April 2018, reporter George Harrison wrote an interesting piece which concerned one of the very first journalists to visit the house, and in this article, Roz Morris, presented her 2018 thoughts on the case. Roz Morris a journalist with BBC radio was very sceptical when she initially entered the house in 1977 believing it all to be a hoax or a prank that was being played out on the mother Peggy Hodgson. Roz in her 2018 thoughts had this to say.

"I recorded the voices and a thumping, knocking noise on the walls. There was this very strange voice coming from near Janet. She wasn't moving her lips, but the voice would just appear, talking for hours. The voice would say a lot of childish stuff swearing as well. It was very disturbing. Something strange was happening which just wasn't normal. Things only got weirder when Janet started having violent trances and claims soon spread that the 11 year-old could levitate, supposedly hoisted into the air by a mischievous energy. But there were lots of independent witnesses and it was the report of the policewoman which really stood the story up. I was a reporter for many years, and it was the weirdest story I've ever

reported on. There was definitely something unusual going on, but I honestly don't know what caused it. "

JUST A PRANK GONE TOO FAR?

There are many that would tell you that this case was just a prank that went too far. There are numerous researchers who have had their say and left their mark on this case. Researchers Anita Gregory and John Beloff members of the committee for Sceptical Inquiry, believed that the girls made the whole thing up. Stage magicians Milbourne Christopher, Bob Couttie and Joe Nickell felt that both Guy Lyon Playfair and Maurice Grosse were falling for the tricks of the girls. Indeed, both Margaret and Janet were caught faking some of the phenomenon and hiding the tape machines of the investigators and were also caught out making the odd noises themselves. Janet was secretly filmed bending a spoon. Of course, both girls defended themselves by saying that whilst yes, they did admit to a bit of trickery here and there, in the main, the phenomenon was real. As a researcher, I have worked on many haunted houses and you always have to be careful of the occupants of so-called haunted houses and their claims! Are they making a ghost story up with a view to get a better council house? Well this possibility was aimed at Peggy Hodgson who was quick to deny these accusations. Peggy lived in the house right up until her death in 2003 still maintaining that all the events were real. And whilst Janet is on record saying that 2% of the events were faked by herself and her sister Margaret, the vast majority of the events were real and were not manufactured. The Enfield poltergeist has gone on to spur many a documentary and even a movie. The Conjuring 2 was based loosely on the Enfield events.

I mentioned in one of my previous books, that in March 1992, I took one of my daughters, Karen Robinson who was eleven years of age at the time, to her very first paranormal lecture. It was on the Enfield Poltergeist case and was presented by researcher Maurice Gross (Sadly Maurice passed to spirit in 2006). The lecture took place on the 5th of March 1992 at the

23

Boyd Orr Building in Glasgow University and was attended by a large audience. The President of the Scottish Society for Psychical Research Archie Roy opened the lecture, after which Maurice took the stage and informed the audience all about this impressive English case. 180 hours of tape recordings were obtained also several hundred pages of written notes. Maurice explained that during the entire haunting, the Hodgson family had the lights 'ON' in the house continually, night and day. Automatic drawing and automatic writing became another facet of events. There was also the facet of a dog barking in the living room, nothing strange about that you might say, but here's the rub, 'no dog was to be seen'! My daughter Karen and I sat transfixed as Maurice continued talking about the events that had transpired in the Hodgson's home.

The infuriating part of this investigation, Maurice stated, was that none of his S.P.R colleagues paid the slightest bit of notice to this case and didn't even question or ask Maurice what was going on! This, Maurice stated, was a big sore point with him. Janet appeared to be the main focus of these strange events. She was continually going into trance states in which she would become extremely violent. Maurice stated that when this went on, he was scared out of his wits! But by far the most bizarre and most amazing incident that occurred was that of Janet being seen by a neighbour who was outside their house, 'levitating up past her own (Janet's) bedroom window! The neighbour stood transfixed at this wondering how on earth this could be. Janet was lying horizontally and yet being forced up and down past the window inside the house. Also, books and toys were seen by this neighbour moving of their own volition going round and round in a circle in the room. (Maurice explained to the audience at this juncture, that the producers of the film Poltergeist actually based part of their film on this incident). A local baker walking outside the Hodgson home was astonished to see coming out of a locked window in the house, a cushion, and a book, which then floated up onto the roof. The baker stood with mouth aghast and was further surprised to see that the curtains were billowing strongly out into the bedroom, (the windows were closed!) Now hearing these verbal accounts from Maurice on the events in the house, were absolutely nothing compared to when Maurice played extracts to the audience from an audio tape. This audio tape contained segments of interviews that Maurice had done with the family. A hushed silence prevailed in the theatre of the Boyd Orr Building which was broken up by the thuds and bangs and raised voices from the audio tape as the poltergeist activity broke out. 53 knocks on the wall was met by the question, *"Is that how old you are"?* More knocks indicated YES, a procedure which was followed to procure more information. Squeaking from the springs of a bed were clearly heard, although no one, it was claimed by Maurice, was anywhere near it. Listening to this voice I found it quite unnerving and even although I have been researching cases like this (although certainly not as eventful), it still sent shivers tingling up and down my spine. After around 16 months the events in the house died down and then faded away completely. As I've stated, a big selling book came out on this case and this case is probably the biggest poltergeist case in the annals of paranormal research here in the UK. After Maurice's talk, Archie Roy of the Scottish Society for Psychical Research gave a vote of thanks to Maurice and he finished by saying that Maurice's talk had clearly been the best talk that the society had ever had in their history, and I for one, would definitely echo this statement. I asked my 11 year old daughter Karen what she had thought about the lecture and she proceeded to ask me a whole range of questions. Yes, a good night and a night that I will remember for a long time to come, simply because of how Maurice presented the lecture, and had the audience on tenterhooks. The playing of the audio tape which held this gruff man's! voice was equally disturbing.

So, the Enfield Poltergeist, true or false? At the end of the day all you can do is to look at the evidence and make your own judgement. I met Guy Lyon Playfair who researched this case many years ago when he attended one of my lectures that I gave in London. After the lecture we got talking about the Enfield case and he certainly was convinced. Oh, how I would have loved to have been on that case!

THE SOUTH SHIELDS POLTERGEIST

Location: South Shields, Tyne & Wear England.
Date: December 2005

The South Shields Poltergeist is probably not as well known as the Enfield Poltergeist, but I'll tell you what, for me personally, it's the biggest case ever in the annals of poltergeist events. What an incredible case this was. Needless to say, a book was written about it entitled, *'The South Shields Poltergeist. One Family's Fight against an Invisible Intruder'* by Darren Ritson & Michael J Hallowell. The History Press, October 2009. ISBN-13: 978-0752452746. Basically, the strange events started in December 2005 to Marc and Marianne and their son (pseudonyms) at their house in South Shields which is a small town in the North East of England. The family, which consisted of husband Marc, his wife Marianne, and their three year old son Robert, were plagued by numerous paranormal events which were not only frightening in the extreme, but were also malicious and actually caused physical harm to one of the residents, more of that in a moment. The house was subject to all the usual terrifying poltergeist effects, namely furniture being moved around, the displacement of household objects. Household objects disappearing then re-appearing in different parts of the house. Chairs were found stacked up upon themselves on top of a table in one of the bedrooms. Young Robert's chest of drawers was found out on the top landing after being moved from his bedroom. Then there was the time when both Marc and Marianne entered Robert's bedroom only to be met with a barrage of Robert's toys being hurled towards them both! I personally know both investigators of this case, Darren Ritson and Mike Hallowell. They were called in to help the family a year later, and we have discussed the case on many occasions, and hearing it from the researchers themselves, well for me it sure made for some disturbing listening.

SIMPLY RIDICULOUS!

I was told by Darren about the time when he walked into young Robert's bedroom and was astonished to see a large toy bunny on a chair which had been placed at the top of the stairs. The bunny was holding a box cutter blade in one of its paws. *(See photograph here in the photographic section)* It would seem that this poltergeist wanted to create fear and alarm to this family, well by staging this scene, it certainly did! Darren also told me of the many other strange events that occurred in the family home, namely some of the doors of the house opening and closing when no one was near them. Then there was the occasion when both he and Mike walked into the kitchen and were amazed to see a small plastic bottle of water balancing on edge on the kitchen table. The bottle wasn't sitting flat on its bottom, it was teetering on edge at an angle that should have seen it fall over, *(see photographic section)* and on another occasion, young Robert's rocking horse was found hanging from one of its reins from the loft hatch in the ceiling at the top of the stairs. Darren also spoke about how the poltergeist upped the ante which surprised all in the family home. The poltergeist started to write threatening messages directed to both Marc and Marianne on young Robert's Doddle Board. Both Darren and Mike were also fortunate to witness cupboard doors swinging open and also light shades swinging back and forward with no observable reason why. They also saw a quilt which was on one of the beds moving of its own accord. (Shades of the Sauchie Poltergeist, more of which later) Incredibly the poltergeist did something that (as far as I know) no other poltergeist had done before, and that was to leave quite threatening messages on Marianne's mobile phone! These messages comprised of, *'Get you Bitch'* and *'You're Dead'* Needless to say after checks with the phone company and more, they were at a loss to explain how they appeared on her phone. This in itself is not that unusual, however. In his book review of this case, Scottish author and investigator Alan Murdie stated the following.

27

"Extraordinary as these incidents sound, they are not wholly without precedent in poltergeist literature. For instance, interference with telephones were a feature of the Rosenheim case in Germany in 1967 (Bender, 1969); similar claims of peculiar messages over the telephone also turn up in unpublished cases sent to the SPR as long ago as 1948 (Case File P55, 1948). Threatening scribbled messages have also been reported in a handful of historic cases".

THE POLTERGEIST ATTACKS!

By this time things were escalating and getting very nasty. The poltergeist started to turn its attention to Marc, where incredibly by some unknown means, left large red scratches and weal's on Marc's torso. These were observed suddenly appearing in front of witnesses! Marc said he felt that his body was feeling warm and uncomfortable, and when he lifted his shirt up, lo and behold, red scratch marks started to appear on his body! As soon as these scratches appeared, they disappeared again! *(See photographic section)*

Here is what the authors Darren and Mike had to say about the violence suffered by Marc, taken from their book 'The South Shields Poltergeist. One Family's Fight against an Invisible Intruder'

"One night, Marc was lying in bed with Marianne when he felt a burning sensation on his torso". "He took off his shirt to have a look, and it was at this point when the poltergeist had decided to take its terror campaign that one step further". "As they both stood there looking at his body, the poltergeist literally 'ripped' Marc's torso to pieces". "From nowhere, cuts and welts appeared across the chest, side and stomach of Marc until his body looked like something from a 'slasher' movie."

Scary stuff. Clearly a new level of violence was in evidence which was disturbing and frightening to all. These attacks on Marc were not isolated, he sadly had to endure these attacks on several occasions. It would appear that it wasn't just Marc that

28

was subject to these frightening episodes, his son Robert, although not physically attacked, was actually moved from one location to another in the house! For instance, the child was found lying on a floor within the house wrapped up tightly in his bed quilt, nothing the matter with that you might think, he could have been sleep walking and decided to sleep on the floor, but he was found with a plastic table 'on top of him'? He appeared to be asleep, but interestingly, his eyes were 'wide open'! On another occasion, both parents could not find their son anywhere in the house and were getting quite alarmed about his disappearance, when eventually, they discovered their son in a closet, with his quilt wrapped firmly around him. Some researchers state that the poltergeist is only feeding off a teenager going through puberty, well, as we know; there were no teenagers in this house. The young child Robert was only three years old at the time. And interestingly enough, with Robert, we 'appear' to have a situation where he had an imaginary friend. Very young children from 3 years of age to 6 years of age claim to speak or see, other children of whom the adults cannot see, and this was the case with Robert. Robert stated to his parents that he was playing with a boy with blue skin and who had blisters all over his body. Both of Robert's parents could not see this 'other blue boy', but Robert was convinced and continued to state that he could 'see' him. It was both Darren and Mike's opinion that the poltergeist was trying to create fear in order to generate emotion that it could feed from. Needless to say, Darren and Mike catalogued as many of the bizarre events as they could both by writing and on audio tape. They also photographed a number of after effects that the poltergeist had left. The investigators knew that this was a big case, probably the biggest that they had ever worked on, and decided to seek out the advice and services of fellow paranormal researchers. They decided not only to include paranormal investigators, but looked for advice from graphologists, medical personnel, University lecturers, some of whom, we are told, witnessed some of these bizarre events themselves.

There is so much more I could tell you about this case, but that's not truly the nature of this book. The above four present day poltergeist cases are only placed here to give you the reader an understanding of how destructive the poltergeist can be, so much different from your usual haunting. In summing up this case, I can do no better than let one of the researcher's who worked on this case give you his own thoughts, over to you Darren W. Ritson.

DARREN W. RITSON'S THOUGHTS.

"South Shields now there was a poltergeist case! This was a case that split opinion right down the middle, either you believed it, or you didn't. Of course, the phenomena that we reported and documented, was so incredible, so farfetched even, that it couldn't possibly have been real, could it? Well, yes it could, and it was. I often say to people when talking about this case that, 'I never thought I would ever see paranormal activity displayed on this level, but I did'. This was the case that ultimately dragged me off the fence that I was sitting on and made me sit up and realise that this kind of paranormal activity does happen. This of course, is merely my opinion but what folk have to remember is this, I was there, and you were not. For those that were not there they have to ponder over this it was either a monumental hoax, or it was a genuine poltergeist infestation, one of the worst in recent history; with one thing more to consider we still have our evidence that suggests the latter. In the South Shields case, there is no grey area, no in-between, you are either for it, or you are against it".

Bedroom 30 East Drive (Pontefract Poltergeist)

Janet is found on top of a piece of furniture.
(Enfield Poltergeist)

31

Janet leaps into the air. (Enfield Poltergeist)

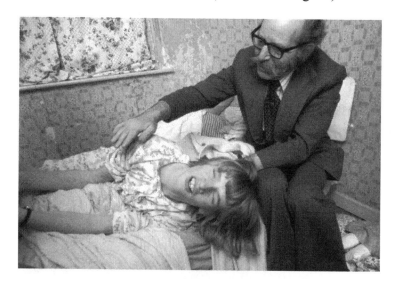

Maurice Gross comforts a disturbed Janet.
(Enfield Poltergeist)

The Hodgsons a troubled family. (Enfield Poltergeist)

A frightened mother watches a poltergeist in action.

33

Enniscorthy Poltergeist. County Wexford July 1910

Tedworth Drummer Poltergeist 1661

Typical Poltergeist Effects

An apport suddenly appeared on the floor.
Rochdale Poltergeist. (c) Steve Mera.

Steve Mera looks up at the mysterious damp patch on the ceiling. Rochdale Poltergeist (c) Steve Mera.

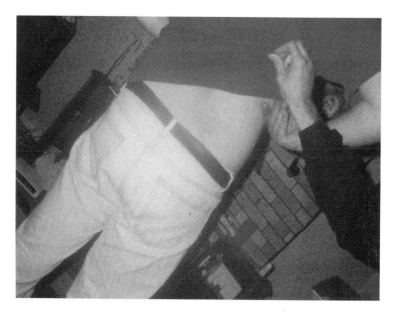

Thumped by the Rochdale Poltergeist. Steve Mera shows
the strange red mark on his back. (c) Steve Mera

The Troubled House in Rochdale. (c) Steve Mera

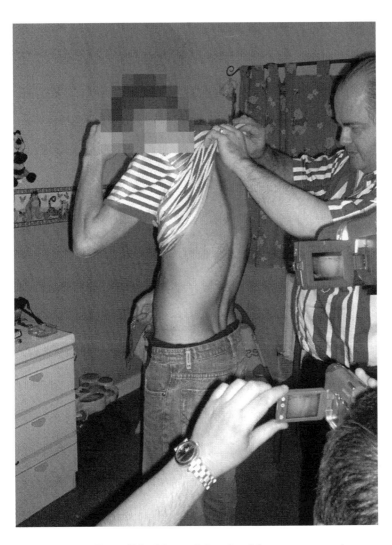

Mike Hallowell holds up Marc's shirt to expose the
scratches on his back. South Shields Poltergeist Case
(c) Darren W. Ritson

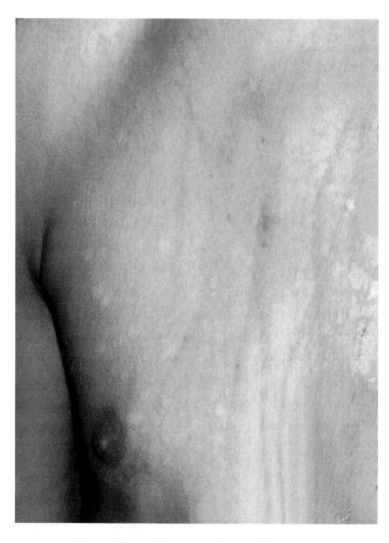

Marc shows the scratches on his chest.
(South Shields Poltergeist Case)
(c) Darren W. Ritson

Mike Hallowell and Darren W. Ritson. Researchers of the South Shields Poltergeist Case.

The South Shields Poltergeist would set up scenes like this. (c) Darren W. Ritson

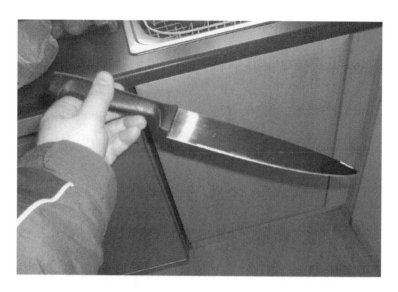

This knife was thrown at researchers in the South Shields
Poltergeist Case (c) Darren W. Ritson

Bottle balancing on kitchen table. South Shields
Poltergeist Case (c) Darren W. Ritson

South Shields Poltergeist Case. Darren Ritson looks at the
upturned table in boy's bedroom (c) Darren W. Ritson

South Shields Poltergeist Case. We are not going. The
poltergeist confirms its stance. (c) Darren W. Ritson

CHAPTER TWO

OTHER FAMOUS SCOTTISH POLTERGEIST AND GHOST CASES

"It was a very humbling experience and I felt we were in the presence of forces hitherto almost unknown that we were just on the edge of a more or less uncharted ocean, that was my own feeling, and I was feeling more or less lost in this quite new experience we sought help from the only power we thought could give us help".

Reverend T.W. Lund (Scope Radio Programme on the Sauchie Poltergeist)

In this chapter I'd like to present to you the reader, some interesting poltergeists cases that I have come across in my research. These cases are predominantly from other authors of which credit is of course given. Most of the Scottish cases that I personally have researched over the years, can be found in my earlier books on these subjects, *Paranormal Case Files of Great Britain (Volumes 1 & 2)* Publish Nation, available through Amazon or lulu.com.

THE BALDARROCH POLTERGEIST

Location: Baldarroch, Aberdeenshire, Scotland.
Date: 5th December 1838

Author Geoff Holder informs us that in Charles Mackay's book, *'Memoirs of Extraordinary Popular Delusions and the Madness of Crowds'* published in 1852 (now there's a title!) We learn that a farmyard in Baldarroch in Aberdeenshire Scotland, witnessed a number of poltergeist effects which started on the 5th of December 1838 and continued for several weeks. The farm lies around two miles east of the town of Banchory, and like a number of poltergeist cases that you will read about in this book, was similar to many other poltergeists cases, namely, stone throwing and also clods of earth being thrown at the property from outside. If that wasn't bad enough, the poltergeist changed its track and decided to have some fun indoors, where it proceeded to throw cutlery, plates, shoes, mortars, mustard pots, rolling pins and warming irons around the family home. The devilment of a poltergeist never ceases to amaze me, and we learn that a servant girl, who worked in the house, was seen by a number of people to place a mustard pot in a cupboard, but a few minutes later, that self same mustard pot came hurtling down a chimney. On another occasion, the poltergeist knocked on the doors and roof of the property and rained down sticks and pebbles on the windows, some of which broke.

THE ARDACHIE LODGE POLTERGEIST

Location: Ardachie Lodge, Loch Ness, Scottish Highlands.
Date: 1952

In their book, *The Poltergeist Phenomenon,* Headline Books, 1996, John and Anne Spencer tell us of an interesting Poltergeist case which was situated in a Lodge right next to the infamous Loch Ness in the Scottish Highlands. It occurred in 1952, to Mr and Mrs MacDonald who worked as housekeepers at Ardachie Lodge. On their very first night at the Lodge, both husband and wife began to hear footsteps which they couldn't explain. Things got steadily worse as Mrs MacDonald witnessed the ghostly shape of an old woman who was beckoning to her. Not surprisingly Mrs MacDonald did not follow her. The MacDonald's then decided to move into another room in the Lodge, no doubt to hopefully get some peace and quiet, but sadly they were awoken by the sounds of rapping noises. Now fully awake, they looked outside the room, and were astonished to see an old woman with a lighted candle, crawling (not walking) along the corridor! It would appear that the previous owner of Ardachie Lodge, one Mrs Brewin, suffered from arthritis and, so we are told, used to crawl around the corridor late at night with a candle in the hope that she could catch other residents out who she believed were stealing from her. Indeed, Mrs MacDonald would later see the ghostly shape of Mrs Brewin again but on this occasion, Mrs MacDonald went into some kind of trance in which she claimed that the spirit of Mrs Brewin was complaining that her favourite tree in the grounds of Ardachie Lodge had been allowed to die, and guess what! This fact was verified by the gardener! A later Investigation into Ardachie Lodge was undertaken by the prestigious Society for Psychical Research of which during their investigation, they heard for themselves, several loud unexplainable knocks.

SANDMAN?

Location: Yorkhill Street, Partick, Glasgow, Scotland.
Date: 1974.

Then following is a case that I presented in my second book, *'Paranormal Case Files of Great Britain (Volume 1)* Published by Publish Nation, available through Amazon or Lulu.com. I present it here again, simply because it has all the hallmarks of a poltergeists visitation, however, it would seem, that it was just a 'one off', and other than you are about to read, the phenomena did not return. See what you make of this.

Here is the story of the Sandman as told by the witness, Kenneth J. Kelly.

"The following is a true and accurate account of what I found in a room in my house early one morning in February 1974". "I was awakened at 08:00am by my wife shaking me violently and saying, "We've been burgled". "I opened my eyes to a scene of mayhem". "The whole room was a shambles, every pane of glass in the window was shattered, and the television was lying on the floor in the opposite corner from where it had been previously". "The sideboard had been pushed over, it had wedged against the back of the heavy sofa,

thus preventing it from fully toppling over, but all the contents were scattered over the floor, but most inexplicable was that almost every piece of glass had been changed to a very fine type of sand. Every cup, saucer, plate, bowl and tumbler, even my wife's collection of Italian glass ornaments which had stood on the high mantelpiece". "There had been eight such pieces, all of heavy multicoloured glass, but in place of each, stood a large mound of brightly coloured sand, the colours synonymous with those of each ornament". "We also had a set of blue and white stripped bowls, but all we found were little mounds of blue and white stripped sand"

"I checked the door and found it still locked, chained and bolted from the inside" "It was this discovery that made me a bit apprehensive". "The rest of the house was untouched, and nothing was missing, if you accept that the mounds of sand were really the glass objects". "We left the house and went to my parents and told them". "My father suggested that I take the dog over to my house and if there was 'something' there, as he put it, the dog would probably sense it and react accordingly" "The dog was a well trained Alsatian guide dog (My parents both being totally blind) "I went back to the house but when I tried to take the dog up to the entrance, he became very agitated and would not enter". "I tried to pull him, but he began snarling and was very panicky". "The dog would not enter the building, let alone the flat". "I returned to tell my father and he said we should not go back to the house, and we didn't". "I did go back a few days later to pick up our belongings and everything was as we had left it, except that the sand had been blown everywhere". "I hope whoever reads this finds something useful in this description of what I have come to call 'the aftermath of a visitation'. "I will simply reiterate that what I have written is what actually happened, make of it what you will".

Kenneth J. Kelly.

I remember this case well. I have met Kenneth several times and he didn't tire of telling me this story, it would have been great to have some photographic evidence to back up this story, but sometimes when you are frightened that's the last thing that goes through your mind. You just want to get out the house without looking back so I can understand the family's feelings on that one. I often wonder what the next tenant of that house had to endure!

THE POLTERGEIST OF PITMILLY HOUSE

Location: Between St Andrews and Kingsbarns in Fife Central Scotland.
Date: 1936

What follows, is, according to researcher Geoff Holder from his book 'Poltergeist Over Scotland'. The History Press 2013. ISBN: 978-0-7524-8283-5 probably one of the longest poltergeist outbreaks that has ever occurred on Scottish soil. As we know, poltergeist outbreaks are usually short lived, anything from a few days to a few weeks, however, this particular poltergeist it would seem, liked to hang around this particular home, as he inhabited it for neigh on thirty years. Admittedly, all this hinges on the truth of the incidents given. Embellishments as we know, more so from many years ago, can tend to grow arms and legs, that said, who knows, maybe the accounts you are about to read in our next case, may have happened exactly as reported. The case was initially investigated by Lord Charles Hope, and I refer in part, to some text from the Society for Psychical Research and a book review on the case written by Lorn Macintyre and reviewed by one Tom Ruffles.

I now take you back to 1936 to a house which stood between St Andrews and Kingsbarns in Fife Central Scotland. A number of tenants had already lived in the house, but we are concerning ourselves with the Jeffrey family who inhabited the house for a period of years from 1936. The Jeffrey family, we are told, also shared the house with a couple of elderly female servants. Probably the first unusual event to have happened was when on one evening as the family all sat down to dinner a piece of coal suddenly and inexplicably appeared on the table. After this,

48

things thankfully abated and very little else of a paranormal nature event happened. However, all this was to change, when on leave from the war (1939-45) Ivan Jeffrey was stunned to see what he described as a Chinese bronze ornament which sailed effortlessly across the hallway and hit him in his "tum-tum", as he so eloquently put it. Things steadily progressed from there, when numerous ornaments were found throughout the house, broken and damaged with no evident accountability for this. A large wardrobe crashed to the floor. Pictures would fall off the wall's household items would disappear never to be found. One bronze item rotated 90 degrees in mid-air. The poltergeist also reserved its outlandish behaviour to bed clothes and pillows, and many a time they would be found in disarray. Numerous objects felt the force of the poltergeist, as billiard balls, vases, and mirrors would all be displaced. Chest of drawers would slide across the room or, would you believe, be moved to other floors in the house! Clearly this was a poltergeist on a mission! Ornaments would fall effortlessly off the family mantelpiece. Small things like this were bad enough, but sadly for the Jeffrey family, it was to get a whole lot worse! Hot coals were found throughout the house which would often cause fires. One such fire in March 1940 went on to affect some twenty rooms. The family put in a claim stating that the fires were caused by a poltergeist, and guess what? Their claim was settled by the insurers who recognised the ongoing poltergeist activity. Of course, all this happened during the war years, and like many large houses, sometimes they were requisitioned by the Army, which was the case here. Between the years 1942 to 1946 the house saw numerous soldiers take up residence throughout, and they too had some strange experiences one of which related to one of the soldiers witnessing the ghost of Captain Jeffrey, who had died in July 1941. Another soldier, Polish man Jan Rostworowski, observed a large wardrobe move towards him and then teetered menacingly on its edge. If that wasn't bad enough, Jan also had the misfortune to witness all his personal belongings piled up in disarray and then at this point an ashtray flew through the air and landed in a fireplace. Around this time, Ivan Jeffrey also remembers seeing soldiers bayonets stuck firmly in the walls.

49

Needless to say, something of this nature did not go unnoticed by the media, and numerous reports about this house was featured in a number of publications including the *American Weekly* a newspaper from the United States dated July 1942 and entitled 'No Rest in the Mansion'. Due to the very nature of these ongoing paranormal events, the family felt it best to seek the services of some psychics and a visiting clergyman and whilst the psychics did claim to have experienced 'things', the exorcism which was carried out by this visiting clergyman sadly had no effect. It would appear however that the poltergeist did not like this clergyman trying to disrupt his play, as it took the clergyman's hat off his head and threw it into the fire. Both the Roman Catholic and the Anglican clergy were involved with conducting services at the house.

Things steadily progressed and there was no let up to these disturbing events. The family found water filled ewers had been deposited all over their beds. The poltergeist had it would seem, a fascination for hot coals, as numerous hot coals were found throughout the house, burning and scorching as it went. Apparently, shovels full of hot coals were deposited on the library sofa. Ivan Jeffery's father, Captain John Arthur on one occasion rose to his feet to beat out a fire which was 'moving' across his bedroom carpet! The flame, we are told, was not hot to the touch and would move out of John's way. More interestingly however, that when the flame disappeared, not one bit of the carpet was scorched or burned in any way! Famed controversial paranormal investigator, Harry Price, actually devoted a full chapter to this case in his 1945 book '*Poltergeist over England*'. However, for some reason he didn't name the actual house, instead, he referred to it as 'Poltergeist Manor'.

FINAL DAYS

As time progressed and people moved on, the Jeffrey family sold the house and in 1947 it became a hotel. But things were not to stop, and this destructive poltergeist was once again up to its old tricks. We learn that further events of a paranormal nature continued to occur, such as a spectral woman who was dressed in green was witnessed in and around the house. Then there is the tale of a pair of gloves! Someone (we are not told who) came into a room and was astonished to see in front of the fireplace, a pair of gloves being held up to the fire, as if filled by invisible hands. No body, just gloves! This same individual also claimed that when he was walking down the stairs at the residence, he was startled to see family portraits come off their chains and spin around. Furthermore, whilst the residence was being used as a hotel, bottles of sealed alcohol would be found empty of their contents, yet their seals were left intact! Not all individuals felt that there were ghosts or poltergeists in the house, writer G W Lambert in his 1964 paper in the Society for Psychical Research Journal, entitled, 'Scottish Haunts and Poltergeists II', was more apt to believe that the disturbances in the house, was caused by the nearby Ochil Fault of which due to the movement of the Earth's crust along this fault line, it caused movement and subsequent 'disturbances', which he further tells us, were prevalent between the years 1936-40, the very years in which events at the house were at their height. Lambert went onto state that in his opinion type of hydraulic pressure, which was in effect caused by underground water action, acted as a mechanism for the so called poltergeist events. And whilst this is a theory shared by a number of modern-day thinkers, fault lines cannot always be the cause of all strange events, and I refer to the floating gloves and apparitions. After a period of years, the building was eventually demolished between the years of 1967/1968. There are no remains of that building at all now, it's all just farmland.

THE VIBRATING BED!

Location: Fife, Central Scotland.
Date: 1998

As I've traversed the length and breadth of the United Kingdom researching weird tales of the weird and wonderful, you also meet many fellow seekers of the truth along the way, one such diamond I met, was the lovely Tricia J. Robertson who is a lifelong member of the Scottish Society for Psychical

51

Research (SSPR) She lectured at our Scottish UFO & Paranormal Conference which was held at the Falkirk Town Hall on Saturday 8th July 2017 (and what a wonderful talk it was) It was all about her ghostly experiences and her many visits to paranormal locations accompanied by the late Professor Archie Roy. Tricia has written two books on ghostly phenomena, *'Things You Can Do When You Are Dead'*. (True Accounts of After Death Communication) and *'More Things You Can Do When You Are Dead'*. (What can you truly believe?) Both books contain a wealth of wonderful supernatural cases and I am going to refer to just one. Now due to witness confidentiality, Tricia does not divulge the names of the witnesses but gives them pseudonyms namely, Anne for the mother, and Jill for the daughter. Tricia also does not reveal the actual location of the events that you are about to read, other than they occurred in Fife, an area in Central Scotland. As usual, Tricia was accompanied on this investigation by her lifelong friend and confidant, Professor Archie Roy, himself a seasoned and well respected researcher. Upon arriving at the property, both Tricia and Archie clearly saw how troubled the family were. Both mother and daughter lived in the family home between Monday and Friday but at the weekend, Anne's daughter Jill, (13) was sent to live with her 80 year old grandmother who lived about a mile away. The reason for this was simply that Anne had a new male companion who stayed with her at weekends and allowed them both to have some 'special time' together. Some weeks later, strange paranormal events started to happen in the grandmother's house. There was only one bed in the house, of which Jill shared with her grandmother, and they were both alarmed when the bed started to vibrate with them in it. It vibrated so much that each leg of the bed would lift off the floor making a tick tick tapping sound on the wooden floor. Strange noises which comprised of banging and cracking sounds were also heard coming from the headboard of the bed. These were not low sounds but were very loud indeed. It was as if the bed had a mind of its own, it shook so violently, that apparently items which were situated on the nearby bedside cabinets would fall off due to the vibrations. Needless to say, this alarmed both women and Jill quickly phoned her mother who rushed to the house, but by this time the events had calmed down. On another occasion, again whilst Jill was staying over with her grandmother, three other male witnesses who were also in the house at this time were privy to these alarming events. Again, the bed shook very violently with both women on it, seeing this; the three men rushed to help and tried to hold the bed down, all to no avail. The women quickly jumped off the bed and joined the three men in the living room where they tried to get some sleep. Jill knew that something of this nature would be hard to prove to people who were not there, so she had the bright idea to place an audio recorder next to the bed in hopes that it would capture its supernatural dance. And capture it she did. She recorded the loud banging's, the tapings and also the noises from the headboard.

A few weekends after this episode, Jill decided to spend the night with an aunt, and guess what? Yes, the knockings and banging's were heard once more, this time in a different house but 'not' from a bed. These noises emanated from the skirting boards of the house. Things escalated in her aunt's house as cups were smashed in the kitchen when no one else was in the room. Furthermore, a feeling of a 'presence' was also experienced in the home. Then, on one occasion, as Jill walked into a room, some papers and items which were sat on the top of a coffee table, suddenly were lifted up into the air and thrown down onto the carpet, this was witnessed by two other people who were there. Noises, as we have learned, play a big part in the poltergeist effect, and it would seem that there were no let up in this house. Jill found that sometimes when she entered a room in her own home, extremely loud banging's were heard, like claps of thunder.

Tricia tells us that things got so bad, that enough was enough, and they sought the services of the Christian Church (after trying a number of other churches with little if any success I imagine!) Anyway, a minster from the Church of England attended the family home and blessed the house, after which he said that all should now be well. Anne asked him,

"But what if it's not all well". "I'd like to ask Jill into the room to see if all is well" The Church minster agreed, and as soon as Jill entered into the room, a tremendous bang pervaded the whole room at which point, this church minister took to his heels and was out the house in a flash. It was after this sequence of events, that Tricia and Archie Roy were called in. Both Tricia and Archie were of the opinion that young Jill, at 13 years of age, could well be the focus of the events. Apparently, she had a lot of pent up energy and had just reached puberty, a combination of which to many paranormal researchers (but not to me) would seem to be the catalyst of all the phenomenon. We will look closely at the puberty and emotional stress factor as an answer to the poltergeist phenomenon in the final chapter of this book. With this case however, both Tricia and Archie advised Jill to restart circuit training (no doubt to channel this pent-up energy) and also for them both to sit quietly together of an evening to try some de-stressing techniques. Both Tricia and Archie stated to the family that by doing all this, things should improve, and they did, for Tricia and Archie never heard from the family again. Tricia is of the opinion that no ghostly spirits were involved with this case. Indeed, her words to me in an e-mail stated, *"You have to remember that the activity was born from stress and resentment there was no 'spirit' involved"* I didn't work on that case, so I can't really comment, it may well have been stress, but then again!

I SAW MY DEAD GRAN, ALIVE!

Location: Inverurie, Scotland.
Date: Mid 1990's

I receive many letters and e-mails from people from all walks of life, each of whom have a story to tell me about their own personal ghostly experience, as the following story now does.

"When I was first married, I had an illness which because of the pain I had, prevented me from sleeping". "My husband

54

Derek was on dayshift and I said goodbye to him at 05:45am then I went back to my bed". "As soon as Derek drove off, I heard someone open and close my bedroom door to my bedside". "My covers were pulled up to my neck and were tucked in at both sides". "At that point I knew it was my Gran (she had died of cancer five years before) "It sounds strange now, but I sat up straight in bed and asked my gran to show herself, which she did". "She was sitting on the edge of my bed she looked incredible, so beautiful". "Her hair was glossy, and her skin was a very healthy looking pink." "She wore her glasses and a coat buttoned up to her neck" "The first thing my gran said to me was 'Are you frightened', are you frightened now'? "I told her I wasn't and gave her a big hug". "She was warm and as solid as you or I". "She told me about my aunt Betty who, for the last 20 years of her life, had been without the use of her legs". "My gran said that she was now walking perfectly". "Gran also spoke about other relatives, 'living and dead'". "After speaking to me for about an hour or so, she lay me down on her bed and put her hand over my eyes, I fell asleep" "It was the best sleep that I've had in weeks". "When my husband came home, I asked him to take me and see my mum, I wanted to let her know that I'd seen and spoken to her mother". "My mum remembered the coat that my gran had on, and she told me something that she had kept to herself for five years". "The day before my gran died, we all went to see her, and we went into her room in sets of two". "My sister and I went in first" " I got just inside the room and had to run out, the person lying in the bed didn't look like the gran I knew, she was so thin and pale" "My gran called for my mum and said, 'I've frightened Christine'. Gran died the following morning". "I know now why my gran had asked me the morning she appeared in my room, 'are you frightened, are you frightened now'?

Christine Ramsay, Inverurie, Scotland.

Wow, what a fantastic story. Now, if we all do survive the death of our physical material bodies (which I believe we do) then isn't this just the perfect example of someone coming back to prove survival? However probably what I found most incredible about this story, was the fact that not only did Christine hold a solid person (spirit) but that she did so for an 'hour or so' Now that is really quite something, it really is. Sceptics would quite rightly say, *"Why didn't you shout for someone else to come and see this"*. Indeed, why not, but I guess when you are in that situation surprise takes over and you don't think rationally. Another feature of this case is that Christine saw her 'dead' gran looking absolutely beautiful and there's the rub. Many people who see their loved ones that have passed on, always state that they looked radiant and lovely. Indeed some people who have passed on and gone to spirit without either an arm or a leg (which they may have lost in an accident) the other world would seem to recreate a new one for you!)

PUSHED DOWNWARDS IN BED!

Location: Dunalistair Hotel in Kinloch Rannoch Perthshire Scotland.
Date: 1980.

Most of my mail comes from people residing here in the U.K. but now and again I sometimes get letters and e-mails from people overseas who want to tell me about their own weird and wonderful experiences. The following comes from an ex Scot, now living in Napier New Zealand who wrote to me to tell me about a strange experience that he had many years ago whilst working in Scotland. Here is his letter to me in its entirety.

"I recently discovered your address in a book on ghosts so I thought I would write to you relating my experiences while working in Scotland back in 1980. I was working at the Dunalistair Hotel in Kinloch Rannoch Perthshire as a barman/cook. One weekend the hotel was fully booked to overflowing for some event or the other, and I had to give up my room for a guest, which meant spending the night in an ex-maid's room, reputedly haunted. It was a stereo-typical haunted room, upstairs, dark and foreboding. The evening of

56

my night there, I had several strong whiskies and headed to bed fearing the worst. Nothing happened. The next night however, when I returned to my room, the night was not so restful. I remember awakening in the early hours of the morning in a semi-conscious state. Something told me that I was about to experience a bad event but that it would all be OK in the end. I was pondering on what that could mean when all of a sudden, I felt myself being pushed downwards in my bed and I was unable to move. I was now fully awake and frankly terrified. This continued for approximately ten seconds or so. I finally sat up and turned on the light, the room was very cold. I then went to one of the maid's rooms (any excuse!) and spent the remainder of the night there. The maid's first words upon seeing me were, "God you look awful, have you seen a ghost?"

THE GARTMORN ROAD POLTERGEIST.

Location: Sauchie, Clackmannanshire Central Scotland.
Date: February to March 1987

Now admittedly this case was featured in one of my previous books, *'Paranormal Case Files of Great Britain Volume 1'* Publish Nation (2010) available through Amazon or lulu. But I present it here simply to show you the reader that the poltergeist can equally cause havoc to not just one stand alone house, but three houses joined together! This case, would you believe, also comes from the same town of Sauchie of which this current book is dedicated to. However, this Sauchie case occurred 27 years after the main Sauchie Poltergeist case, 1987 to be precise. On the 8th of February 1987, fellow Scottish researcher Ron Halliday and I began our research into claims that three houses joined together in Gartmorn Road Sauchie, a town near Alloa in Clackmannanshire Central Scotland, were haunted. Early research showed that these houses which were built around 1937 were, for the past six months, subject to strange footsteps, noises, bangs, smells, and all the usual phenomenon associated with haunted buildings. Many of these noises it must be said were reported to have come from the loft.

57

Interviews were conducted on audio tape with Cindy Hope (pseudonym) where she told me that ever since she had first moved into the property she just didn't feel at home, that there was something not quite right about it. Cindy's first experience was that of standing on a certain stair on the staircase in which she experienced strange sensations, dizziness being the main one. This, incidentally, was not a medical condition on Cindy as we checked for this. Cindy's 18 year-old daughter Laura (pseudonym) had to sleep with the light on owing to constant bad dreams. Cindy's next door neighbour Mrs Elaine Peters, also related much of the same events only these events were happening to her in her own home, again with most of the noises coming from the loft area.

THE INVESTIGATION BEGINS

Our society Strange Phenomena Investigations (SPI) consulted Tony Cornell of Cambridge University, and also Professor Archie Roy of Glasgow University, asking them if they could offer any form of assistance, unfortunately they were both too tied up with other commitments to be able to offer any help. SPI also contacted other Scottish researchers but again with little effect. So, it looked like we were on our own with this one. And so, SPI began one of their most intriguing cases that we would talk about for a very long time. When our Investigative team appeared on the scene, we found much to our surprise, that the two families who lived at either side of Cindy's house, had had enough of the ghostly events that were happening in their house, they had abandoned their houses and joined up with Cindy whose house was the middle house of the three. And when we walked into Cindy's house, well it was like a battle zone. There were camp beds and air beds everywhere in the living room where the two guest families had came to stay (strength in numbers as they say) Apparently what had capped it all off, was when Cindy's neighbours had come round to visit, and they were all sitting in the living room discussing all the weird events, when all of a sudden the sound of 'thumping' was heard coming from upstairs, probably from the loft again they surmised. That was it, enough was enough, sick to the back teeth of these disturbances, they decided to face their fears, and they all got up out of their chairs and angrily headed out into the hall area and looked up the stairs. Their fears were doubly enhanced for when they all looked up the empty stairs, they all clearly heard the unmistakable sound of heavy footsteps coming towards them, and nobody, absolutely nobody, was there. Needless to say, they broke all speed records as they quickly took to their heels jamming themselves in a door as they all tried to get out at the same time. That was the last straw Cindy said, that's when her next door neighbours on both sides joined forces with them. The following is a combination of but some of the strange events to have transpired in the house.

(1)   Cold spots would suddenly appear in various parts of the house even in the summer.

(2)   Many strange noises came from the loft.

(3)   A kitchen drawer opened by itself and a knife and fork sailed through mid air without anyone touching them. Both utensils then fell to the floor, thankfully without coming near or injuring anyone.

(4)   The family dog (of the Hope family) refused to go upstairs, and anytime anyone tried to lead it upstairs it would suddenly try and bite you.   One day it was found in an 'upstairs' bedroom locked in (from the inside!)   The dog had tried to claw its way through the door and had bloodied its paws in the attempt. The bedroom door was full of scratches.

(5)   A doppelganger of one of the women was seen to walk down the stairs but that particular lady was not in the house at that time. (More of that one in a moment)

(6)   During one point in our Investigation as we were interviewing one of the ladies, she went into a trance and started speaking in a different language which no one had heard

before. I was sitting right in front of this lady and I can tell you, this was pretty scary.

Mrs Peter's 11-year-old son Dane claimed that he was being visited in the night by a strange man and woman, the woman was carrying a small baby in her arms. Both people he said, looked real and solid. On one occasion the ghostly woman snatched the pillow beneath the head of young Dane and placed it at the bottom of the bed! Not only that, this woman continually asked young Dane what his name was, and also asked him not to be frightened of them. She went on to say that they didn't like the dog next door and that it was her that had locked the dog in the room so that it wouldn't bite us or the baby. *(Ghosts being frightened of earthly dogs, whatever next?)* We ascertained that young Dane was 'NOT' aware that the dog was found locked inside the bedroom.

When I happened to mention to Dane's mother about her son's visitors in the night, the man and woman holding the baby, she blurted out.

"That would explain it. I've had strange dreams of a man and woman with a baby".

Elaine Peters, the next door neighbour, later explained that she has lost two babies in childbirth. On a later date, young Dane told us that he was still seeing the strange man and woman appear in his bedroom, and this time they stated to him that they were only 'looking after the baby' until the owners stopped being mad at it? Dane said that the woman kept trying to insert a strange looking dummy tit into the baby's mouth as she turned around and headed towards his mum's room. Was this all fantasy in the mind of a young boy who must surely have been aware of what his family and friends had been speaking about for days? Well that's a possibility that we have to consider, but then again, what if it 'is true'. Just because something sounds ridiculous does not necessarily mean that it is so.

Now with any haunted house we must be very careful, careful in the sense that it might not be haunted at all? That it all might be one big joke for ego publicity, or, more realistically, it might be a case of, 'let's make up a ghost story in order to get out of the house' (believe you me some people will try anything in order to get better housing, although admittedly, we as a research team, have never come across this before.) But as with any case, we still had to ascertain for sure, whether or not this was a genuine haunting or just some people out to pull the wool over our eyes. We need not have worried on that point, as later events would clearly show us that this case was the 'real deal'. As the investigation continued, we also found out from Cindy, that one day as she walked into the kitchen, she heard a distinct 'swishing' sound come from above the kitchen table, a sound that she couldn't account for. It wasn't long before electrical items such as televisions and radios were switching themselves on and off. Elaine explained to the author, that one of the most unnerving episodes that she herself personally witnessed, was the day when she saw a reflection of a man's face in the stacking stereo system. This wasn't a reflection from the TV, as it wasn't switched on at the time, nor was it a reflection of anyone else in the room, for there was only her and her small son. She did not recognise this face at all. Marie Hope (Cindy's daughter) stated to SPI, that on one occasion when her boyfriend paid a visit to her house, he claimed that he heard Marie's voice calling him to come upstairs (he had only just come into the house) whereupon he did so, but upon entering Marie's bedroom, she wasn't there, he found her fast asleep downstairs on the living room settee! Further to this, along the same lines, Cindy herself heard her 21 year old son Timmy, calling out to her, but Timmy wasn't home. This 'mimicking' of voices is not that uncommon in hauntings and is reported quite often. It would appear that spirits get quite a kick of pretending to be someone they are not!

Probably one of the strangest things that occurred in Cindy's house was the day when Cindy's mother happened to spend the night. The mother was downstairs in the kitchen making a cup of tea when she saw her daughter Cindy walk down the stairs in a flowered night gown. She asked her daughter as she was descending the stairs, if she would like a cup of tea, to which her daughter did not respond, indeed the 'daughter' coming down the stairs, stopped, then turned around and went back up the stairs. Later the daughter came back downstairs to which her mother said,

"Hey, why did you not answer me when you were coming down the stairs"?

Cindy replied, *"But I'm just up, I just got up this second".*

Cindy's mother went on to mention her daughter's nice night gown to which Cindy replied,

"But mum, I haven't got a night gown like that, I don't own one like that"

So, we have to ask ourselves, if that wasn't Cindy coming down the stairs, then who was it! Most of us will have heard about Doppelgangers which is someone that looks exactly like you but then suddenly disappears, was that the case here? Was Cindy just sleepwalking and didn't know it, but if so, where did the night gown come from if she states that she doesn't own one like that? We also learned in our Investigation that strange 'growling' noises were heard coming from a cupboard in Cindy's home, a noise that she never investigated for fear of what she might find.

SPI SPEND THE NIGHT

After taking notes of all the recent strange occurrences, I asked Cindy if our research team (SPI) could spend the night in the family home to see if we could document these events ourselves, this request was accepted, and so my colleague Kevin Cole and I, arranged to spend the night there the following evening. Upon entering the property, Kevin and I began to set up our equipment. We were all alone in the house as the Hope family had gone next door to be with the Peters family, and also the other family to give us free reign of her property. We decided to set up most of the equipment in Marie's bedroom which we were told, was the chilliest room in the whole house (even in the summer) But before Kevin and I sat down for our night time vigil we decided to check the loft space of both Cindy and Elaine's house. So, with some trepidation we gingerly entered Cindy's loft, and that was spooky I can tell you. And with our flashlights we looked in every nook and cranny. We didn't find any hidden devices that could make these banging noises, nor did we find any birds' nests that could account for birds perhaps getting into the loft and making noises. We also never found any evidence of any mice or rats which could have made scurrying sounds in the loft, which might have been misconstrued as something else. It was just an ordinary loft which contained the usual bits and bobs of household junk. Satisfied, we quickly (and I mean quickly!) got out of the loft and went next door to do the same in Elaine's loft.

Sadly, we didn't see, hear or sense a thing on that particular night, which I must admit was most disappointing. In the morning, we were joined again by all three families where they were disappointed to learn that we hadn't seen anything. (They were probably not as disappointed as us)

THE EMPTY AND LOCKED ROOM

I then took the decision to take the Hope family and some members of the other families, along to my local Spiritualist Church in Alloa to see if they could help. The Alloa Christian Spiritualist Church meetings were held at that time, in an upper room in the Alloa Town Hall. (I must state that I gave the Church committee members minimal details about what was going on, as I was hoping that at a later date, we could perhaps get some of their psychics to attend the houses). Sadly, I had to leave later that night as I was working night shift at the local Glassworks Factory which was a bit of a pain but there you go. The following day I took a phone call at home from one of the ladies of the church who stated excitedly that just 10 minutes after I had left, loud banging noises could be heard coming from above their heads. They knew that above their heads was a locked room, so they all got up out of their seats, went upstairs, and peered through the two oblong windows of the door into the seemingly empty locked room. Everything was in order, there was nobody there. The noises had stopped. They tried the door handle; it was securely locked. Seeing that all was in place, they all trooped back downstairs and sat back in their seats where they began to tell the church people about what had been happening to them, no sooner had they started talking, then all hell let loose again, banging's and thumps coming from above their head. There were also sounds like falling stones falling down between the walls of the building. They jumped up off their seats and raced upstairs only to be met with the same sight, a locked room and nobody there. The family explained to the church committee people that this was nothing unusual, as these types of crashes and bangs were a regular occurrence in the family home. The committee members stated to the family that nothing like this had ever occurred in the Alloa Christian Spiritualist Church before, whereupon Cindy smiled and stated,

"Well this type of thing goes on all the time back at our house".

THE CLEANSING!

Having convinced the Alloa Christian Spiritualist Church of the seriousness of this case, some church members, along with some SPI members, attended the Hope house on the 16th of February 1987 to see what we could do. The following information is taken from notes that I took of this Investigation at that time. After some brief introductions as to what the Alloa Church did and what they hoped to achieve by them being there, we separated into groups, some went upstairs and some downstairs. Prayers were said in each of these rooms by mediums of the church. Audio recordings were taken by me of these prayers. John Allardice, a local medium, stated that he felt

64

extreme heaviness in his head and also heat throughout his body. Mr Allardice then said that he perceived a voice which was asking for love. He then got two spirit people come through saying that they, 'didn't want to be sent away'! Now I was at this time in Marie's bedroom in which local Alloa medium Emily Manini was saying some prayers. I remember that the whole room was bitterly cold, but it was February after all. But I do recall that my teeth were clattering quite loudly as I shivered in this room, (which was a wee bit embarrassing) Anyway, after Emily had finished saying her prayer, the silence in the room was broken by the sound of a woman bounding up the stairs shouting at the top of her voice that Cindy had been pushed off a wooden bench in the living room with nobody near her.

Elaine Peters who was in the bedroom with me, stated that just before this woman came bounding up the stairs; she felt that the room was getting warmer, as if whatever might had been in the room with us, had left, and went elsewhere, downstairs perhaps! We all at once quickly abandoned the bedroom and rushed downstairs. After the excitement of what previously had happened, a church member administered psychic healing to Cindy and Elaine and the other neighbour. All was quiet for now, and the relaxed psychic healing seemed to ease the tense situation. Now this is where I made a big mistake. I stupidly turned off the audio tape recorder. And typically, some minutes later, the most strange and alarming look came over Elaine Peters face. It was a menacing piercing look, in which one felt they had to turn away from, I know I certainly did? Suddenly, Elaine stood up and started speaking out in the most strangest voice, this was definitely unlike her own voice. From my notes, and sadly not from my audio tape, this is what Elaine said.

"They took Lawrence away, they threw him down a hole, threw logs over him". "I like it here; I don't want to go". "They keep taking away my friends, my mum's name is Victoria. Men are going to get me, the men that threw Lawrence down the hole". "They said that he was dead, we

*are not dead". "Elona is the name of the baby, Lawrence is 30
now, I'm 25, I can't look around the room because the men will
get me. Please don't let me go away" "If mummy comes they'll
put her down the hole" "I've got spots, but she and Lawrence
can't be dead because of this baby".*

I would point out to you the reader that the name Elona was
the name of a baby that Elaine had lost in childbirth some four
years previously. Incidentally, the girl's name Elona \e-lo-na\ is
a variant of Alona (Hebrew) and Ilona (Hungarian, Greek), and
the meaning of Elona is 'oak tree; light'. All eyes were fixed
on Elaine as she continued to whirl about the room and speak
out in this strange voice; it surely was one of the strangest
sights that I've seen in all my years of 'paranormal research'.
Eventually, after about five minutes, Elaine slumped down into
a nearby chair. Wow, this was something else and totally
unexpected, all of which had not been captured on audio tape, I
could have kicked myself. The hole that Elaine spoke about
bothered me. I was aware that quite near this housing scheme,
was a number of old mine shafts (now bricked up) At a later
date myself and a fellow investigator visited some of these
mine shafts, and although we couldn't gain access, we took a
number of photographs of them. Of course, these mine shafts
might have had nothing at all to do with what Elaine was
speaking about when she was 'taken over,' if indeed taken over
she was! could these 'holes' that Elaine referred to, be
anything to do with plague pits? A number of plagues spread
throughout Central Scotland hundreds of years ago, could this
have a bearing on what she was referring to? SPI did find a pit
of sorts a half mile or so from her house. It was covered up
(see photographic section)

The following day SPI secured the services of a well know
Stirling medium, Mrs Jean Glenn. Jean visited the homes of the
families concerned, but other that her picking up some strong
psychic impressions from their homes, nothing else was
ascertained. On the 18th of February, a colleague and I were
again given permission to spend the night in the house. We did
all the usual checks starting from the loft then going through to

every room in the house, and all seemed in proper order. I recall sitting on the top stair of the stairs in the house in total darkness and other than a faint moonlight beam which tumbled in through a chink in the curtain of the top landing window casting its soft diffused glow at the bottom of the stairs, I never felt anything untoward. Dust particles caught in this sparkling light beam, majestically danced around as they hit the foot of the stairs. All was quiet in the house. It was at this point that I thought to myself,

"Why do I do this? I very rarely see anything in haunted houses it always happens when I'm not there".

As I sat at the top of the stairs, I placed a quilt which I borrowed from one of the bedrooms and placed it around my shoulders. I then slowly brought it up to my face as the cold February air bit into my very soul. Sadly, nothing happened that night, and for the second time, SPI had experienced nothing in the house. When we told all the family members that we hadn't experienced anything, they just couldn't believe it. Indeed, they were quite angry that we hadn't experienced anything. We told the families that we would be back in touch and asked them to keep us informed of any new phenomena that might take place.

One amusing incident that occurred during this Investigation (well its amusing now it certainly wasn't at the time) was the following.

ASSAULTED ON AN INVESTIGATION!

I was sitting having a quiet drink with a friend in the Royal Oak bar in Alloa when a man that I didn't know, came up to me and grabbed me by the throat. Now I could see that he was extremely annoyed. I hadn't a clue who this chap was, I had never seen him before in my life, and by way of introducing himself, he had me by the throat, pinned to the wall, and honestly my feet were dangling in mid-air. It was seriously like a Tom & Jerry cartoon. I tried to speak but I couldn't, he was compressing my windpipe. He then said, (And I'm being extremely conservative here)

"I'm going to kill you; you're the guy that's seeing my girl".

Not quite what he said, but this is a family book! Now, like I say, I don't know who this chap was but he's angrier than a grizzly bear whose meal has been taken away from him. Eventually I managed to ease out a few words in my mid air dilemma. I asked him who he was on about, and he stated that I had been seeing Cindy Hope his ex-girlfriend who lives (He gave me the house number and street at this point) Gartmorn Road Sauchie.

Now this was beginning to make sense, but he clearly had the wrong end of the stick. I said that I was a paranormal researcher and I was Investigating the claims made to us by Mrs Hope and that I was attending her house in a research capacity, he thundered by saying,

"Well I've heard a lot of good lines in my time, but you mate take the biscuit, a paranormal researcher, are you taking the mick"?

I informed him that I wasn't taking the mick and I could prove who I was with my SPI card and that he could also check my story out with his estranged girlfriend. Eventually as I told him more about myself and the other people who were involved in the case, he released his grip. I fell to the floor like a sack of potatoes. If I had had been watching this I would have been in hysterics, but there you are, that's a true story of my one and only time (so far!) of almost getting beaten up in the line of his paranormal duties. As I say, I can laugh about it now, but I certainly couldn't at the time.

The outcome of this Investigation was that we later conducted a 'cleansing ceremony' in the house where our resident psychic Helen Walters and other members of SPI made contact with those spirit entities that were 'occupying' the house and made sure that they went to the light. We hope that it worked. All families moved away from the district soon after, and I couldn't really knock on the new tenant's door and say,

"Excuse me, but your house used to be haunted, can you tell me if it still is"?

I don't think that would have gone down so well. All in all then, this was a most interesting case, and although we researchers never saw or heard anything unusual ourselves, (Apart from Elaine's strange trance like state) it was nonetheless an interesting experience for us all.

MORE GHOSTS FROM THE SAUCHIE AREA

The following was sent to me via e-mail from a lady, who, after reading about the Gartmorn Poltergeist, decided to get in touch with me. Here is what she said.

"Hi Malcolm.

"I have just read your article in Sauchie Legends regarding the poltergeist.

(Author's note). Sauchie Legends is a Facebook site dedicated to the town of Sauchie in Clackmannanshire Central Scotland, providing old photographs to local stories and events) the lady continued.

"I found it a very interesting read. This led me to also read your articles regarding the houses in Gartmorn Road, now this interested me greatly as I grew up in a house on Mount William which is a side street to Gartmorn Road. Growing up, the events in this house terrified me. Several visitors to our house saw a small boy dressed in Victorian clothing that would appear from behind the Living room curtains, and he was also seen in the hallway. My mum often saw a man upstairs on the landing that used to disappear round the corner in the direction

of my bedroom. My brother also saw a man standing at the bottom of his bed one night, it was so clear that he thought it was a burglar and he launched himself at the figure knocking over his C.D. collection in the process. One night in my bedroom I was trying to add up some figures in my head, a man's voice spoke out and told me the answer as clear as a bell. I used to hear footsteps walking across my floor all the time. We had two cats when we lived at that house, they used to go into the airing cupboard to snooze and my mum would leave the door open a little for them to get in as the door was on a catch, and you had to give it a bit of a tug to open it, it always made a bit of a squeak as it opened. When the cats were leaving the cupboard, you would hear the squeak and then the thump on the floor as they jumped out. After the cats passed away you would still hear these noises, firstly the catch, then the squeak followed by the thump, it used to terrify me."

"Our hoover and television would turn on by themselves. I had to sleep with the light on from about the age of 12 as I used to be so frightened at night that it would send shivers down my spine. We got a dog when I was about 15, I was really struggling to sleep at night and thought it would help to have a bit of company in my room at night, the dog used to go crazy for no apparent reason, he would stare fixedly at an area and bark and shake with all the fur on his back standing up. I truly believe the goings on in that house drove the dog crazy and we eventually had to get rid of the dog as one day it just went completely berserk and ripped the house to shreds for no apparent reason. Sorry if I am rambling a bit but I am just typing it as I am remembering it. One of the scariest things was on my birthday one year, I think I was 11, someone singing woke me up, and when I opened my eyes, there was a man sat next to my bed gently singing happy birthday, I remember squeezing my eyes shut and saying out loud for him to go away and when I opened my eyes again he was gone. It's strange because I haven't mentioned these events to many people as when I have told people I usually get the impression that they don't believe me, but I 100% know for sure what I have seen and heard in that house. I am curious if you heard of any other

70

goings on in that area and also what number the houses were in Gartmorn Road and what the proximity of them were to my house. Sorry if I have bored you! I just felt the need to share. Have a good day"
Kind Regards, Molly Donaldson". (Pseudonym)

In a further e-mail that I received from Mary, she stated the following.

"I couldn't get out of that house quick enough. It would appear that this was happening at the same time as the incidents in Gartmorn Road. I had a chat with my brother over messenger about this yesterday, he also told me things that he had saw which I wasn't aware he knew about and basically backed up what I was saying. My mum and I didn't really discuss it with my brother as he was younger, and we didn't want to frighten him, but it transpires that he had seen and heard a lot of it too. He also reminded me of a time when he went home to an empty house but heard voices and loud banging coming from upstairs. He ran next door and got the neighbour to go upstairs with him as he thought it was an intruder, needless to say there was nobody there. I'm going to mention something else although you might think I am mad, it seemed an awful coincidence! Whilst myself and my brother were discussing this yesterday, his son who was out at the time, sent him a picture of a ghost, and my daughter who was at a school rehearsal, texted me to say that her teacher had just asked her to take on the part of a ghost and she didn't want to do it"!
Kind Regards, Molly Donaldson.

The good thing with doing research for a book, is that you come across some mind blowing quotes, words that carry immense thought and feeling and one such quote that I came across, I found in Scottish researcher Tricia Robertson's book, *'More Things You Can Do When You Are Dead' (What can you truly believe?) White Crow Books 2015.* The quote comes from the Reverend Mervyn Stockwood, Lord Bishop of Southwark, and is taken from his book, which concerned itself with the life and times of famous English medium, Ena Twigg. *'The Woman Who Stunned the World'* in this quote, the Reverend Stockman is talking about Life After Death and its implications to us all. He states,

"The Church ought to provide the answer for its followers, but I doubt whether it does, except in a minority of cases. My knowledge suggests that most priests are all ill qualified to provide knowledge, comfort, and assurance, instead they content themselves with a routine 'death patter' they picked up in their theological college. My contention is that if we were to take psychic studies seriously, we would learn to appreciate that our experience in this world is not the consummation; instead we live now sub specie aeternitatis. There are other worlds and dimensions, and this should be taught in schools as part of our general education. We must concentrate on psychic studies insofar as they impinge upon our life now and in the future. I would hope that t might affect his (man's) values and behaviour in this world, for what is the purpose of survival unless those who survive are prepared for it?"

As for my own thoughts on life after death and Spiritualism I would say this,

"The greatness of being a Spiritualist is knowing for sure, that when it is our time to pass to spirit, we know that we will see those family members who have gone before us (and our pets) Spiritualism and this knowledge is a great comfort to me. Yes of course we miss the physical presence of that person that goes without saying but to see them again in the afterlife is a wonderful thought. I have just lost an uncle but then I will find him again in spirit. Nobody but nobody can ever take this sure-fire knowledge away from me. And what with being a paranormal researcher who has investigated claims of the afterlife, who has spoken and interviewed members of the medical profession who have related their dying patients last visions, all confirm, that we go to a better place when we die. But please folks, live this life to the full, be good, be honest and give it your best shot. God bless you all".

Alloa Town Hall. Scene of some mysterious knockings.
(Gartmorn Road Poltergeist)

Sauchie Gartmorn Road Case 1987 (c) Malcolm Robinson

Terrified neighbours in the Gartmorn Road Case.
(c) Malcolm Robinson.

Witnesses in the Gartmorn Road Case (c) Malcolm Robinson

The three middle houses were subject to poltergeist activity.
Gartmorn Road Case. 1987

CHAPTER THREE

CLACKMANNANSHIRE
AND SAUCHIE
A BRIEF HISTORY

"I saw these bedclothes moving with a sort of rippling movement as if they were being tugged up towards the girl".

Dr. Nisbet States. (Scope Radio Programme on the Sauchie Poltergeist)

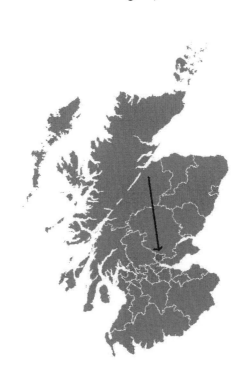

Black Arrow points to Clackmannanshire, Central Scotland.

OK before we move into the Sauchie Poltergeist proper, let me provide you the reader (and more so for those readers overseas) with some information about the county of Clackmannanshire in Scotland and also the small town of Sauchie that the principle witness Virginia Campbell and her family would leave Moville in County Donegal in Ireland for.

Clackmannanshire is a historic county in Scotland, which borders the areas of Stirling, Fife, Perth, and Kinross. The name is derived from three languages the first Scottish Gaelic: Clach meaning 'Stone', and Mannan, which is a derivative of the Brythonic name of the Iron Age tribe, the Manaw, who inhabited the area, and added the English word shire. The Mannan stone can be found placed on a larger stone beside the Tollbooth and Mercat Cross situated at the top of Main Street in Clackmannan. Clackmannanshire is Britain's smallest historic county and is often nicknamed 'The Wee County'. Historically, Clackmannanshire was well known for its weaving mills which were powered by the local Hillfoots burns which run down from the Ochil Hills. The motto of the County Arms is *"Look aboot ye."* This story allegedly came about when King Robert the Bruce lost his glove whilst he was out hunting near the town of Clackmannan. The Bruce sent people out to look for his glove with the instruction *"Look aboot ye"*. The glove is said to have been found on the 'Look aboot ye Brae', near Clackmannan. Whether this story is true, is anyone's guess, but it is written into the folklore of Clackmannan. There are several towns and villages spread throughout Clackmannanshire, namely, Alloa, Tullibody, Cambus, Clackmannan, Kennet, Sauchie, Fishcross, Coalsnaughton, Forestmill, Glenochil, Tillicoultry, Dollar, Pool of Muckhart and Yetts of Muckhart to name but a few.

BREWING IN CLACKMANNANSHIRE.

Some of the industries in Clackmannanshire, included brewing, and the town of Alloa was well known throughout not just Scotland, but also the United Kingdom as one of the major players in the brewing industry. At its height, Alloa was host to

78

nine major breweries, some of which are as follows, Robert Henderson (Mills Brewery), Robert Knox (Forth Brewery), George Younger (Meadow & Candleriggs Breweries), Robert Meiklejohn (Candleriggs Brewery), James Calder (Shore Brewery), Blair & Co. (Townhead Brewery), Maclay & Co. (Thistle Brewery), and Archibald Arrol (Alloa Brewery) Probably the first brewing firms in the town of Alloa were Younger in 1762, and Meiklejohn in 1784. The success of Alloa ales was such that it was sent to the city of London, and moreover, George Younger traded his Alloa Ales as far afield as the West Indies, Egypt, and the Far East. The Alloa Brewery Company produced a tasteful ale called, 'Graham's Golden Lager' in 1927, of which would later be renamed as Skol in the 1950s. The Skol brewery was situated right in the heart of Alloa at one of the major ring roads. Sadly, due to a combination of closures and mergers, many of the local brewing industries went into decline, and by 1999, after the closure of MacLay's Thistle Brewery, only one brewery remained, the Forth Brewery which became Williams Brothers in 2003. That said the Harviestoun Brewery (est. 1984 by Ken Brooker in Dollar) at Alva, is still going strong, and I should point out that the Mansfield Arms in Sauchie, have been brewing ales under the Devon Ales name since 1992, and the pub itself has been a haven and still is, for real ales.

BOTTLE MANUFACTURING

Another major manufacturer in Clackmannanshire was the Alloa Glassworks, a company that I personally gave 21 years of my working life to (but that's another story)! Glassmaking in Alloa started way back in the 18th century. In her article '*A Walk in the Past' The History of Alloa Glassworks,* Valerie Forsyth informed her readers that the construction of the works in Alloa was overseen by Lady Frances Erskine, who was the daughter of John Erskine, 6th Earl of Mar, known as Bobbing John, who led the Jacobites at the Battle of Sheriffmuir. Lady Erskine had the consent of her brother Thomas, and construction work at the Alloa site took around 18 months to complete, and the production of the Glassworks began in 1750.

Lady Erskine knew that Alloa was ideally placed for trade and commerce, and thankfully the raw materials to make glass were close at hand. Salt could be brought in from nearby Kennetpans, although this dried up in the latter part of the 18th century. Sand and kelp were taken from the River Forth. Coal to drive the whole process could be easily transported to the site from the local Mar collieries thanks to the laying of the wagonway, initiated by Lady Frances, to the harbour. The factory has come a long way from those days, and its modern production is now producing millions of whisky and beer bottles 24/7. Its managed by O.I. (Owens Illinois) an American company and is still going strong. I, Malcolm Robinson, left the factory in 1998.

Wikipedia tells us that by 1822, neighbouring Alloa had outgrown Clackmannan and replaced it as the county town. In 1889 and 1890, there was a major 'shake up' of the county boundaries so much so, that in 1971, the Muckhart and Glendevon areas, which were formerly in Perthshire, were transferred to Clackmannanshire. In 1975, Clackmannanshire was renamed the Clackmannan District. It became part of the Central Region, together with Stirling District and Falkirk District. In terms of population, Clackmannanshire is the smallest council area in mainland Scotland, with a population of 51,400 (census 2017), around half of whom live in the main town and administrative centre, Alloa.

THE TOWN OF SAUCHIE

So that's Clackmannanshire (the Wee County) let us now learn about the town of Sauchie where young Virginia Campbell and her family relocated to. From that font of knowledge that is Wikipedia, I take the following.

Sauchie is a town in the Central Lowlands of Scotland. It lies north of the River Forth and south of the Ochil Hills, within the council area of Clackmannanshire. Sauchie has a population of around 6000 and is located 1.0 mile (1.6 km) north-east of Alloa and 2.1 miles (3.4 km) east-southeast of Tullibody. The name Sauchie means the place or field of the willows. The land originally belonged to Clan Campbell, being mentioned in connection with Cailean Mór and Gilleasbaig of Menstrie. In 1321 Robert the Bruce granted the lands of Sauchie to Henry de Annand, former Sheriff of Clackmannan. A tower was built in 1335, and the present Sauchie Tower is on the same site. The extant tower was built before 1431 when Mary de Annand, the co-heiress to the estate, married Sir James Schaw of Greenock. The tower is all that remains of the village which developed within its protective radius. In the early 18th century the Schaw family moved from the tower to the more comfortable Newtonshaw. The village developed a brick works by the River Devon which fell into disuse following the collapse of the local mining industry. Sauchie has seen a lot of changes throughout the years and the Sauchie of today effectively grew from Holton Village which was built in 1710. This village was built to house the Earl of Mar's colliers at the nearby Holton mine. Newtonshaw house, also in Sauchie, was built to accommodate the servants of the notable Schaw family. The Schaw family initially lived in Sauchie Tower, but after a number of years they all moved into their new house at Schawpark in the 1700s. Schawpark was a substantial large mansion and was situated in what is now currently Schawpark Golf Course. No evidence at all can be found of this once impressive mansion house. As the country grew, so did the villages, and the two villages of Newtonschaw and Holton eventually merged into one of which the area then became, 'New Sauchie'. The author's mother was born and raised in Sauchie Main Street which was completely re-developed in the 1960s. Another big feature near the town of Sauchie is the Gartmorn Dam, which is the oldest man made reservoir in the whole of Scotland and is still, to this day, providing the local area as a Public Water Supply. The Dam itself was constructed around 1713 by the Earl of Mar, this was to provide waterpower, via a lade to help drain his coal mines at nearby Holton. The town of Sauchie has its own football team founded in 1960 who play in the East of Scotland League. Some of the footballing stars to have come through the ranks of Sauchie Juniors have been, Alan Hansen who played for Patrick Thistle, Liverpool F.C. and Scotland, and after his career finished, would later go onto the BBC Match of the Day programme as a television pundit. Alan's Brother John Hansen also played for Patrick Thistle and Scotland. Willie Morgan also from Sauchie played for Burnley, Manchester United, Bolton Wanderers, Chicago Sting, Minnesota Kicks, Blackpool, and Scotland.

SCOTLAND IN THE 1960'S

But what was Scotland like back in the 1960's? when Virginia and her parents moved. Well here are a few facts which I am sure will raise an eyebrow! Firstly, the population of Scotland back in 1960 was around 5.178 million. On the 1st of December 1960, Paul McCartney and Pete Best from an up and coming pop band called the Beatles, were arrested, and deported from Hamburg, Germany where they had been touring accused of attempted arson. On December 2nd, Paleoanthropologist Louis Leakey, discovered a 1.4-million-year-old Homo erectus, entitled, Olduvai Hominid 9 in Olduvai Gorge, Tanzania. And for all you soap fans, on December 9th, 1960 we had the very first broadcast of 'Coronation Street' on ITV, which, as we know, is still going strong today. The average house price back in 1960 was just £2,530 and, would you believe, a pint of beer cost just 8 pence, a loaf of bread was just 5 pence, and a packet of 20 cigarettes was less than 25 pence. If you were a fan of Manchester United back then, a season ticket to see United in 1960, was just £8:50, a match programme was just 2 pence. Oh, for those same prices today!

The mid to late 1960's, would see a rise in British pop culture, and would introduce what would come to be known as 'the swinging 60's' where bands such as the Pink Floyd, The Kinks, The Hollies, The Who, The Yardbirds and the Cream, to name but a few, propelled the music industry to an astonishing level with British bands domineering the American charts for the first time which was unheard of before. Apparently, the Hillman Imp car was, for many Scots, their first car, and the Hillman Imp factory which was opened at Linwood near Glasgow in 1963 employed mostly Scottish people even although the design company was based in Coventry. Come what may, many people felt this to be a 'Scottish car'. A total of, 440,013 cars were built before the factory was shut down in 1976.

OK, we have now had a look at Clackmannanshire and Sauchie. It's always nice to get a bit of background on the location of an incident such as this, and it gives you the reader, a bit of the social and cultural history of the area where the Campbell family moved into. We have also taken a quick look at some of the things that were occurring in Great Britain during 1960. The scene is now set, a family from Ireland were about to move to Scotland of which unbeknown to them would change their lives dramatically.

CHAPTER FOUR

THE SAUCHIE POLTERGEIST

"Virginia is not responsible for what has happened". "The child is innocent". "What has taken place was not conjured by the child herself, an outside agent is responsible". "Believe me, something unfortunate has been going on in that house". "The girl was hysterical all the time the phenomenon was appearing".

Dr. Nisbet. The Campbell's Local G.P

THE SAUCHIE POLTERGEIST

Location: Sauchie, Alloa, Clackmannanshire, Central Scotland,
Date: November-December 1960.
Sauchie Pronounced (Saw-Key)

For me, this is undoubtedly the biggest poltergeist case of its kind in Scotland, and that's a fact. It occurred just a few miles from where I lived at the time in a town called Sauchie in Clackmannanshire, Central Scotland. There is not a case in Scotland that comes anywhere near it. Sadly, it was a case that was way before my time, as I was only 3 years old when it was occurring, how I wish I was old enough to be involved in this one. This was a momentous case and I often wondered what happened to the little girl who was the main focus of the poltergeist events (Virginia Campbell) and did the classmates of Virginia still remember those bizarre events from all those years ago? Now admittedly I mentioned this case in my second book, *'Paranormal Case Files of Great Britain' (Volume 1)* Publish Nation (2010 & 2017) ISBN: 978-1-907126-06-2

But as this case has always fascinated me, I thought I'd give it one more go, and in 2019 and in the early part of 2020, I decided to seek out any further potential witnesses who might still be alive. This would be my third Investigation into this famous case, the first one being in 1987 where I managed to track down and speak with, a few of Virginia Campbell's classmates who informed me in no uncertain terms that they 'too' witnessed some amazing bizarre paranormal happenings in the classroom. However, when I tried to interview the aunty of Virginia Campbell who lived just a few hundred yards away from me at that time in Woodlea Park Sauchie, the door was slammed firmly shut in my face, something that in all my years of Investigation has never ever happened to me before. These are things that one just has to accept, but saying that, I did write a letter to Virginia's aunty and popped it through her door, hoping that perhaps, she might just grant me an interview. Here is that letter that I wrote, dated, December 7th, 1987.

Dear Bella,

I felt I had to write to you to explain more fully the reasons for my partner and I's visit to your door on Sunday 6th December. Before I do, may I begin by informing you that I am the founder member of the research group Strange Phenomena Investigations, (SPI). Basically, we research cases relating to strange paranormal events up and down the country. We recognise that there is indeed a vast amount of data relating to strange phenomena throughout the U.K. which ought to be documented. We do not go into our research with any pre-conceived ideas, but with an open mind, documenting the facts as they are given. I personally have interviewed a good number of witnesses relating to their perception of apparitions and have found many of them very reliable and sincere.

As a serious researcher, I do not mock or ridicule these witnesses, I respect their views in what they have perceived, and if they wish that their name, or indeed their experience does not go any further, then I readily agree. The witness is my main concern, and I would never research a case if the witness did not wish me to. The reason then Bella for trying to get in touch with you, was to discuss the events in Park Crescent Sauchie relating to the 'poltergeist'. I was aware whilst coming to your door that you may not wish to discuss the matter, and I would like to state that it is not my intention to stir up any more memories of that time if you do not wish it so. I would respect your wish if this was the case.

SPI felt that the events in Park Crescent should be fairly documented, and, as a research group, we felt that a re-appraisal of the 1960 events should be re-documented by interviews with classmates of Virginia etc, whereby compiling the information into a booklet for possible inclusion in the Alloa Library. (Author's note, this was my intention at the time) *As the case was the biggest in the annals of Scottish Psychical research, we felt that as it was a local event, it should be portrayed in booklet form whereby the people of Clackmannanshire would realise that there still are things in the 20th century which man cannot explain but is certainly trying to. Obviously for any person not wishing to disclose their true name in the booklet, a pseudonym would be used. SPI as a group, feel that this important psychical event should be correctly told with no pre-conceived ideas or speculative conclusions, just disclose the facts as they stand. I have been clearly convinced, largely through my exposure to the facts of this case that these events were real and were not fraudulent in any way. The veracity of the evidence that has been accumulated in support of this type of phenomenon is impressive, and clearly this is the case regarding the Sauchie event. We feel that people are more or less left in the dark regarding knowledge of this type of phenomenon, and this is why we feel we should inform people that these things do occur. However, as I have said, if you feel that further research, or indeed a possible date to speak with you personally would be upsetting, then we would readily drop the whole matter. For witnesses of the family come before anything, and, as SPI have a code of conduct whereby, we do not infringe upon the witness if they wish it so, then we would respect their wishes.*

*So, in conclusion then Bella, we hope that you my realise
that we are a serious research group who's aims primarily are
to document the facts of this important case. People should be
made aware that these things do occur. Science should find
answers for them. Witnesses and researchers should work
together in harmony whereby hopefully discovering the key
answer which would unlock the poltergeist mystery. Is Virginia
now back in Ireland? Where can the audio and cine tapes of
this event be found? Would you be prepared to discuss these
events with us? We do hope so, but we will respect your wishes
if you do not. I have enclosed a stamped addressed envelope
for your reply, or you may telephone me at my home on the
number at the top of this page.*

Yours Very Sincerely,
Malcolm Robinson
Strange Phenomena Investigations.

Well sadly I never received a reply to that letter, which,
admittedly is understandable. My guess is that they just wanted
to file all this away and not bring it up ever again, in any way
shape or form. And whilst writing this book people have said to
me, shouldn't I just leave all this alone, that its best left in the
past and let Virginia get on with her life? Yes, to a degree that
is true. But we have to remind ourselves that the Sauchie
Poltergeist didn't just feature in Scottish and English
newspapers, it went right around the world. It's been featured
on radio broadcasts and the principle and only serious
researcher who was involved in this case. Mr A.R.G. Owen
included it in his book, 'Can We Explain the Poltergeist' (1964.
New York Garrett) so in effect, it really is public knowledge.
All I am trying to do with this book is to bring the Sauchie
Poltergeist up to speed and present some new and very
interesting facts that I have accrued over the years. With any
historical event, if one has uncovered some new and relevant
facts, either on any UFO or Paranormal story, or indeed any
historical event, then it's that person's duty to provide those
facts. Knowledge is for the people, and to retain, or hide away
any information which might prove relevant to the study of the
poltergeist, then that individual is not doing themselves any

favours. Information is for the people, and not for filing cabinets.

Somewhat disheartened after the door being slammed firmly in my face and not receiving a response to my letter, I foolishly abandoned all plans to keep searching for further people involved. However, thankfully that passion and desire to find out more, re-surfaced, and seven years later (1994) I was once more chasing potential witnesses to those events of yester year.

But first, and before I get into my re-investigation of this most impressive case, let me take you the reader, a trip down paranormal lane, and take a look at those horrible and alarming events that occurred to the Campbell household in those winter months of 1960.

THE EVENTS AS THEY HAPPENED.

The Sauchie Poltergeist effectively began back in November 1960 when an eleven girl by the name of Virginia Campbell came to Scotland with her mother, leaving behind other family and friends from the small village of Moville in County Donegal Ireland. Virginia's mother Annie had come to Sauchie (a small town near Alloa in Central Scotland) in October 1960 to live with her married 30 year old brother Thomas and his wife Isabella at a house in Park Crescent Sauchie. Virginia's father James remained back in Moville for a while to sell the family farm. Virginia's mother wasn't always at home, as she had found a job in the nearby town of Dollar which offered accommodation, this of course, didn't help the already distressed feelings of young Virginia, who at this point in her young life, had her father over in Ireland, and her mother being out of the house most days whilst at work. Not only was her life upside down at this point, what accentuated her distress even further, was the fact that she had to leave behind in Ireland, her beloved wee dog Toby, and also her friend Annie. So here we have Virginia living in a strange country away from her friends and pet dog with just her mother, it goes without saying, that for those early months where she was settling down to it all, it must have been difficult to adjust. What made matters worse, was that Virginia didn't even have her own bed in Sauchie she had to share a bed with her niece Margaret (9). Isabella's other son Derek (6) had his own room in the house. Indeed, someone who knew the Campbell's at that time was reported as saying.

"They gave the impression of people who had lived for a long time in a remote and isolated place"

Virginia was an attractive girl with blonde hair and sparkling blue eyes. As with any young child leaving behind their family and friends and moving to a strange place, Virginia was at first most unhappy but at the same time accepted that her parents wanted the best for her, as this move was also a big move for the rest of her family. The first few weeks were fine and trouble free, but soon the peace was broken by numerous scratching noises which came from various parts of the house, noises that no family member could account for. However, as the weeks progressed the strange noises increased in intensity and proved quite unsettling. As if the noises were not bad enough, the family noticed that various household items would disappear only to return at a later date. Ornaments would move of their own accord with no one near them. But probably the most unsettling and terrifying occurrence during these early weeks, was when the furniture starting to move around the living room of their own volition, and various doors throughout the house would open and close when no one was near them.

A TABLE OF EVENTS

Tuesday November 22nd, 1960

Below, are but some of the many bizarre events that occurred in the Campbell household, as you will see, something happened on a daily basis over 7 days. As far as we know, the bizarre and inexplicable events began on November 22nd, 1960. A short while after both Virginia and her nine year old niece Margaret had gone to bed, they complained of some strange noises that were occurring in their room. Virginia's aunt and uncle were both sitting downstairs and heard all this commotion and the uncle shouted up to the children to be quiet, that it was just their imagination. Deciding that enough was enough, both girls quickly jumped out of bed and ran downstairs, as they did so, what sounded like a large invisible ball, was heard bouncing down behind them, hitting every step. Both girls then rushed into the living room in an extremely frightened state but were told to go straight back to bed by Virginia's aunt and uncle. Reluctantly both girls slowly walked back upstairs to their bedroom, and were tucked in. However, no sooner had both Virginia's aunt and uncle shut the door, then they too, heard these knocking sounds. Rushing in, they could see that the sounds were emanating from the girls headboard, and yet both girls' arms were under the covers! Seeing this, both the aunt and uncle decided to place both girls in another bedroom in the house, but yet again, as soon as both girls were in bed, the bizarre knocking sounds once more rattled out from the headboard. Thankfully, the noises abated when young Virginia fell asleep.

Wednesday November 23rd, 1960

The following day, November 23rd, it was decided to keep Virginia off school, however, if the Campbell family felt that they would be getting any peace from all these unusual disturbances, then they were to be proved wrong. It was the early part of the evening, and members of the Campbell family were all congregated in the living room. Virginia was sitting in an armchair next to a sideboard, when all of a sudden, this sideboard started to move five inches out from the wall all by itself then gently move back to where it had came from. Although Virginia was sitting near it, it was noted than she did not touch it. More knockings were heard coming from all over the house of which apparently even the neighbours heard!

Eventually both girls (Virginia and Margaret) were sent to bed. Thomas and Isabella knew that strange things were afoot and decided to get in touch with their local reverend; the Reverend Mr. T. W. Lund, a minister from the local Church of Scotland. I'm sure the Revered Lund must have been wondering what he was getting himself into as he approached the front door of the Campbell house just after midnight. Reverend Lund was then briefed about what was taking place in the family home and decided to see if he could offer any help, and more importantly, find out for himself, exactly what was going on. As Reverend Lund entered Virginia and Margaret's room, he was astounded to hear these strange knocking sounds himself. These knocking sounds were clearly coming from the headboard and thinking that perhaps Virginia was somehow making these noises herself, he asked her to move down the bed to ensure that her head did not touch the headboard, believing that perhaps she had somehow been hitting the headboard with her head. However, even although Virginia was now away from the headboard, the noises still occurred. The Reverend Lund was more astonished to conclude that as the headboard was not actually touching the wall, then it couldn't even be people from next door who might be banging on the walls of which somehow might have reverberated through the wall making Virginia's headboard move, quite an improbable possibility, but one in which he may well have considered. It was therefore clear, that the knockings were actually coming from the headboard itself! To convince himself of this, the Reverend Lund actually placed his hand on the headboard itself and could feel the vibrations coming from it. Virginia was becoming upset at this point, and in a way to calm her down, The Reverend Lund joked that perhaps it was her boyfriend knocking on the headboard to get her attention, and jokingly stated to Virginia that perhaps she should knock back to him? It's not recorded what happened after this suggestion.

As if things could not get any more bizarre, they did! For at this point a large and heavy linen chest that stood near the foot of Virginia's bed, began to mysteriously, rock back and forth. The Reverend Lund stood transfixed at this peculiar sight, and was no doubt trying to fathom out what was going on. The linen chest then began to 'rise up from the floor' and in a jerking movement, moved towards Virginia's bed, almost toppling over as it did so. With eyes fixed on this bizarre scene, the linen chest then moved slowly back in the same wobbly manner to whence it came. Seeing this, Virginia was quite hysterical and Reverend Lund quickly moved over to Virginia to comfort her. After speaking with her a while, Virginia, become more relaxed and began to calm down. Then he suggested that Margaret should get back into bed with Virginia, and that both girls should try to get some sleep. No sooner had he said that, than violent consistent knocking began again, very insistently, as if to say that Margaret was not wanted in Virginia's bed. At this point, Margaret used another bed which was situated in the same room, and upon doing so, the knocking stopped for the night, and both girls fell soundly asleep.

Doing research for this book, I came across some further information about this particular night, which lends even more interest to this particular evening. Author Michael Clarkson describes more of what happened that night from his book, *'Poltergeist Phenomenon, an In-depth Investigation into Floating Beds'* published by Career Press/New Page Books (20 Jan. 2011) He had this to say about that particular night.

"The Reverend Lund Church of Scotland said he saw a large linen chest 27 inches by 17 inches weighing 50 lbs which was near the bed, rock sideways, it then raised itself off the floor, and travelled in a jerky motion parallel to the bed to a distance of around 18 inches and then move back to where it had come from. Reverend Lund and a neighbour, who did not want to be identified, said that they lifted the linen chest out of the bedroom and out into the top hallway. At this, very loud knocking was heard by both, coming from Virginia's headboard".

Thursday November 24th, 1960

A new day, but sadly another day where things were not letting up, the noises in the family home continued. Some china vases were seen to move by themselves when no one was near them. Not only that, during a period when Virginia's father was staying at the house, (by now, he had sold the family farm over in Ireland and was now in Sauchie himself) he too was suddenly subject to the antics of the poltergeist, where he stood aghast as he witnessed an apple rise out of a bowl of fruit. Not only this, he witnessed a sewing machine starting all by itself. I am pretty sure that all those in the house at this time, including young Virginia herself must have been terrified, what on Earth could be causing all this? That night, the Reverend Lund attended the family home, however on this occasion he was accompanied by local practitioner, Doctor W. H. Nisbet. Both men were about to witness some astonishing paranormal events, which no doubt would have tested their credulity to the max. Whilst both men were in Virginia's bedroom, (Virginia being in bed ready to go to sleep), they were both amazed to witness Virginia's pillow rotating about 60 degrees underneath Virginia's head whilst her head was resting upon it! Whilst all this was going on, there were more rappings and knockings heard throughout the room. The heavy linen chest again rocked and moved, then the lid of this linen chest opened and closed several times of its own accord, and on this particular night, a strange 'sawing noise' was heard. But probably the most incredible thing that both men saw on this particular night, was a strange 'rippling movement' which moved up and down the top bedcover of Virginia's bed. Virginia at this point, had the bedcovers pulled up tight, firmly against her chin and did not look to be in a position to be doing this herself.

Friday November 25th, 1960

When you thought things could not get any more bizarre 'they did'! Due to the frightening events that were occurring in the Campbell home, Virginia's aunt and uncle had, over the past few days, kept Virginia off school; believing no doubt, that she was in no fit state to concentrate on her school work. However, come what may, school beckoned, and on Friday the 25th of November, Virginia attended school probably in hopes of some peace and quiet, some time away from the house, where hopefully she could make new friends and settle down. Well not quite! Sadly, the poltergeist decided to follow her to school. More of that in a moment, but later on this day, Dr. Nisbet, again paid a visit to the Campbell home where he too, was astonished to see the large linen chest in Virginia's bedroom move about 12 inches from its original position with its lid opening and shutting several times of its own accord, not only that, he too saw this unusual rippling movement of Virginia's bed covers rippling up and down as if it was a was a small wave hitting the beach. Dr. Nisbet however, described this motion of the bedcovers, as more of a 'puckering' movement.

THE POLTERGEIST GOES TO SCHOOL!
Friday November 25th, 1960.

Sauchie Primary School was not all that far away from where the Campbell house was located in Park Crescent, probably less than a quarter mile. Apparently, Virginia's teacher, Miss Margaret Stewart, had initial difficulty in trying to communicate with Virginia, due to Virginia's strong Irish accent and her somewhat shyness. Let us not forget, Virginia was in a strange country and was about to mix with a whole load of school children all of whom she didn't know, so her apprehension of her new found situation may well have caused her to withdraw within herself. Other than that, there was no denying that Virginia was a normal young girl with average intelligence.

So, on Friday 25th November 1960 Virginia attended her local school for the very first time, hoping no doubt that all those strange and disturbing events were behind her. All was going well that day for a while, but then things started to change. Now back in the 1960's, school classrooms had way more children in them than we have today. On some occasions, there were upwards of 40 children in the one class. On this particular day, all the children in Virginia's class had their heads bent down busily writing away on their school jotters, apart that is, for young Virginia. Virginia was struggling with her desk lid, as it seemed to have a life of its own. With her forearms, Virginia was pushing down firmly on her desk lid, at which point her class teacher, Mrs Margaret Stewart, looked up and saw this strange spectacle. She could clearly see that Virginia was struggling with her desk lid but was unsure what

94

was going on. Thinking that perhaps Virginia was 'fooling around' and that perhaps Virginia had her knees up under the desk trying to force it into the air, she gave Virginia a stare as if to say stop it, then shouted out;

"Virginia what are you doing"? To which Virginia replied, *"Nothing Miss honest"* To which the teacher replied, *"Stop that at once Virginia."*

As soon as Virginia took her forearms away from the desk, the desk lid was flapping up and down. The screams of Virginia's classmates as they looked upon this spectacle, resounded throughout the room. Virginia's teacher looked on, open mouthed in disbelief. After no doubt settling the classroom down, the teacher resumed with that day's studies but it would appear that the poltergeist was not finished yet, for later that day a girl who sat behind Virginia had asked the teacher's permission to return her library book. She stood up and left her desk approaching Miss Stewart. At this point, Miss Stewart watched astonished, as the girl's empty desk, began to rise slowly upwards, until it was around an inch off the floor. It stayed there, suspended in the air for a moment, and then gently lowered itself back down to the floor. At this juncture, Miss Stewart got out of her chair and went over to the empty desk to see if she could find any way in which this desk could have risen up into the air all by itself, needless to say, she couldn't find any cause for this desk to have managed this feat on its own! As Miss Stewart returned to her own desk, she approached Virginia surmising that perhaps all these strange events had something to do with her, said.

"Are you feeling better Virginia"? To which Virginia is reported to have said, *"There's nothing wrong with me, Miss Stewart."*

Later that same day, the Reverend T.W. Lund paid another visit to the Campbell home to see how Virginia had got on at school, and proceeded to ask her how her day had been, to which she was reported to have said;

95

"All right, but something funny happened when I was there. When my teacher was standing near my desk, the lid of another desk went up all by itself."

I will come back to those strange events in Virginia's school shortly, but for now let us continue with our timeline of strange and daily events.

Saturday November 26th, 1960

As far as we know 'that has been recorded for this day', other than Virginia's pillow once more rotating underneath her head, and her bedcovers rippling up and down, Saturday was pretty quiet.

Sunday November 27th, 1960

On Sunday November 27th, Virginia was observed to go into some kind of weird trance and became hysterical. She was calling out for her dog Toby and her friend Anna, whom we have learned, were back in Ireland. This wasn't the only occasion where Virginia had gone into a trance like state.

Monday November 28th, 1960

After Friday the 25th of November's strange happenings in the school, Virginia was I dare say, would be hoping that those strange events would not repeat themselves. Well sadly, that was not to be. On this particular day Virginia approached her teacher's desk to lay down her school essay which she had been working on, at which point a long cane blackboard pointer which was lying on the teacher's desk, began to vibrate, moving until it fell on the floor. The teacher's desk then started to vibrate, at which point the teacher placed her hands down onto the desk's surface and could feel these strange vibrations. Then, as if by magic, the teacher's desk slowly began to lift a few inches off the floor then swung around 90 degrees counter clockwise and moved away from the teacher. Virginia at this point was just a foot or so away from the teacher's desk, looking on at this amazing spectacle whereupon she burst out crying saying.

"Please Miss, I'm not doing it, honest I'm not"

To which Miss Stewart calmly said,

"It's all right, just help me straighten up my desk"

I should point out here that my cousin, June Robinson (Murray) sadly no longer with us, was in Virginia's class and she told me that she saw some papers floating up from Virginia's teacher's desk. She was also in the class the day that Virginia's teacher's cane started to vibrate, rise up, and fall off the table followed by the teacher's desk rising up from the floor a few inches, then turning around 90 degrees at which the whole class screamed and ran for the class room door.

Later that afternoon, after school, it was decided no doubt by Virginia's parents, to allow Virginia some respite, and it was agreed that she should stay for a few days, with an aunt over at the town of Dollar, which was six miles away. Sadly, like the school, the poltergeist, or whatever was causing these effects, followed her to Dollar and the usual knockings and rapping's could be heard coming from all over that house as well.

Thursday December 1st, 1960

By now the Campbell family were at their wits end, and they once more sought the help of their local G.Ps. Dr. W.H. Nisbet, who lived in the nearby village of Tillicoultry. He attended the home, as did fellow practitioner Dr. William Logan. Joining them on this night, were three Church of Scotland Ministers, including the Reverend T.H. Lund, who had already attended the family home. On this occasion they were to do things differently! At around 11:00pm The Reverend Lund and three other Church of Scotland Ministers conducted a divine intercession service. This they later stressed was 'not' an exorcism, but a completely separate service. During this fifteen minute 'service,' many loud knocking and sawing like noises were heard. Also, on this particular night, Dr. Nisbet and Dr. Logan brought along with them, an audio tape recorder and a cine camera in hopes that they could manage to record these sounds as proof for those who were doubtful. This proved successful, as they managed to capture a number of strange audio noises comprising of 'rasping and sawing sounds' as well as loud knocks. More disturbingly however was when both the doctors and the ministers observed Virginia having some kind of hysteria where she was observed to be babbling and in some kind of trance. These recordings were later broadcast on a BBC radio Scotland programme called 'Scope'. (More of which later) It should also be pointed out, that Dr. William Logan's wife Sheila, herself also a doctor, also attended the Campbell home, but not, as far as I am to believe, on that occasion. (More from Dr. Sheila Logan later) It's been stated elsewhere, that after this 'service,' both doctors decided that in order to stop any further publicity surrounding the family, they stated that they had affected a 'cure' on young Virginia. That may well have been the case, because after that 'service', things did appear to settle down and were less frequent in their intensity. Virginia eventually made a friend at Sauchie School by the name of Elizabeth Brown, and, as children are often want to do, a name was given to Virginia's poltergeist, she called it, *'Wee Hughie'*.

Of course, bizarre events of this nature do not go unnoticed, and soon all these strange occurrences were the talk of Sauchie. We have to remind ourselves that there were no mobile phones or internet back in 1960, but that didn't stop word spreading around all the other Clackmannanshire towns and villages, and soon it was big news. Not just locally, but soon to be, nationally. Soon reporters were knocking on the door of not just the Campbell household, but neighbours doors as well. Pressmen appeared at the school, each one looking for an exclusive. We shall cover the newspaper involvement shortly.

1961
Monday January 23rd, 1961

Things were slowly quieting down, but one notable thing that did transpire, was again back in Virginia's classroom, where a bowl of bulbs flew off teacher Margaret Stewart's desk, and guess who placed those bulbs on Miss Stewart's desk? Yes, Virginia. Other than some sporadic strange happenings back at home, which consisted of pretty much as before, knockings and rapping's and on one occasion there was the sound of someone walking along the bedroom floor, things were getting quieter, that said, there was the occasional invisible poke on the bodies and legs of both Virginia and her niece Margaret, which, apparently also happened to a visitor in the house, although I can't substantiate that. It's been stated by others that by March 1961, the poltergeist effects had completely disappeared, much I dare say, to the joy of the Campbell Household. Virginia's dog Toby was eventually reunited with her, and overall, Virginia appeared to be more of her old self.

HOW THE LOCAL NEWSPAPERS COVERED THE STORY IN 1960

Before I present my updates on this story, let me give you the reader the events as they were transcribed by the local newspaper at the time, 'The Alloa Journal'. For this, I had to delve into the microfilm archives at the local Alloa library a small town near to Sauchie. Boy, what an afternoon that was, phew, it was like going back in time, well in a sense it was! A full afternoon was spent in the library going through page after page of microfilm. The following are but extracts from both the Alloa Advertiser and the Alloa Journal, the full transcripts can be found later in this book which extends the bizarreness of these puzzling events. The following are extracts from the Alloa Journal of 2nd December 1960. In part it reads.

"Just over a week ago strange things began to happen to Virginia. Heavy pieces of furniture were seen to move when

99

she entered a room, doors opened when she approached them and then were found difficult to shut. Worried and anxious, Virginia's brother asked the Reverend T. Lund to try and help and also Doctor W.H. Nisbet of Tillicoultry who was the Campbell's family doctor. Both men have been greatly impressed with what they have been told and with what they themselves have seen". "Their concern for the well being of Virginia and their family had increased during the past week because of the effect which gossip, and publicity are having upon them". "Before she came to Scotland, Virginia lost a pet dog of which she was very fond of and a little girlfriend died. Both of these occurrences upset her very much. One night when sitting on the edge of Virginia's bed, Mrs Campbell was roughly pushed off, and as she stood watching, she saw the blankets and sheets rising and falling above Virginia while the child made little moaning sounds like someone in pain"

The Alloa Journal in this very large article goes on at great length to state that Reverend Lund and Doctor Nisbet refused to make any public statements or comments regarding this case. As the days wore on, further and more worrying strange events occurred within the Campbell household. The National press soon got wind of the story, and soon the village of Sauchie was awash with reporters. The Alloa Journal in this 2nd of December 1960 article goes on...

"Mr James Henderson, Secretary of the Alloa Spiritualist Church said, "In my opinion, this little girl has certain unusual psychic qualities and I am convinced that some person who has passed on is trying to communicate through her". "I believe that a responsible medium should be taken to see the little girl, for such a person could certainly help her". "The medium might be able to take over from Virginia, the pressure which is being put on her from the other side, and so bring relief to her". "I am convinced that this little girl, if properly looked after spiritually, might be able to help many hundreds of people as the late Helen Duncan did"

(Helen Duncan was a famous Scottish psychic medium that was arrested and charged with witchcraft during the Second World War). Her 'crime' was to channel information allegedly from the spirit world concerning a British warship that had been sunk '**before**' the Admiralty had even released the news to the public.)

Also mentioned in the Alloa Journal of 1960, was Mr James McNee, a spokesperson for the Spiritualist National Church. He was quoted as saying.

"Happenings such as are taking place with this little girl are not nearly so unusual as many people think, and contrary to much popular opinion they are not necessarily evil in nature. Children are much more alive psychically than are adults and are often although unconsciously, real mediums. If much of what is called their 'blethers' (stories) was seriously examined, they would be discovered to contain communications from people who have passed on."

From the Alloa Journal's sister paper the Alloa Advertiser, I take the following quotes.

"Dr Nisbet said, "Virginia is not responsible for what has happened". "The child is innocent". "What has taken place was not conjured by the child herself, an outside agent is responsible". "Believe me, something unfortunate has been going on in that house". "The girl was hysterical all the time the phenomenon was appearing". "We decided then to try sedation". "Virginia was given mild tranquillisers to quieten her". "If the phenomenon were being conjured by her own imagination, they would no longer appear if her brain was dulled". "But even though the brain was not working normally, the phenomenon 'STILL APPEARED'"

It didn't take long before the story leaked out in the national press and it became the case that the Campbell's were virtually prisoners in their own home. Other family members as well as friends were tracked down by the national media hacks, all of

101

whom were out for a good story, and if they couldn't get it, I dare say they would make it up! And try as they might, Virginia's family were unable to protect her from the continuous pressure, and inevitably the strain began to tell. Meanwhile, the events intensified. The Alloa Journal of 16th Dec. 1960 reports,

"Two Tillicoultry doctors used a tape recording of sound phenomena that had been heard during the 'psychic illness' of little Virginia Campbell, In the Scottish Home Service programme 'Scope on Tuesday'. The sounds in themselves were not terrifying, but when a child's voice started screaming 'Mummy, Mummy'; that happened when Virginia saw the lid of a linen basket starting to open, the doctors explained that it was then that the listeners realised that something unusual was happening" *"Mr. MacDonald, Reverend of St. George's West Church, in Edinburgh, described the sounds and movements witnessed, and he considered that there were two possible explanations, and he favoured the explanation that the phenomena were caused by some 'lower forms of intelligence"*

It's fair to say that whilst all this was going on the Church of Scotland throughout all these traumatic events was non-committal which is no real surprise I suppose, as the Church tends to distance themselves from events such as this. An official at the Kirk's Edinburgh headquarters said,

"The girl is entirely in the care of her doctor and minister. Her whole future and mental stability will depend on peace and quiet. This is entirely a personal thing".

Even after all that the Reverend Lund had witnessed, he was still of the opinion that the poltergeist originated from within Virginia Campbell herself, and did not believe that it was an 'outside agent' a poltergeist, spirit, call it what you will. Apparently, his view was also shared by both Miss Margaret Stewart (Virginia's school teacher) and Dr. Logan too. Incidentally it's worth noting that Dr. Logan's wife (also a doctor) attended the Campbell home, on one occasion, along with her husband, and whilst she was quite sceptical of what was going on, after hearing these bizarre knocking and sawing sounds herself, she quickly came to realise that 'something' was going on, but what that 'something' was, was open to conjecture. One thing to also note, was that Dr. Sheila Logan traced these strange sounds to a point in mid air, near Virginia's bed! We will hear more from former Doctor Sheila Logan in this book.

After my fact finding afternoon in the Alloa Library looking back through the old micro fiche files of the Alloa Advertiser, I decided to start a re-investigation of the facts in an attempt to find out for sure, if all which was said before on this case was true and factual. Local people were still talking about this most fascinating case, and in 1994 I decided to look back into this case once more, and see what I could find, I was not to be disappointed.

THE AUTHOR'S 1994 RE-INVESTIGATION OF THE SAUCHIE POLTERGEIST.

I initially looked at this case in 1987 but never got anywhere, however, I had more success in 1994 when I looked at it again. I first of all decided to launch an appeal through the local Alloa newspapers for anyone who knew Virginia Campbell to come forward with any information concerning the events of 1960/61, fortunately a local lady, (who wished to remain anonymous), who although had not been in Virginia's class, was friendly with her teacher at Sauchie Primary School she kindly supplied me with the telephone number of the teacher, formerly Miss Margaret Stewart, but since her marriage to a minister, was now Mrs Margaret Davidson. I remember that call well. As I lifted up the receiver and started to dial the number, I thought that if anyone could confirm or deny these amazing claims, then it would certainly have been Virginia's teacher, I was not to be disappointed. Here is what transpired on that telephone call when I spoke to Margaret (Virginia's teacher) Margaret stated.

"Virginia was a shy withdrawn girl, but very pleasant and although she wasn't really forthcoming, she was in every other way quite normal. She was also good at her lessons. I had never really heard the word poltergeist before, indeed, I thought it was the name of some kind of medicine, that's how naïve I was. The first time I became aware of anything strange, was when I had given the class an essay to do. The class was quiet, and all the children had their heads bent down over their jotters busily writing away. In 1960 we still had the old desks that had a lid top. Anyway, I looked over at Virginia and noticed that she was sitting with both hands pressed firmly down on top of her desk lid. I rose from my chair and walked over to Virginia. I was then surprised to see the desk lid rise and fall with Virginia trying her best to keep it shut with her hands".

"At this point a child in front of Virginia rose to take her jotter over to my desk, no sooner had she left her seat, than her desk rose a few inches off the floor on its four legs. I then explained to the class that I would be back I a few minutes, and during this time I went to see the school headmaster, a Mr. Peter Hill. I told him that there was something funny going on in my classroom and explained to him what I had just seen. Mr. Hill said that he had heard talk of strange things going on in the Campbell household. He then asked to see Virginia and asked me to explain to her classmates that Virginia would be going home for a few days because she was feeling unwell. I was also to say that there might be talk from others of ghosts centred around her, but they were not to believe this, that they were just rumours, this is what he more or less told me to say"

"Anyway, I went back to the classroom and summoned Virginia over and told her the headmaster wanted to talk to her. As Virginia left the room, I found that I could not shut the door behind her and had to summon help from three of the children to help me push the door shut. I remember saying to the class, "It must be very windy today!" Virginia was not distressed at this time. I then mentioned to the class of what the headmaster *had told me to say, and I found that the class was quite responsive and very supportive".*

THE VIBRATING TABLE
(Monday 28th November 1960)

Margaret went on to tell me.

"The most unnerving thing that I experienced in the classroom, was when on one occasion, I was sitting behind my large oak table, Virginia was standing at the other side of the table with her hands clasped firmly behind her back. Suddenly, a large blackboard pointer cane which was lying flat on my table, started to 'vibrate'. At first it vibrated slowly, and then increased as the seconds wore on. I sat transfixed looking at this, then the table, which was quite heavy, started to rise up slowly into the air, and also vibrated. I put my hands on the table and tried to push it back down but with no success. I was quite horrified, but it did not stop there. The table continued to vibrate as it hovered a few inches off the floor. Then the table rotated through 90 degrees, so that where I had moments before sat behind the long edge of the table, the table had rotated so that its narrow edge was now directly in front of my stomach. I looked up at Virginia and saw that she was quite distressed, and I remember her saying, "Please miss, I'm not doing that honest I'm not". I calmed her down, just then, a bowl of flower bulbs shot straight across the table".

Margaret went on to discuss with me, other aspects of strange events that had occurred within the classroom, more so the school jotters (books) which would rise up into the air and move away from the direction of where Virginia was at the time. These objects never seemed to move towards Virginia, they always moved in a direction 'away' from her. Margaret also informed me that she had noticed that strange things seemed to occur on a 28-day cycle!

SUPPORTIVE CLASSMATES.

During this time, the newspaper hacks hounded poor Virginia at school but thankfully Virginia's classmates were incredibly supportive to her. Indeed, on one occasion as the pressmen gathered at the school gates, a classmate of Virginia's who bore a striking resemblance to Virginia, put on Virginia's coat and rushed from the school building going towards a different direction from where Virginia lived. Hot on the heels of this masquerading Virginia, were the merry band of pressmen hot in pursuit, what happened when they caught up with the copycat Virginia was not stated. Margaret also mentioned to me, that she too was hounded by the press, and went on to say that there were two incidents that stood out at the time both of which were complete and utter crazy

One story concerned a woman who asked if she could touch her (Virginia) because she was, *"One of God's chosen ones"*. She also recalls receiving a letter from a Witch doctor in Africa who advised her to, *"Pound down some bones and dance over them"*, this, she was told, might get rid of Virginia's ghosts. The Church of Scotland arrived at Sauchie Primary School and held a service in the classroom, this was not an exorcism Margaret explained, this however failed to work. And events continued in their absurdity. Margaret concluded the interview with me on the phone by saying,

"These events really did happen, Mr Robinson, I remember them as if it was yesterday, I'll never forget them".

A MAJOR WITNESS RECOLLECTS.

As stated earlier in this book, I did partly mention the Sauchie Poltergeist case in my second book, Paranormal Case Files of Great Britain (Volume 1) Published by Publish Nation and available on Amazon and Lulu, and the following of which you are about to read was presented in that book. It is the testimony of one James Carruthers, not his real name, but a pseudonym. I stated in my second book that the reason that I gave him a pseudonym, was simply because, and I quote.

"I must humbly confess to the reader that the identity of Mr Carruthers I have now lost through time and various house moves. I am meticulous when it comes to investigations and the like, with the recording of names and addresses, but this one, seems to have been lost".

Well whilst doing research for this book, I uncovered in some packed away files, the identity of Mr Carruthers, and his testimony matched to a tee what I wrote about him in my second book. Mr Carruthers was none other than Dr. Logan, yes, that's right, I DID speak to Dr. Logan, and looking through my notes, I have the date of the 14th of February 1994 when I spoke to him. When I had briefly wrote about the Sauchie Poltergeist in my second book (Paranormal Case Files of Great Britain (Volume 1) my papers and notes on that case got mislaid, and to find them again after all these years was a blessing whilst compiling all the new evidence for this book. Dr. Logan as we know was one of the main witnesses to the strange phenomenon in the Campbell home, and the following comes from a telephone call that I made to him. He stated.

"On one occasion, I was in Virginia's bedroom with a number of other individuals and I was standing close to the bed in which Virginia was lying, she had the bedcovers pulled up to her chin. Suddenly I observed the covers making a' rippling movement' from the bottom of the bed right up to her chin. I am convinced that Virginia did not produce this effect, there was no movement from below the covers, i.e. from her legs, just this peculiar rippling movement running up and down the top bedcover".

Dr. Logan continued...

"Seconds later, I then observed the pillow next to Virginia which had been plumped up, suddenly take on what appeared to me the shape of someone's head. A clear indentation of the

107

pillow was seen by myself and others in the room. Now during this time, strange knockings, banging's, and scratchings and what sounded like 'sawing noises,' were coming from all over the room, you couldn't really pin point the exact source of the noise, 'it was coming from everywhere'. Most unusual was the sound of what appeared to be like a ping pong ball constantly being bounced. Virginia was quite distressed by all this. On another occasion when the Church of Scotland were in attendance in the home, these noises, these banging's and rapping's intensified during the exorcism ceremony, they were really loud I remembered the church members started singing 'The Lord is my Shepherd".

Dr. Logan went on,

"Someone mentioned at this time that animals are to some degree psychic, so I decided to test this theory and I took my pet dog along to the Campbell house and even although these same knockings and rappings could be heard in Virginia's bedroom, my dog was at no time disturbed by it all. My feelings on the matter are that these events have nothing to do with ghosts or spirits. I believe that the shift in environment from a rural farming community life in Ireland, leaving behind her friends and such and coming over to Scotland, was, in a sense, a bit of a trauma and that somehow, this suppressed emotion was externalised to objects and items close to Virginia".

Dr. Logan also stated to me during this phone call, that he remembered seeing a diary, which was kept by an uncle of Virginia at that time, and there was an entry in it that stated that marks 'appeared and disappeared' on Virginia's hands but he had never seen these marks himself.

I must admit that I had hoped for a better response from the readers of the Alloa Advertiser to my request for people to contact me with information on this case, but we have to consider the fact that any witnesses to this phenomenon, may have moved away from the area, I myself now live in Hastings.

Also, you will have people who are reluctant to talk about what they themselves saw. I did, however, track down and interview two of Virginia's classmates who, confirmed the events of which their teacher had experienced.

AFTER THOUGHTS ON MY 1994
RE-INVESTIGATION

I must admit I really enjoyed looking back at the Sauchie Poltergeist case (Probably Scotland's biggest ever case of its kind). My telephone call to Virginia's school teacher proved very illuminating, 'how I wish that I had have been in Virginia's class at that time to see all these weird and paranormal events'. Now whether you subscribe to the belief that 'spirits' were involved here, or, as Dr. Logan puts it, that Virginia 'herself' through this 'suppressed emotion', somehow caused these events to occur, is a matter of some debate. What is abundantly clear is the fact that these events DID occur, and they were witnessed by sound and very reliable high standing people in the community. The village of Sauchie was, as the Alloa Advertiser so aptly put it, 'Descended' upon by swarms of the press like one of the plagues of Egypt'

And me, what do I believe regarding this 'suppressed emotion'? Well considering the state that the world is in right now, there must be countless millions of people suffering from this so called, 'suppressed emotion' and I don't think that strange events are occurring to them. Dr. Nisbet, who attended Virginia, saw a heavy linen chest rise up from the floor. Now dear reader, I'm sure you would agree that it would take some 'suppressed emotion' to cause that! 'Suppressed Emotion' or Poltergeist? We could argue about it all day. Whether it's one or the other, or a combination of both, one thing is for sure, these events are so fascinating to researchers the world over, but obviously not so to the people involved. It should also be noted, that another researcher, one Michael Clarkson, also noted that both Virginia and Margaret's pyjamas were rolled up across their bodies whilst in bed, however, I have been unable to substantiate that particular claim with any other testimony that I have come across. The events eventually decreased in their intensity and by March 1961, they had stopped entirely. Virginia was more settled at school, and she had made a friend by the name of Elizabeth Brown and was re-united with her little dog Toby.

Before we look at my 2020 re-investigation of the Sauchie case I should point out here that this case was investigated my Mr. A.R.G. Owen as the following will showcase.

ALAN ROBERT GEORGE OWEN'S INVOLVEMENT IN THE SAUCHIE POLTERGEIST.

As stated earlier in the book, I was only three years old at the time when the Sauchie Poltergeist was plying its trade; I would not be involved in paranormal research for another 19 to 20 years. A case like this would have been paranormal gold for me, but there you are, too young, too soon. One man who did come to Scotland to research this case, certainly had the pedigree to do so, his name was Alan Robert George Owen. But before we go into what Mr Owen thought about the Sauchie Poltergeist case, let us find out a little about this man himself.

Mr Owen was certainly the man for the job when it came to look for poltergeists. He was a University lecturer, a geneticist, and a mathematician but before he would look to the paranormal world, he played his part in World War 11 where he invented a radar aerial for the British Army. Educated at Cambridge University, he graduated with a Bachelor of Arts in Mathematics and also physics and received a Master of Arts as well as a Ph.D. in mathematical genetics. Later in life, Mr Owen would have a particular strong interest in matters pertaining to the unexplained, and would go on to write three books on these subjects, the most well known being, 'Can We Explain the Poltergeist?' (1964) in which the Sauchie case is mentioned. But it was to the poltergeist effect that Mr Owen was mostly interested in, and this interest saw him becoming a member of the prestigious British Society for Psychical Research (SPR) and also the American Society for Psychical Research.

110

Doing research for this book, I came across an interesting account written by A.R.G. Owen and his colleague Victor Sims in an article entitled, 'Science and the Spook' published in 1971. I felt it relevant to quote from it here, as it details Mr Owens trip north to Scotland

"In late November and early December 1960, accounts appeared in the national press of what seemed to be poltergeist doings that took place in Virginia's presence. Until that time, I was a sceptic, but I was impressed by something in the tone of the newspaper reports which conveyed to me that for once this was the real thing. I corresponded with the people who had been mentioned in the papers as being concerned with the case in their professional capacity, and after Christmas, went up to Sauchie, the suburb of Alloa where Virginia lived. I discovered incidentally that a letter seems to take as long to get to Scotland now as it did in the time of that pioneer parapsychologist Charles l namely, three days!"

"When I arrived at Alloa I found that, not untypically, things had died down before the investigator had reached the scene. But instead of wending south again in disgust, as some researchers have been known to do, I took the precaution to take down detailed and circumstantial accounts from eyewitnesses. These were five in number, professional people whose contact with the family had previously been very remote or non-existent. I then realised that I had stumbled on a scientific treasure beyond price, incontrovertible testimony as to the reality of poltergeist phenomena. It was agreed by all, that a change of scene might be beneficial, and so Virginia was sent for a few days to her aunt at the nearby town of Dollar. Here no objects moved but each evening knockings sounded all over the house".

After his investigation, Mr Owen headed back south to England, realising that there was indeed something strange happening in the Campbell household, but that this 'force' was somehow connected to young Virginia herself. He of course wrote up his thoughts on the Sauchie case in the book that I have mentioned above *'Can We Explain the Poltergeist?'* which also featured other bewildering poltergeist cases. And he has been quoted as saying the following about his involvement with the Sauchie case.

"In my opinion the Sauchie case must be regarded as establishing beyond all reasonable doubt the objective reality of some poltergeist phenomena. There is no evidence indicating the separate existence of 'the poltergeist' as a discarnate entity. The phenomena are consistent with production by forces emanating from the child or else resident in space and 'triggered off' by some influence emanating from her. Regarding the supply of energy required for the manifestations, it is clear that this is within the physiological capacity of a healthy girl of eleven. However, it is quite conceivable that she provided no appreciable amount of energy this may have come from the potential energy of some unknown force field in the space around her. Virginia's contribution may, mechanically speaking, has been to trigger off the operation of this force field at certain points. "It seems evident that the physical phenomena observed by the key witnesses are incompatible with trickery by Virginia, or by other children or adults".

What I have also learned about Mr Owen's investigation into this case, was his meticulous digging into other potential answers to account for what went on in the Campbell house. Some of these theories may sound outlandish, but I too, certainly would have investigated them, for not to do so, would have been foolish and not in keeping with professional paranormal research. For instance, he checked for any medical condition with Virginia, such as, was she prone to hallucinations etc? He also looked at atmospheric conditions, could they have played a part in being misconstrued as paranormal effects? He also looked at the geology of the Park Crescent area to see if perhaps some of these paranormal effects were the result of earth tremors. And whilst is his statement that the Sauchie case must be regarded as establishing beyond all reasonable doubt the objective reality of some poltergeist phenomena, he still felt that the emotional aspect surrounding

112

Virginia and the stress of leaving Ireland to come to Scotland had made things more difficult for young Virginia to adjust. She would often talk in her sleep, there was also the fact that both her parents would be out the house working on their respective jobs. She was going through puberty, and whilst these in themselves might not be reasons to cause poltergeist phenomena, they had to be considered. And whilst Mr Owen was at Sauchie to get to the truth of the matter, he was not there to 'get rid' of the poltergeist, although I dare say that if he could, he would have. The Sauchie case played a big part in Mr Owen's life, and it was a case that he would regularly talk about on the lecture circuit. I dare say that the Sauchie case left a lasting impression on him. He would later marry his sweetheart Iris and retire to Canada. But I am not entirely finished with Mr Owen. Whilst compiling this book, a fellow UFO and Paranormal researcher by the name of Steve Wills from Warminster in Wilshire England, kindly placed on my Facebook page, a You Tube Video entitled, *'Can We Explain the Poltergeist'?* It was a BBC documentary filmed in 1965, four years after the Sauchie Poltergeist. The presenter of this intriguing documentary was none other than Mr. A.R.G. Owen. George Owen, (as we have read earlier) was the only professional researcher into the Sauchie Poltergeist case. The following is a short transcript of that programme which features the Sauchie segment, other parts of this intriguing documentary, contained interviews with other people who had in one-way shape or form, encountered the wrath of the poltergeist. Mr. Owen starts off by stating to the viewer.

"In Scotland, in Sauchie, a few years back. A little girl, 11 years old, Virginia Campbell was the centre of intense poltergeist activity observed by many reliable witnesses including the family physician, Doctor William Logan. He was called into the case because at school, a teacher had seen a desk rise and float about two inches above the ground. Doctor Logan recalls some of his experiences of five years ago"

Doctor William Logan now takes up the story.

"My first involvement with the Virginia Campbell poltergeist was on the evening of Saturday the 26th of November 1961".

(Author's note, this is of course incorrect, Doctor Logan is a year out, his first visit was on the 26th of November 1960)

"I was called to the house because of the incidents and happenings that had been taken place there during that night, and as it turned out, on previous nights. When I arrived at the house, the householders were in a state of excitement and tension, and they informed me that there had been knockings and noises and pieces of furniture being moved, and that something odd was going on. So, I went up to see the child who was lying in bed looking fairly relaxed despite the obvious commotion that had been going on. And I asked her to try and forget as much as possible that I was in the room beside her. After I had been in the room for oh say, 10 or 15 minutes, I noticed that one of the pillows beside Virginia was beginning to move in rather an unusual fashion"

(Author's note. Dr. Logan describes to the viewers what he saw next)

"If you imagine Virginia lying with her head on this pillow here, (Author's note Dr. Logan pointed to a pillow) *and another pillow beside her and this pillow started to turn in a rotatory fashion. In addition, I noticed that there was an impression, or indentation beginning to occur as if something was either pulling, from the inside or pushing, but there was no obvious physical force being moved about. I checked thoroughly that Virginia herself was in no position to bring about these odd movements both by observation and by checking her position, her hands, and feet. Furthermore, there was no other person close enough to Virginia or the pillow to bring this about. I waited for a little while and only one other phenomenon occurred, and this was a 'puckering' of the bed clothes. Again, if you can imagine that this piece of cloth",* (Author's note, Dr. Logan holds a pillow and makes some noises on it) *"as part of*

the coverlet on Virginia's bed the bed clothes appeared to be 'pulled up' and pulled towards Virginia as if some force was trying to pull this coverlet. One of the noises was a very characteristic sawing sound" (Author's note. Dr. Logan then brushed his fingers over the pillow to try and recreate the sound for the viewer) *"The other noise that was present, was a knocking tapping noise similar to this"*

(Author's note). Again Dr. Logan tried to recreate this sound for the viewer as he tapped the side of the chair he was sitting on.

"After a short while we decided to go home, thinking that perhaps Virginia would settle down and go to sleep once we had left. Just as we were going out the door a very unusual thing happened, well it seemed unusual at the time, that was that the noises and knockings appeared to take on a character, in that they became extremely hurried and agitated, as if something was trying to get us to stay in the room or attract attention to the child in the bed. The noises became as I said, agitated, something like this",

(Author's note. Again Dr. Logan tried to recreate this sound for the viewer as he tapped the side of the chair he was sitting on)

"Now that is the end of my own personal contact with these phenomena but I have been given permission to read extracts from a diary that I suggested a close relative of the child should keep, shortly after the events started".

THE DIARY

Now, I was not aware that a diary was being kept of all the strange incidents that were occurring in the Campbell household until I watched this 1965 BBC Documentary and was astounded by what I heard. We see Doctor Logan flicking through a diary of the events reading out pieces from different days. As to who kept and wrote in the diary, I'm not entirely sure, however, there is a strong possibility that the diary entries were made by Virginia's Uncle Thomas, or Virginia's Aunty, Isabella, although as yet I haven't been able to confirm that.

Let me set the scene for you dear reader. We have Doctor Logan sat down holding a small black diary. He looks to the camera and says.

"She noted down very carefully in her own words. By the way, this diary has never been published or read in any form before to the public and she was very kind in allowing me to read some extracts from it tonight. I would like to read the first description of the first night of which the phenomena started. It's dated Tuesday the 22nd of November 1960".

"At about 10:30pm Margaret and Virginia were lying in bed. There was a noise like a ball bouncing on the floor. I looked under the beds in the room but couldn't see anything. No sooner had I left the room when it started again. Margaret and Virginia went downstairs for a brush thinking that perhaps a mouse was under the bed. The 'thing' seemed to follow them downstairs".

(Author's note. After reading this entry, Dr. Logan flicked through the diary reading bits and pieces as he went along, so the following is not necessarily in chronological order.)

"A friend had just been visiting the house and after he left, (and I quote) an apple jumped out of a dish, Virginia eat it. I went away to the phone, Virginia was in the house with dad, and he said that while I was away, an apple came out of the dish three times. The clock came off the cabinet and hit Virginia on the nose, settling on the chair just before I came back. (Again, we read) A piece of chocolate jumped off the sideboard, also a pencil. A brillo pad came out of the kitchen, into the living room. The light went on twice, Virginia was using the cleaner, it went off, and the rubber flew off the handle. There was a knocking under the table. Virginia gave three knocks, then there were three knocks back. Later she said, nothing

happened this day. There was knocking on the table at dinner time, someone was punching the girls in bed. And on another occasion, the top of the hot water bottle was open and there were scrapings. The girls were getting pinched sore. Virginia's leg was being tickled. There has been writing on the girls' faces for the past three nights. Virginia's lips went bright red three times, and there was the noise like a ball bouncing".

(Author's note, Doctor Logan stressed to the watching viewer the following information.)

"Incidentally, this bright red description, really, as far as I can make out, what she really intended to express, was to express that Virginia's lips appeared to 'glow bright red' and this she saw herself".

"The bed cover turned red; it was a green cover".

(Author's note. Please note that the bedcovers changing colour is important and we will come back to this later and I will explain why.)

"There was a noise like somebody walking across the floor. There was knocking on the bed, also on the mattress. And on occasions she writes, all went well during the past two weeks. Then she goes on again. There was a lot of knocking on the bed this morning and Virginia was getting nipped. Until we come to the last statement in the book, which she simply states, and it's dated Sunday 23rd of April 1961, there was a knocking on the cupboard door"

The scene then changes back to programme narrator Mr. A.R.G. Owen, who stated to the watching viewers.

"The Sauchie Poltergeist case is to my mind, a wonderfully diagnostic one. A living person, Virginia Campbell was, for some weeks, at no wish of her own, the centre of a mysterious force. This force was fitful and capricious. Sometimes it moved

117

solid objects at other times it produced strange sounds. Here is a tape recording made by Dr. Logan"

The scene then changes to Doctor William Logan who plays a short extract from the reel to reel audio tape in which one can hear young Virginia screaming "mama" followed by some sharp knocking sounds.

The scene once more changes back to programme narrator Mr. A.R.G. Owen who stated.

"But, unlike the good people of Tidworth"

(Author's note, Mr. A.R.G. Owen is referring to another poltergeist case which he has already mentioned in this BBC documentary)

A.R.G. Owen continues.

"I do not think that it was a Demon or a Goblin or a disembodied spirit. I think it was a force, a force admittedly unknown to orthodox science but yet a force proceeding in some way from Virginia herself. Until recently, in fact until a few weeks ago, I thought of the Sauchie Poltergeist case as the very pattern and type of all poltergeist cases. Now I have to tell you, that I am beginning to think that there may be yet another kind of case of this sort, and in some ways different, and in some ways akin to the old notion of the haunted house".

At this point A.R.G. Owen takes the viewer to another poltergeist case in Northfleet in Kent, where Mr Owen believes that the poltergeist effect was somehow due to the very house itself, rather than the occupants who resided in it. This was the difference between the Sauchie and the Northfleet case. One centred on a young girl (Virginia) whilst the other was centred on the very house itself. We may therefore ask ourselves the question, as no doubt A.R.G. Owen did, what is the true definition of a poltergeist, what is the main route cause? Is there a 'one size fits all' approach, or are there other alternative elements that go into producing the poltergeist effect? A.R.G. Owen went on to inform the viewers of this documentary, and I quote.

"But do the scientists really know all the forces that are in nature? When I was young, they admitted to only two, magnetism and gravity, now they tell us that there are two more, the atomic forces with strong and weak interaction. All this I think, must make the layman ask, is this the lot, or are there other powers at work in the universe? But the scientists are right in requiring us only to believe in the two which there is real evidence. Evidence on poltergeists has not been easy to collect for the reason that poltergeist out breaks actually occur, far more rarely than even the more uncommon crime of murder. But statistics do disclose to us, curious facts. It seems that in every afflicted household the strange happenings tend to be mysteriously connected with just one member of the family. This person is usually a young person, someone in the age group of 11 years up to 21 years old. And here perhaps, we ought to pause for thought. Perhaps it really is all trickery. Perhaps it is just the kind of mischief that a young lad, like that (points to a young boy throwing a ball) might want to get up to"

At the end of this interesting 1965 documentary on poltergeists, Mr Owen summed up by saying.

"Is it possible that sometimes, a place and the people in it, should conspire together, to generate some poltergeist energy? One big question hangs over the whole subject. Why is it that some people and not others can be sensitive to the poltergeist force? We know little about this. We know that they tend to be young and are more likely to be girls than boys. We know that they are basically healthy, indeed, rather intelligent, and possibly a trifle highly strung. Stress it seems, and emotional tension, can act as triggers, helping to set off the manifestations. But clearly, this cannot possibly be all, for otherwise the poltergeist would afflict every home in the land. One thing is certain, these stories have happy endings. The

119

effects are short lived. Virginia Campbell today, is a normal happy and charming teenager. What is the origin of the poltergeist force? I wish I knew I regret I cannot tell you. All I know is that it exists. Why has it stayed unrecognised for so long? Perhaps it is because of the great variability of poltergeist cases. A milk bottle flew up said Mrs Howells, an apple rose up out of as dish said Doctor Logan. There were noises galore at Sauchie, and yet everything happened in complete silence at Swansea. Yet, when sounds did happen, it's very striking for several of them were the scratching and the bouncing, long ago at Tidworth, and, in our own time, in Northfleet and in Scotland".

"I think myself, that although its physics and its mode of application are mysterious and obscure, the poltergeist force itself has its origins in living human beings and not in ghosts or haunting. However, the Northfleet case remains very puzzling to me and something of an exception to my theoretical scheme. There, the poltergeist activity, the physical phenomena were all it seems attached to the house, and not with particular people in it. Just what influence it is, and what awoke it to activity at 16 Waterdale, and why it has brooded over the house, these 4 years past, is something that is going to remain for the time being, unknown".

2020 THOUGHTS AND A RESPONSE FROM FACEBOOK.

Social media and Facebook are a wonderful thing, it can connect people the world over and bring people together, sharing stories, thoughts, photographs and a whole lot more. I decided to use the power of Facebook to try and see if I could locate anyone who might have been in Virginia Campbell's class, or indeed anyone who knew her current whereabouts. In part it worked, but not to the degree that I hoped it would. Here is what some of them had to say from the Sauchie Legends Facebook page. Pseudonyms have been given to some individuals who did not want to be name in the book.

Sarah Aitkins stated.

"Malcolm Robinson I was at Sauchie School at the time and remember all the reporters at the school gates".

Barbara Mason stated,

"I remember that too. I was at same school when this happened but not the same class, I remember it well. All true she lived in Park Crescent"

Then I heard from Nancy Harrison who stated.

"I lived there a while back and moved quickly".

Janice Millen joined the thread and asked Nancy why she had moved so quickly!

To which Nancy Harrison replied.

"My son had nightmare's every night in that house, in the back bedroom, he was 4 at the time, he said a woman used to sit on the end of his bed and laughed at him? I switched rooms but there was a horrible atmosphere in there".

Of course, not everyone on the Sauchie Legends page believed in the Sauchie poltergeist, one Isa Sinclair stated,

"Daft nonsense! I was at my Gran's at the time, Mary Kincaid, and there were all kinds of stories circulating. All of them made no sense at all, physical impossibilities. It seemed like a lot of attention seeking to me. Is this all being dug up again because someone is writing a book? I think it was all about making money in the first place".

Needless to say, I quickly responded to Isa and stated,

"Hi Isa. How I wish it were nonsense, but sadly it's all true. Witnessed by the local G.P. and the local minister and school teacher, they all saw these things happening".

Alex Holden came on the thread saying, *"True story".*

Cathy Sharples stated,

"It was a good school to go to. Happy times spent there. Remember reading about this, it gets your mind thinking though, real or not".

Alice Rushton stated.

"I was in the same class, but I don't remember much, I just felt so sorry for that little girl"

Kathy Jones stated.

"She lived round the corner from me in Park Crescent I was in number **"

Christopher Simpson stated,

"My wife knew Virginia, but she never witnessed any strange phenomenon only heard odd noises. When this happened, the class was ushered from the classroom, the teacher was Miss Stewart, red haired and quite stout, she lived in Tillicoultry. My wife feels that they were being shielded from what was going on by the school staff. Having now talked to my wife about Virginia, she tells me that they were school friends and played together she was never in her house but played at my wife's. My wife is Jane Oldfield, she stayed in Posthill at the time".

Caroline Aspel stated,

"My cousin George was in her class and confirmed that it happened".

Sally Harper stated,

"I knew both Mr. Hill and Mrs Davidson both very reliable people. That was Sauchie School though".

Ivor Haines stated,

"I remember it well. I think at the time I was in primary 4 or 5 at the Hallpark annex. I can remember the minister Tom Lund, speaking about it on the radio".

I received an e-mail back in August 2004 from an ex reporter who worked for the Alloa Advertiser, the newspaper that reported the Sauchie Poltergeist events of 1960. Here is what he said to me.

Dear Malcolm Robinson,

"I was fascinated to encounter you on various websites tonight, during casual browsing. In the high and far off days, I was a reporter on the Alloa Advertiser and the Alloa Circular and was involved with Wee Hughie, the Sauchie poltergeist. (Author's note, Wee Hughie was the nickname given to the Sauchie Poltergeist by Virginia) *The information on the web seems to be full and accurate. I confirmed the incidents in Sauchie School in an interesting way. I asked the headmaster, Mr Hill, if the things reported had been happening, the round ruler rolling up the desk, and so forth and he said, "I haven't seen anything". When an honest man answers a question you haven't asked him, a reporter knows that the truthful answer to the question you did ask him is embarrassing"!*
With best wishes. Duncan Gillespie.

I take from this that Duncan is implying that Mr Hill might have been covering himself by saying that he didn't see anything, that said, he may not have seen anything, as being the headmaster, his office would have been in a different part of the school, and other than being called to the class room when these disturbing events happened, he may have missed them and just caught the tail end of the mayhem!

ANOTHER WITNESS RECOLLECTS

Back in 2010 I contacted another lady who said that she could tell me a little bit about the Sauchie Poltergeist. Here is what she said to me.

"My name is Allison Whitton Ramage and I wanted to let you know that I was at the same school as Virginia Campbell although she was in a class two years above me along with my sister Helen, who was incidentally her best friend at the time. Many times, my sister and I would be at the house and let me say, some of the things we saw I can still vividly remember to this day. Also, a lot of the activity when we were all at school, still freaks me out when I think of it. Nobody believed us, at first our families put it down to the three of us playing pranks and tricks, those thoughts were soon dispelled, when the activity started to happen at our primary school. I do remember the local Minister at the time was a Reverend Lund, who was eventually asked to attend both the girl's home and school, whereupon he blessed them. With hindsight I guess it would be a sort of exorcism, although I'm not certain of that".
Yours Sincerely.
Allison Whitton Ramage.

In a further e-mail to Allison, I asked her about the school desk lids moving up and down of their own accord and if her sister saw any evidence of this? She replied,

Hi Malcolm,

"Ah, the desks, well you have to imagine an old school class with rows and rows of desks and chairs, the desks with the lift up lid. Virginia always sat next to my sister. Not all the time, but very regularly when she was there, all the desktops 'would lift up', and on occasion, the whole desks would rise. I should

124

say at this point, Virginia and my sister and everyone else, was scared"

"Then there were the sleep overs where my sister Helen would go to Virginia's house. On several occasions, when Virginia went to bed, there was a complete shape next to her where it looked like an indent of someone sleeping on their side".

I also telephoned Allison on a few occasions and during one of those calls, she mentioned something that had happened when she and her sister visited the Campbell home and were sitting down at the dinner table. Here is what she related to me in an e-mail.

"The dinner was when I was invited along with my sister Helen. The table would be set and when we sat down, the knife and fork next to Virginia would move as if eating, as did the glass as if drinking. Virginia and her family mostly ignored all these things. Yes, she did try very hard to ignore all of the 'happenings' however the more she did that the more the poltergeist would throw things all over the place, including in the school. From what I remember, she was just an ordinary, very popular nice girl, had no family problems. What I would consider the most important thing at the time was our local Minister Mr. Lund was called in to see if he would help. That I remember vividly since he spoke of things that I didn't understand at the time. It made most of the papers. It was shortly after that, that Virginia Campbell and all the family left and went back to Ireland".

Best regards Allison Whitton Ramage
P.S.
"I forgot about the morning assembly incident which happened when the whole school was singing and one row of the desks from front to back was tipped over. I believe it was after that the Minister Reverend Lund was brought in. Unfortunately, my sister is no longer with us".

The following comments also come from people on social media who reacted to my request, and also the sister of one of my friend's, about trying to locate some potential witnesses of the Sauchie Poltergeist events that might still be living in the Clackmannanshire area. Linda, my friend's sister, received three replies, one from someone who didn't leave their name, and I have given the other two pseudonyms. Here is what they had to say.

Hello Linda,

"I can certainly remember when it happened but didn't witness anything first hand because she was in the other class in our year. I remember Miss Stewart, her teacher running into our class to tell our teacher what she had seen pencils flying and desks moving. Reporters would surround the school. I remember Jessie Pollock knocking a camera out of a photographer's hand! Mr Lund the minister was asked to go to her home. I can remember exactly what she looked like but sorry didn't witness anything personally".
From Mrs Cook

Hello Linda,

"I can certainly remember when it happened but didn't witness anything first hand, because she was in the other class in our year. I remember Miss Stewart, her teacher running into our class to tell our teacher what she had seen, pencils flying and desks moving. Reporters would surround the school. I remember Jessie Pollock knocking a camera out of a photographer's hand! Mr Lund the minister was asked to go to her home. I'm sure Margaret Harrison (Reid) was in her class. I can remember exactly what she looked like but sorry didn't witness anything personally". (Name not given)

Needless to say that during my 2020 research on this case, I was hoping to talk to any members of Virginia Campbell's class, it was a long shot, but I managed to track down Peter

MacGregor who was actually 'in' Virginia's class. The following comes from two e-mails from Peter where I asked him various questions, he stated.

Hi Malcolm,

*"Here is the answer to some of your questions about the Sauchie Poltergeist. My birth name is Peter MacGregor Anderson Johnstone. I am 69, and I was born in Airthrey Castle Maternity home which is now in the grounds of Stirling University on the 17 July 1950. I was brought up in Posthill Sauchie and went to Sauchie Primary and was in the same class as Virginia Campbell. I wasn't sitting near Virginia when the disturbances took place, but I did see the desk lid banging up and down and Virginia shouting "stop it stop it" and then the desk started lifting off the ground without Virginia touching it, strangely I wasn't frightened, but I thought Virginia is going to be in trouble with the teacher Miss Stewart and the Headmaster. Remember this was the time when you got the Belt if you got into trouble. I remember the teacher Miss Margaret Stewart, she had Ginger hair. I think she later married when we went to Forebraes, **(another school in Sauchie no longer standing, author's italics in bold)** I didn't know Virginia well, my pal in the class was Archie Napier **(pseudonym, author's italics in bold)** Archie stayed in Park Crescent near Virginia Campbell. Archie is still living but has Dementia. I remember My Mum talking to a neighbour about other neighbours living next to Virginia hearing banging noises and furniture moving. I also remember when our Parish Minister got involved Mr Lund but I can't remember when the Campbell Family moved away. Virginia was a shy quiet girl really, it is a shame this happened, but as far as I am concerned it was real, and all the people in the village thought so to at the time. Remember Sauchie was a small village then and it was soon the talk of the village. I remember my Mum saying to Mrs Bateman our neighbour in Posthill where we stayed about Mr Lund our Minister from Sauchie Parish Church got involved and also a Doctor. Then it got into the Alloa Advertiser and the National Newspapers. It is a shame so many of our class have passed away. We were all*

witnesses and there will still be Sauchie Folk of my age or a bit older who will remember it well"

"I have no photos of Virginia or class photos. I can remember some of those in my class but they have all passed away. I can't recall anything about a piano lid falling down on a teacher; in fact, I don't think we had any music classes at that time". **(Author's Italics in bold, this was in reference to my question that someone recalled a lid falling down on a piano teacher's hand in Virginia's class)**
Peter Macgregor.

BUT DID THE POLTEREGIST LEAVE WHEN VIRGINIA DID?

The Sauchie Legends Facebook page proved very helpful in tracking down some more people who either knew Virginia and were in her class or were aware of the strange experiences surrounding her. But probably one of the biggest pieces of information to come through the Sauchie Legends Facebook site was when I was contacted by a lady who had actually moved into Virginia's old house at 19 Park Crescent many years later, 2003 to be precise. She too had her fair share of bizarre and frightening stories. An in an e-mail that I received from Nicola Bernard dated 27th February 2020, she had this to say.

Hi Malcolm

*"Yes, I lived there round about 2003. With my two boys (Michael) who was 2 at the time and (John) who was 5 at the time. They shared the back bedroom and my eldest son John had constant nightmares saying there was a lady talking to him when he was falling asleep and that his **bed covers were changing colour?** He was so distressed that I swapped rooms with the boys. The back bedroom had a horrible thick feeling in the air quite hard to describe it. Not nice at all. I suffer with sleep paralysis and hadn't had it in a long time but seemed to have it nightly in that house. My husband worked offshore at*

*the time, and I was there alone with the boys most of the time.
There were always strange and very loud bangs and noises, and
my kettle used to turn on and off by itself on a daily basis. Also,
putrid smells now and again that would disappear on their
own! I spoke to one of my neighbours about my kettle, and she
told me that I carried a presence with me wherever I went? We
moved shortly after that. My father in law was at school with
Virginia Campbell and he told me that he remembered the desk
lifting up and down in the classroom. Sadly, he passed away a
few years ago so can't get any more information from him. Yes
of course you can use these comments and I don't mind my
name being used or any of my son's.
Many thanks.
Nicola Bernard.*

This was dynamite to me. Everyone had believed that when
Virginia and her family had moved away from the Sauchie area,
the poltergeist either went with her (as it did when it followed
her to the nearby town of Dollar) or it just disappeared. Now
here we have testimony from someone who took residence in
the property, admittedly many years later, but who seemingly
was still feeling a presence. I decided to ask Nicola some more
questions.

Hi Nicola,

*"Many thanks for providing me with this information I'd
just like to ask you a couple of quick questions that I'd love you
to answer if you can?"*

1) *"Why did you leave, was it because of what was going
on"?*

2) *"Did you know about the house and its reputation before
you moved in, and if so, did it bother you"?*

3) *"Did you ever see your son's bed covers changing
colour?*

129

4) *"Did you ever see this 'lady' that your son spoke about"?*

5) *"Since you moved out of there has everything been fine in your new home"?*

Nicola was quick to reply, and in a further e-mail from her dated the same day, she stated.

Hi Malcolm

"I didn't leave because of this as it didn't really bother me. My son seemed to be fine when I moved them into the front room. We moved to a bought property in Tullibody. I read a lot of ghost story books and recognised the address in one of them, but it didn't deter me from moving there. It was a brief chapter about Virginia. I lent this out to a friend and never got it back. I never seen the covers change colour, but my son was so upset, and I thought it was a very strange thing to say? He remembers it to this day. I seen a lady on the corner of my bed a few times, but she was dark, and I couldn't make out a face. She didn't scare me. But I understand why a 5 year old would have been scared. I haven't felt anything as strange as this since I moved. As I say, the only room that felt uncomfortable was definitely the back bedroom. The smells I used to experience were always at the back door of the house where there was an old coal cellar cupboard. I will have pictures of inside the house so I'll look them out and email them to you.
Many thanks
Nicola Bernard

THE PARK CRESCENT DIARY

I mentioned earlier in this book about the diary that was kept by the Campbell family to record all the strange events that were going on in the house, and that there was an entry in the book which stated;

"The bed cover turned red; it was a green cover".

130

As we have read above in the account from Nicola Bernard who stated that her son's bedcovers changed colour, I wanted to know what colour her son's bedcover was, and what colour it changed to. She replied by stating.

"Hi Malcolm.
"He always had red bed covers, as this was his favourite colour. He said they always changed to blue and that it made him feel cold. But he always kicked them off the bed with fright. I personally never seem them change colour".

Now admittedly as we can see, there are different colours allegedly changing on the bed covers in the same house 43 years later. With Virginia in 1960, her bed cover changed from green to red, whilst Nicola's son's bedcover in 2003, changed from red to blue! I have never ever heard of this type of phenomenon happening in any poltergeist case before. I may of course be wrong, and if so, I would like to know. My contact details are at the end of this book.

So, 43 years later we still have paranormal happenings occurring in this house. Poltergeist phenomenon does not last this long, usually poltergeist phenomena is of a short duration from a day to a matter of weeks, but 43 years!

Strangely, the next person to occupy the house was a couple named Ellen and James Mcleish, they moved into the house during 2003, and stayed there for 14 years, leaving in 2017 after which a Polish couple took over residence of the house, and in point of fact, at the time of writing this book, (April 2020) are still there. On the 29th of February 2020, I telephoned Ellen to ask if she too, might have had some strange experiences in that house, here is but some of that conversation.

Abbreviations
(MR) Malcolm Robinson
(EM) Ellen Mcleish

(MR) *"Hi Ellen. I believe that you stayed at number 19 Park Crescent, is that correct?"*

(EM) *"Yes"*

(MR) *"What year did you move in and what year did you leave"?*

(EM) *"2003 to 2017"*

(MR) *"Before you moved in, were you aware of the reputation of that house or what had gone on in that house before"?*

(EM) *"When I went down to view it, a couple of the neighbours said that there had been a poltergeist in it".*

(MR) *"Right"*

(EM) *"And that was just because she wanted her son to get it"* (Author's note, it would appear this other person was looking to put Ellen, as a potential buyer, from buying the house)

(MR) *"Did that put you off at all, I mean, how did you feel?"*

(EM) *"I'll tell you what I said to her I said that if there is any spirit in there I'll drink it"*

(MR) *"Laughs" So it didn't bother you at all obviously"?*

(EM) *"No"*

132

(MR) *"Now did anything strange happen to you in the house at all"?*

(EM) *"I can honestly say, that in the 14 years that Jim and I stayed there, there was not a thing. My grandchildren stayed there, and not a thing"*

ANOTHER PARK CRESCENT GHOST!

During my research for this book, I was introduced to another person who had experienced ghostly occurrences at their home in Park Crescent. Now admittedly, this wasn't the main poltergeist house that Virginia stayed in, it was a house in the next block up! I was contacted by a chap called David MacDonald who had this to tell me.

"Hi Malcolm"

"My mum moved into that house in late 1969, she thinks 17 Park Crescent and lived there 14 years. My mum said there were always activities, but when we first moved in, the sockets used to fly out the walls, and doors would open and close. We heard scratching noises like a mouse behind the units, cold eerie feelings. My aunt would not come in the house she said that the hairs stood up on her neck and arms. I used to sleep walk in the house and had an imaginary friend, which I believe was all linked, it was an eerie place".

I e-mailed David back saying that what he was telling me might be a ghost rather than a poltergeist as there was a marked difference. He replied with.

"This might sound daft but what is a haunting compared to a poltergeist? What I can remember, as I was very young, was that I would be floating down the stairs unable to scream for help. It was like it was in slow motion, my feet not touching the ground. I used to hear footsteps running around the upstairs of the house, mostly but never down stairs. I used to get up in the middle of the night and I would be outside playing in the

133

garden but still sleeping if that makes sense. My mum took me to the doctor's, and I was put on medication to help me sleep after it went on for some time. It may or may not be linked to the house, but it all stopped when we moved house".

I asked David if it would be alright if I contacted his mother to have a chat about what went on in that house (17 Park Crescent Sauchie) to which he said yes, that his mother would be more than happy to speak to me. So, I called that very same day, and the following is some of what was said.

Interview with Avril MacDonald 9th March 2020
Abbreviations
(MR) Malcolm Robinson
(AM) Avril MacDonald

(MR) *"Hi Avril. I was asked to give you a call by David"*

(AM) *"Ah yes, my son"*

(MR) *"Did he tell you that I might be calling"?*

(AM) *"Yes he did"*

(MR) *"I won't keep you long Avril as I'm sure you are busy. As you know, I am writing a book about the Sauchie Poltergeist and I am also giving a lecture in Sauchie Hall later in the year about it. Now David said that you used to live in that house or was it next door"*

(AM) *"Yes we stayed in the house, number 17. And, as far as I know, there was a poltergeist in that house"*

(MR) *"OK. Well the Sauchie Poltergeist is known more for being at number 19 Park Crescent, but certainly if there was one at number 17 as well that makes it even more bizarre"*

(AM) *"Yes there definitely was something strange about the house"*

(MR) *"Uh huh. And you were definitely in number 17 Avril, yeah?"*

(AM) *"Yes"*

(MR) *"Tell me what you experienced living at number 17, what was going on?"*

(AM) *"Well the plugs used to just fly out of the sockets as you were walking past, they would just fly out for no reason. And there was always a sort of strange clawing or scratching noises, and David, my son used to have a lot of strange dreams when he was younger. My sister used to come through and stay with me and said that she would not stay in that house on her own"*

(MR) *"So she just didn't like it then. Was that a feeling she got"?*

(AM) *"I think so yeah"*

(MR) *"And you stayed there in 1969, is that correct, or was it later"?*

(AM) *"My oldest son was born in October 69 and he was about 5 or 6 month old when I moved in there, that would be 1970.*

(MR) *"1970"?*

(AM) *"Yes"*

(MR) *"And were you aware that things were happening straight away, or did somebody tell you that things were happening?"*

(AM) *"It was more or less after a week, or two weeks after I moved in. You know, sort of strange noises. As I said, the plugs* *just used to fly out of their sockets, but I never felt threatened. Other people felt it when they came into the house but I personally, didn't".*

(MR) *"Other than the plugs coming out of the sockets, did you experience anything else? Did you see or hear anything"?*

(AM) *"It was just noises, like scratching and clawing and like creaking of floorboards when there was no one walking about. You know that sort of thing"*

(MR) *"Do you remember where the scratching noises came from"?*

(AM) *"It used to be mainly from the living room"*

(MR) *"Was that coming from the walls or skirting boards"?*

(AM) *"Well we used to have a back hall with a cupboard that went under the stairs, and of course that wall was in the living room as well, and it was definitely coming from that area. And I used to empty the cupboard, oh I don't know how many times, to check that there wasn't anything in there, and there was never anything"*

(MR) *"So there were no mice or anything like that, you never saw any mice droppings"?*

(AM) *"No, nothing at all"*

(MR) *"So that was a couple of weeks into your tenancy, how long did the events last for and when did they stop?*

(AM) *"I would say that it would more or less have gone on the whole time that I was there. I was there, oh, 14, 15 years"*

(MR) *"Was your house an end house, or was it in a block"?*

(AM) *"It was semi-detached"*

(MR) *"Now I've got to get this right, as it has always been known that number 19 was the main poltergeist house. You were number 17, was that next door"?*

(AM) *"Yes, that would have been the next two houses"*

(MR) *"The next two houses up, yeah?"*

(AM) *"Yes"*

(MR) *"And were you aware that when you moved into that house that people were talking about 'that' house 10 years before, because it was 1960 that the young girl got bother in the house. So, were you aware of that?"* **(Author's note. I was of course referring to number 19 Park Crescent and wondering if she was aware of the stories concerning that house, prior to moving into number 17)**

(AM) *"No, or I might not have gone" (laughs)*

(MR) *"So your son had dreams in your house you said"?*

(AM) *"Yes, he used to sleep walk"*

(MR) *"And is MacDonald your surname is that correct?"*

(AM) *"It is now. But when I moved in there, it was Leishman".*

(MR) *"And would you be happy if I used some of what you have said in my book. It's to let my readers known that someone else has experienced this as well"?*

(AM) *"Yes. Years ago, oh, I must have been in the house maybe 9 years or something, and somebody actually came to do a report. I mean, I didn't speak to them they were just filming the house for some magazine or something, I don't know"*

137

(MR) *"And did they ask for you by name, or did they just knock the door"?*

(AM) *"No, they just asked if it was OK to film the house and I said yes, certainly, but they didn't come in, they just filmed from the front to the back. But I don't know what it was for really"*

(MR) *"You mentioned the living room and scratching noises. Were there any bother in the upstairs bedrooms, any noises?"*

(AM) *"Well I didn't hear any in my room. But I don't know if it was the noises that were disturbing David"*

(MR) *"Do you know who got the house after you, the name of the family"?*

(AM) *"No, I'm not sure"*

(MR) *"That's OK, that's fine. Is there anything else that you can tell me about your house that you can tell me"?*

(AM) *"No nothing else. As I say, I never felt threatened, but some people would come in and must obviously have felt some kind of atmosphere, and said to me, 'I don't know how you can live here'. But I never ever felt threatened by it"*

(MR) *"Well I must thank you for being upfront and honest with me Avril and letting me know about this. You have been very helpful. Best wishes and God bless".*

So not only did we have the Sauchie Poltergeist at 19 Park Crescent, we also had ghostly phenomenon at numbers 17 and 30 Park Crescent! (We shall come back to 30 Park Crescent later in the book) Why is this? Is it something to do with the area where the houses were built on? To find out more, I sought the advice from some members of the Sauchie Legends Facebook page.

WHAT WAS ON THE PARK CRESCENT LAND
BEFORE THE HOUSES?

Needless to say, the lovely people who contribute to the Sauchie Legends Facebook page didn't let me down. Nearly everyone remembers the land before Park Crescent was built, as initially farm land and then later used for football, Highland Games, and local Gala's, as the following commentators recollect. Here are but a few of their comments.

"I believe it was farm land. In more recent memory, new houses were built near Park Crescent, where once grew rapeseed plants. I remember the bright yellow plants which could be seen from Fairfield Park".

Another commentator stated.

"I don't remember it as farm land but there certainly were loads of fields where we used to play along side of the railway line. I do remember it. As kids we would steal the turnips to make Halloween lanterns"!

It would appear that after the fields, some land was reclaimed in order to provide the Sauchie people, a public park, and a place where local events could be staged, as the following commentators stated.

"It was a park. My grandpa had photos when it was a park playing football"

"It was the public park and the path that runs up beside the school led to the Hennings. We used to call the woman that owned all the hen sheds, 'Hen Mary'. It's funny when you start to think about it. I can picture it all, they were care free days".

Phil Diane Brownlie was kind enough to send me some old aerial photographs showing this football park, (see photographic section) Phil stated.

"Here is the proof showing the football pitch. This was where Park Crescent is now. The row of houses below it is Fairfield".

Another commentator spoke about those care free days, she stated;

"I lived in Holton Crescent when Park Crescent was being built. My memory was of playing in the small play park and fields next to it where we rolled our Easter eggs. I used to watch flocks of birds rising and settling of an evening something you don't see now or am I just not looking".

Another gentleman remembers the Highland Games being staged at the park. He stated.

"Prior to Park Crescent it was a public park. The highland games were held there every year. Sauchie Juveniles played there before moving to Fairfield Park. We used to sit up on the hill and watch the games. You entered from the Mansfield Arms Road".

The local football team, Sauchie Juniors, started their football journey on this public park as our next commentator stated.

"Before Park Crescent, this was a public park where Sauchie Juniors played, managed by Jimmy Miller".

It would appear that not only was football played at the park, it was also a stage for the Highland Games. Local Gala's were also held at the park as well, as our next commentator recollects.

"It was Sauchie Park where they held the highland games and the children's galas were also held there"

So, as we can see from the above, there was nothing in the land as such which might contribute to paranormal events occurring, and I am alluding to old graveyards etc. A number of researchers believe that poltergeists are simply the result of children going through puberty and somehow, this sexual energy gets expanded out of their body to cause disruption. And whilst admittedly Virginia was at an age going through puberty, the other two houses in Park Crescent which also had ghostly disturbances, did not have teenagers, young children yes, but not in their teenage years. This is of course presuming that these other researchers are correct in their assumptions, and that the poltergeist is nothing ghostly and mysterious, but just a human faculty which is yet to be understood. I'll be writing more on this later.

I had a few more people from the Sauchie Legends Facebook page come forward, but when they did, it was to tell me that the people I would need to speak to, didn't want to talk to me about it, which was fair enough. I was also told by some people that the person they were referring to in their e-mails that I was enquiring about on Facebook, had sadly passed away. One of my main contributors for sourcing information on the Sauchie Poltergeist, was Peter Macgregor Anderson Johnstone, who I have mentioned earlier in this book and who has given his own recollections. Peter, as we have learned earlier, was actually in Virginia Campbell's class at that time. The following are some more comments taken from the Sauchie Legends Facebook site from what Peter, remembers from that time.

"It was all very real Malcolm. I am a Christian now, and I believe it was demonic. And for whatever reason, the desk lifted 6 to 7 feet off the ground, and then just dropped down. Nobody was near it at the time, because the lid had been banging noisily before it maybe for about a minute, and Virginia was shouting "go away" "go away" Then it suddenly all stopped of course. It was the talk of the village then and it got into the paper the Advertiser, and then there were the neighbours who heard banging and things getting thrown about. I remember my

mum saying there was a Priest that was going to have an Exorcism, but I can't remember what happened Malcolm"

Of course, I was keen to know if either Peter, or anyone he knew, had photographs of Virginia or inside the school, he replied with.

"No Unfortunately not Malcolm. In those days hardly anyone had a camera and I don't even have a class photo at all, but if there was one, I would recognize Virginia. Malcolm, I have been in contact with friends from Sauchie Primary on the group Sauchie Legends and a lot of my class have passed away. My younger sister lives in Alloa, and the family talked about it a lot. My sister is two years younger than me and was at Sauchie Primary. Her friend lived just along from Virginia in Park Crescent and I heard her friend saying to my sister, that they had heard banging noises coming from the house as if furniture was being thrown about"

INTERVIEW WITH COLIN ATKINS
February 3rd, 2020 Regarding the Sauchie Poltergeist.
Abbreviations:

(CA)   Colin Atkins.
(MR)   Malcolm Robinson

The following comes from a telephone conversation that I had with Colin Atkins (pseudonym) whose mother was in Virginia Campbell's class at school. Sadly, Colin's mother passed away last year (2019) Colin told me that there would be many occasions when the Sauchie Poltergeist would come up in conversation, and he remembers those conversations well. The following is but some of the recollections that Colin recalls.

(MR) *"So Colin, tell me about some of those conversations that you and your mother had about the Sauchie Poltergeist".*

(CA) *"Well you know how your mum would sit you down at Halloween and tell you spooky ghost stories? Well I remember when I was quite young, my mum would refer to this thing that happened, and as I gradually got older, I would say to her, are you winding me up, is this a lie? and she went no, it absolutely happened. And we had numerous conversations over the years about it. Moreover, there would be something about it in the local press, as there has been in the Alloa Advertiser, 'Looking Back Through Time'* **(Author's Italics in bold. This is a part of the newspaper that looks back to stories that appeared in the Alloa Advertiser 100 to 50 to 25 years ago)** *So we often had conversations surrounding it, and the reason that I know that it's not a lie, is like anybody else, your mum wouldn't lie to you about these sort of things".*

(MR) *"No"*

(CA) *"But my mum's memories were very vivid, and as I said to you on the phone last week, the information that I've got is third hand, so I don't know if the time, dates and accuracies of it all, are correct, but I am happy to recount from what I recall".*

(MR) *"Do you remember something about a piano teacher that"……..*

(CA) *"Yeah. The story that I remember about the piano teacher, was that in those days, and I don't know what it's like in high school now, there would be a piano teacher, a separate teacher and the piano would be wheeled into the classroom. So, on this particular day the piano came into the classroom and all the kids would be sitting at their desks. And the piano, according to my mum, levitated a bit, (Now I'm not talking about 10 foot) it was just a few inches, and everybody was screaming, and I think the head teacher or other teachers came into the room. I don't know what sort of timeline, but during all that, the piano teacher was playing after it (the levitation) sort of went away, and then the lid of the piano keys slammed shut on her fingers. And I don't know if there was an injury or if*

143

there were any breakages or anything like that, but my mum recalls the teacher leaving the classroom quite abruptly because of that had happened".

(MR) *"And was Virginia in the class at the time"?*

(CA) *"That I don't know Malcolm. I definitely know that this was in relation to Virginia Campbell, because that is the name that my mum often referred to. So, if that is what you are asking me about then what I am telling you about is about Virginia Campbell and nothing separate from that".*

(MR) *"And what was the story about the blinds in the classroom"?*

(CA) *"Yes, well what I do know, and this is from what my mother told me. If you think about an old school classroom with double height windows along the one wall in the one room, the blinds, the venetian blinds do you call them? Well they would periodically throughout the day when Virginia was in the class, they would rise and fall, rise, and fall, very very quickly. The blinds wouldn't open up so that you could see through them, they physically went up and down, and that is what my mother recalls. My mother also spoke about an incident where a small boy was violently sick, projectile vomiting. I don't know if it was because of what he saw, or if he was potentially possessed, I don't know, I don't know how these things work. She recalls that vividly. My mother never saw this, but she heard that when Virginia was at home lying in her bed, she was often pulled out of her bed, and thrown about in the air, again, this will be fourth hand, because my mother heard this from someone else so we don't know how much truth can be placed on this. My mum never witnessed that. The other story with Virginia and her house, was that the wallpaper would peel off the walls in sheets, but again I don't know how much truth there is in that. One thing that my mother does recall vividly, and this is when I realised that there was something to it, was at some point after all of this, or during it, the local authorities were involved, but it escalated, and my mum recalls American people coming in to*

144

the class and interviewing everyone. And there were a lot of American psychologists or doctors, and my mum just remembers a lot of American accents and being interviewed, and a lot of questions being asked of that class surrounding what they had witnessed".

(MR) *"Did your mother have any photographs of the school and Virginia's classroom, or perhaps of Virginia herself"?*

(CA) *"No, there was nothing in her possessions".*

(MR) *"Did you ever find out where Virginia Campbell and her family relocated to?"*

(CA) *"The story that my mum heard was that everything stopped, all the activity when Virginia left the class. I asked my mother where she went to and she said that she didn't know, but the understanding is that she went back to Ireland. And the rumour was from those that knew her, was that the entity or whatever was disrupting her life in Scotland, was that they didn't want her in Scotland, they wanted her back in Ireland".*

(MR) *"Is there anything else that you can recall from what your mother told you?"*

(CA) *"I don't have anything else really that I can recall, other than what I have said. But with all those conversations that I had with my mother, she said that it was absolutely true, that she had seen it with her own eyes. And you don't disbelieve your mum".*

(MR) *"Well Colin I'd like to thank you very much for your time this evening and your recollections have been very helpful".*

(CA) *"You are more than welcome Malcolm".*

At the end of the day the above information from Colin is still valuable, and his conversations with his mother regarding the Sauchie Poltergeist is still etched very firmly on his mind. That said, there were certain things in Colin's conversation with me, which Colin himself admits is fourth hand that I should take with a pinch of salt, and I refer to the wallpaper coming off the walls in the Campbell household, and also that Virginia was thrown out of her bed. We know from historic record that Virginia was pinched in bed and that the covers on her bed were seen to move in a rippling movement. As for the American psychologists or doctors coming over to Sauchie, I haven't as yet clarified that, if true, it sure sounds interesting if not incredible that they would travel all the way from the U.S.A. just to talk to Virginia and her class mates, more so when one considers that surely there would be a number of good American poltergeist cases that they could get their teeth into.

JUST FOR THE RECORD

Regarding venetian blinds being in Sauchie Primary School, it should be noted that Wikipedia tells us that in 1769 Englishman Edward Bevan patented the first Venetian blind. In 1841 American John Hampson invented a mechanism for controlling the angle of the horizontal slats. Nearly all blinds hanging today operate using Hampson's invention. Although the early history of Venetian window blinds is mostly conjectural, they are thought to have originated in Persia, not Venice. Venetian traders discovered the window coverings through their trade interactions in the East and brought them back to Venice and Paris. In the late 19th and early 20th centuries, Venetian blinds were widely adopted in office buildings to regulate light and air. According to Peter Anderson Macgregor Johnstone who was in Virginia's class at the time of the poltergeist events, he stated to me in an e-mail that he cannot ever remember venetian blinds being in Sauchie Primary School. He remembers venetian blinds being in his secondary school Forebraes and them being closed for film shows but cannot remember them being in Sauchie Primary. In a further e-mail to me he stated.

146

"Malcolm the main railway line between Alloa and Dollar was right next to the School, clearly visible as a right of way now. I can still visualise the steam trains with around 40 coal wagons going to Dollar coal mine and taking the coal to Kincardine Power Station (We used to count the coal wagons) Now you can imagine the noise of the steam train and 40 coal wagons make, the whole school trembled. The point I am making is I knew the difference between that noise and a desk lid banging on its own and lifting of the ground. There was a wee corridor door on each side of our classroom which was in the centre. It was back in the days when the boys and girls went out of different doors although classes were all mixed".

THE AUDIO TIME CAPSULE OF THE SAUCHIE POLTERGEIST!

B.B.C. Radio Scotland. Scope Programme, December 1960

When I did some research on the Sauchie poltergeist case back in 1994, I tried ever so hard to locate the famous audio tape that was recorded by Dr. Logan of the poltergeist sounds that they all heard in Virginia's bedroom. Part of that recording was used by BBC Radio Scotland for a short thirty minute programme on the Sauchie Poltergeist called, *'Scope'*. I had requested a copy of this recording from BBC Radio Scotland at Queen Margaret Drive in Glasgow, but they told me that they couldn't locate it.

Then whilst working with One Tribe T.V. during February 2020 for a short piece on the Sauchie Poltergeist, I mentioned to them that there was audio tape of the Sauchie Poltergeist sounds and that I had tried but failed to locate it. Well, lo and behold, their researchers managed to track it down at the BBC Radio Scotland Archive Department in Glasgow. Anyway, to say I was pleased would be an understatement, I was absolutely ecstatic. Cameron Howells, one of the researchers for One Tribe T.V. sent me the link for that recording, and that same night, I sat in front of my home P.C. and listened intently to this

147

half hour programme. I sat enthralled listening to the interviews with the Reverend Lund, Dr. Nisbet and other people associated with the case, and when I heard the actual taped recordings of the poltergeist sounds, those strange knockings and sawing like sounds, well, it was truly breath taking. Probably no one had heard this show since its first (and I guess only) broadcast back in December 1960. So, 60 years had elapsed, and I was hearing it for the first time. When this initial broadcast was made, I was only 3 years of age!

I have been given permission by BBC Radio Scotland to transcribe this tape for inclusion in this book, so here it is in its entirety, word for word. I'm sure like me, you will be stunned.

BBC RADIO SCOTLAND PROGRAMME SCOPE.
DECEMBER 1960

Taking part were the Reverend T.W. Lund, Reverend Ewan Murdo MacDonald, Dr. Nisbet and Dr. Logan. The programme starts with some bouncy pleasant introduction music, whereupon the show's presenter makes himself known. Unfortunately, try as I might, I couldn't make out the presenter's name on the audio. I've tried to Google the show and tried to find out through the internet who this was, but so far have been unsuccessful. So, the following, is word for word, what was said on that radio show about the Sauchie Poltergeist.

SCOPE PROGRAMME

This is *(Author's italics. Name not made out on sound file)* presenting Scope. The word itself is German, its first part means noise racket, hub bub, its second part signifies ghost. The poltergeist has a long literary history. One is mentioned in the gossip from the J. Hall a Chinese work of a thousand years ago. Probably the first one to intrigue a scientist was the Demon Drummer of Tidworth which was investigated in 1662 by a fellow of the Royal Society, the reverend Joseph Granville. Books on psychic phenomena and research are filled with

148

equally alarming if less romantic report of mischievous spirits. Like all trouble, the poltergeist is nothing if not international a quick flick of the record, shows China, America, the Dutch East Indies, France, Germany, England, and just the other day, Scotland. And to localise it still further in Scotland, a little village called Sauchie.

(Brief dramatic music at this point)

Narrator: There is a suggestion that the Sauchie poltergeist may have been imported. In September of this year, Mrs Annie Campbell, a woman in her 50's, came across from Moville in County Donegal to live with her son who has a council house in Park Crescent Sauchie. With Mrs Campbell, came her youngest child eleven year old Virginia, the central character in the whole curious affair. Their journey has been represented as a flight from the things that were already happening to Virginia, but this is not exactly clear.

(Author's italics in bold, well, this was the first I've heard of this. The suggestion that they left Ireland because of the possibility of the poltergeist disturbances happening there!)

Narrator: If it was a flight, then it was completely futile for Virginia's surroundings continued to be energised in the most strangest and inexplicable way. In her classroom at school, a table rose 3 or 4 inches from the floor and drifted sideways. Desk lids rose and fell of their own accord. Doors near her opened and declined obstinately to close again. Rumours began to fly around the village. Virginia's schoolteacher tried to check these rumours but later admitted witnessing the phenomena described.

(Brief dramatic music)

Narrator: The things that were happening to the eleven-year-old girl, did not confine themselves to the school room, they followed her home. There was the sound of knocking; vases fell over when no one was near them. A linen basket

149

opened and shut itself violently. An apple rose from a dish and rolled itself roundly out of the room. The word got round and the reverend Ewan MacDonald from Edinburgh was one of the many people who saw for themselves.

Reverend Ewan MacDonald states: *"In Sauchie along with two minister friends, I was asked to go up, and the three of us actually witnessed some of the visual and auditory phenomena. We heard the knockings, a few of the noises, and we also saw with our own eyes the rippling of the bed clothes. After a talk with the two doctors, and the Parish Minister, who were in on this all along, we held a simple service, two of us, and since then I believe, the child has not been disturbed at all"*

Narrator: The Parish Minister, the Reverend T.W. Lund, was first summoned to the Campbell household on Wednesday the 23rd of November, eight neighbours were already present, all were adults.

Reverend T.W. Lund States: *"As I was going up the stairs to where the girl was, I heard distinct knockings which seemed to come from a bed or some other wooden object, and when I entered the room, I found these eight people seated about the room, some on a small bed near the door of which the daughter of the house was sleeping and others on chairs, and one or two near the bed where the girl Virginia was herself lying, not asleep of course. As I stood there, I listened and heard repeated knockings on the head of the bed. I held the bed head and felt the vibration of the wood as the knocks, came. And then to my amazement I saw a linen box which had been reported to me, move. I saw it begin to shuggle about from side to side and give little spasmodic jerks, movements, and then I saw it move about 18 inches and move back again, which was certainly very strange to say the least. So, I put my hand on the box to see if I could feel any pressure of which the movement stopped at once. I stayed for some time, and again the knockings persisted. I finally had a word of prayer with the family I tried to relieve some of the tension which they all felt, to begin with, I tried to make light of it by suggesting to the girl, that this was her*

150

boyfriend knocking for her and she should knock back again on the head of the bed, at which certainly caused a laugh and relieved some of the tension".

Narrator: The following evening, Mr Lund returned, this time he was accompanied by two medical men, Dr. Nisbet and Dr. Logan, and another minister.

Reverend T.W. Lund States: *"We went along, I was there just a few moments before the rest and went upstairs and sat beside the girl's bed, she was in the small bed at this time, and I heard subdued knockings in the bed itself, and to my astonishment, I saw the pillow move from its normal horizontal position to an angle of about 50 degrees and move back again. These things had been reported to me but of course I hadn't seen the pillow moving until now. When Dr. Nisbet came up and his colleague and my own colleague, the four of us stayed in the room having put everyone else out. We watched intently and listened for some time but nothing remarkable happened. And then Dr. Nisbet's colleague and my own colleague went off, they had been rather sceptical about the whole thing I think, and as they had seen and heard nothing, perhaps they were in the same frame of mind when they went away. However, Dr. Nisbet and I stayed, and we did then see ourselves, the linen box begin to move and we heard some of the knockings and we saw the lid of the box raise by no human hands certainly and fall again. And all along we had taken what precautions we could to make sure that the girl herself was not instrumental in this, and on the first night I had seen that her head was away from the head of the bed that she couldn't be possibly knocking on it with her own head. And I had seen to that her hands were out of the bedclothes and that she wasn't knocking on the bed herself and I seen that her feet were closely tucked in, that she couldn't possibly be pushing the linen basket".*

Narrator: The narrative now moves onto the Saturday night.

Reverend T.W. Lund States: *"Well on the Saturday the vigil was kept at night by Dr. Logan who had went along and he reported that he had heard certain knocking sounds. And on the Sunday afternoon he took along with him his dog, because we know that dogs seem to be aware of psychic phenomenon more than humans sometimes. Nothing apparently happened in the afternoon, although the girl was fairly interested in Dr. Logan's dog, as she had a dog Toby herself in Ireland which she seemed to be missing and also her friend Annie, who she spoke about and she missed her too. Well at night I went along myself and about half past eleven I found the girl downstairs with her folks and I was told that she had, what seemed to me, like a term of hysteria, although I must say that she was herself withdrawn, quite reserved sort of girl not a hysterical girl in anyway. I wondered if this was just some secondary emotional disturbance. They told me that in the bed she had been rolling about when she went to bed with her eyes closed and as they said was in a trance like state and had been calling for her dog Toby and her friend Annie, and intermittently she had been barking herself like a dog. So, they had got her up, they were so disturbed by this, and she was downstairs having a cup of tea when I went in".*

Narrator: The girl then went back to bed and a strange little interlude followed.

Reverend T.W. Lund States: *"As I watched beside the girl's bed, and she was still in this state of mind and her eyes closed and continually calling for her dog, we thought we'd do something about it and we offered her a teddy bear. And whenever she got it she, with her eyes still closed of course, she felt the teddy bear and said, "Ah this is Toby" And then unfortunately her hand, as it went over the bear, found the brass button on the bear's tummy and she said, "Ah, this is not Toby at all" and she flung the teddy bear away and I'm afraid she hit out with her hand at those of us who were near. And I said, you know, this looks like to me perhaps a bit like hysteria, and maybe if Virginia didn't have an audience it would be the best thing that can happen, at which point I got a violent blow* *from Virginia who still had her eyes closed. However, I left them then, and as far as I know they had a quiet night".*

Narrator: At this point, someone came up with the idea that a change of location might be the solution for whatever ailed Virginia. It wasn't! She was taken to Dollar for a few days *(A nearby town, author's italics)* But all that happened was that different surroundings were soon energised so back she came to Sauchie and the fair view of Mr Lund.

Reverend T.W. Lund States: *"On the Thursday night, Dr. Nisbet Dr. Logan and myself, and three ministers in fact from Edinburgh went along, and we went upstairs and stayed in the room for quite a time we heard and saw nothing unusual except that we did hear some subdued knockings in the bed and certain scraping sounds which did occur now and again, and also sawing noises that were also heard by Dr. Nisbet and myself. And during a short service of prayer these knocking sensations continued. On the Friday we were back again and it was reported that there had been no disturbances of any kind, the girl seemed to sleep well. When she eventually fell to sleep on the Friday night when Dr. Nisbet and I had called, we were convinced that the manifestations were ceasing and that we would probably wouldn't see or hear anymore phenomenal happenings at all, and that the girl would soon be restored to a normal way of life just the same as any other adolescent girl".*

Narrator: The phrase adolescent girl may be important here, but we will hold it over until later. What we will not hold over any longer are actual tape recordings made in Virginia Campbell's bedroom during the course of the phenomena mentioned. Dr. Logan recorded these, and it is through his courtesy that we are now able to present them. The commentary is his too.

Dr. Logan States: *"The first recording that you are going to hear or the first part of the recording, is that in which the knocking or tapping sound is heard. This knocking and tapping was quite typical of the type of sounds heard during the nights*

153

in which the phenomenon was present, and they really are self explanatory. I would like to state here, that I satisfied myself that there was no possible outside source causing these sounds. The microphone at this stage was just beside the bed of the child standing on the linen basket as a matter of fact that features so prominently in many of the phenomena".

Audio Recording: At this point the knocking sounds are played to the radio audience. These were very sharp and quite distinct striking sounds.

Dr. Logan States: *"The sound appeared to come from somewhere in the region of the bed at that stage where Virginia was lying. I couldn't localise it, I looked under the bed, I stood at both ends of the bed, and I stood at either side of the bed, but I couldn't definitely pin point an exact source for the location of the sound".*

Audio Recording: Again, more of the knocking sounds are played to the radio audience.

Dr. Logan States: *"I was sure that there was nothing in the room and I made sure as far as possible that the child was quite immobile and that she had no part to play in the knocking, in fact I am quite convinced on that particular point, that the amount of noise that would have had to have been produced by the child, by quite a great deal I would say of physical activity and she was completely immobile. The next recording was made shortly after the service by the Church of Scotland Ministers. The mother and father had been with the chid for a time and they had gone out of the room for an instant, when this present sequence of events took place".*

Audio Recording: The audio tape is then played again to the radio audience only on this occasion you can hear a very loud scream by Virginia screaming out what sounds like, *"Ah mama/mother...look"*

Dr. Logan States: *"What actually happened there, was that the lid of the linen basket had risen up its full height and remained there until after the mother and father had came into the room, and I personally saw it and replaced it into its normal position. Now, I must point out at this stage that the microphone had been moved to a point on the wardrobe on top of the wardrobe just behind the door. Most of the manifestations were designed to attract the attention of people although this particular instance there was no one in the room when something visible did happen but the child's reaction was sufficient to attract the attention of everyone in the house. The microphone for this recording was placed on top of the wardrobe just behind the door. Dr. Nisbet had just left and was going down the stairs when the following sawing noise was heard. You'll hear the clock chiming in the background, the time was ten o clock, but you will only hear the end of the chimes".*

Audio Recording: The audio tape is then played again to the radio audience. The knockings that you can clearly hear are not so sharp as the previous ones. These knocking sounds seemed more of a dull knock and were quite rapid. For the record, I'm pretty sure that I heard the word *"Yes"* being uttered during these knockings, it was definitely a female voice and not, (for me) a young child's voice!

Dr. Logan States: *"Those are some knocking noises they are different in quality from the ones previously recorded".*

Narrator: The sound portrait of a poltergeist. Colour films were also taken of various uncanny instances. We asked Dr. Nisbet who is also a Baptist Lay Preacher, to describe his reactions to the events he had witnessed.

Dr. Nisbet States: *"I observed actually only on one occasion but that's indisputable, the lid of the linen basket rising up and then slamming shut. Before this happened, I myself having been warned that such a thing might occur, had seen to it that the linen basket was well away from any contact*

155

either with any person or with any surrounding object. And standing in the clear open floor to see this force, was something which no one could dispute, and which has to be accepted. I had always been brought up as a child to believe that in the world around about us, there was a spiritual force as well as a material force. Whether one wants to use the word spiritual force or simply force, is not to my mind terribly important. Our evidence was clearly that there was some force of which we were unaware or incognisant at least, existing in and about the room because of the affect of that force which we could hear and see"

Narrator: In the past, many other poltergeists have been abruptly disenthorned from supernatural status.   Some have been exposed as the product of conscious fraud, others have been fraud of the unconscious variety. In some cases, poltergeist phenomena, both visual and auditory, have turned up to be susceptible to coldly reasonable explanations escapes of natural gas, earth tremors, underground streams, carelessly disconnected wires and so on. Dr. Nisbet was not certain that reason applied to the Sauchie episode.

Dr. Nisbet States: *"When one sees it move about in the presence of a certain person, and only in the presence of that certain person, albeit not either nor connected to that person, it seems to me that anyone who gives that sort of explanation really is just too credulous for words. I took particular care in seeing that many of the events which I was a witness to were substantiated by the normal reason of sight and hearing. I was extremely careful with the linen basket which I've already said. I was also careful with some of the knockings and sounds around her bed (Virginia) and on one or two occasions, I actually had her uncovered in bed that is, she had no bed clothes on her when the knockings sounded, her hands being perfectly visible and also her feet. In these circumstances it seems to me that it is quite indisputable".*

Narrator: Nevertheless, there are those who will still dispute. And inevitably they will point out the recurrence in poltergeist history, of young girls reaching the stage of puberty.

Dr. Nisbet States: *"A very important matter arises there because in this particular type of experience as far as I know, this is my only experience, but having read some articles on the matter, it appears that this is related only to a girl in an adolescent stage. And that of course, we have to confirm from our observation in Sauchie".*

Narrator: One of Sauchie's most famous Scottish historical precedents happened towards the end of the 17th century. At that time, the woman who was to be responsible eventually for the pre-eminence of Paisley as a weaving centre was a young adolescent girl. Her name was Christian Shaw of Bargarron (*) her symptoms were more colourful than those of Virginia Campbell but have certain correspondences. Virginia's poltergeist, however, was much less deadly, since Christian Shaw's illness or possession, or whatever one cares to call it, led to the deaths of several people as Witches. The Sauchie Phenomena were observed much more scientifically but the eyewitnesses were equally emphatic.

Dr. Nisbet States: *"I saw these bedclothes moving and when I did so I was able to confirm that the girl's hands were not in fact underneath the clothes. Whether she could have done it with her hands underneath the clothes or not I'm very doubtful. But in fact, I was in a position to see her hands having previously asked her to put her hands outside the bed clothes and lay them on top. And even at that stage I watched these bed clothes moving with a sort of rippling movement as if they were being tugged up towards the girl usually".*

Narrator: Dr. Logan confirmed this empirically.

Dr. Logan States: *"I tried myself to make a similar movement when I got home but I found that the thickness of the* *blankets prohibited the reduplication of any similar movements that I had witnessed".*

Narrator: Still harping on the physiology of the adolescence theory, we asked Dr. Nisbet about the girls' medical history, was she a hysteric?

Dr. Nisbet States: *"I examined her medically on one or two occasions I have attended her medically for some minor infection at one stage. I do know that there is nothing abnormal in her medical set up".*

Narrator: Dr. Logan added a footnote on the girl's reaction to the experiences she had just undergone.

Dr. Logan States: *"I would say that she reacted in a normal manner towards something very unusual, but she showed fear and some alarm according to the degree of the manifestation. The knocks for example, didn't appear to upset her unduly. The rising of the linen basket caused her to scream out in terror, but she was quickly reassured. During one of the manifestations that happened, which hasn't been discussed so far is, oh I believe Mr Lund may have mentioned it, the sort of hysterical talking that she had just as she fell asleep. I took her pulse, and although she was quite agitated both physically and emotionally, her pulse rate was quite normal, slow and normal. I thought this rather unusual, but I can't explain it in any physiological way whatsoever".*

Narrator: Unless of course you postulate she expected the phenomenon. The Reverend Murdo Ewan MacDonald gave his summing up.

Reverend Ewan MacDonald States: *"I think the explanation of the phenomena is either what I would call an objective one or a subjective one. By an objective one I mean that these disturbances are caused by spirits not necessarily evil spirits, but spirits of a mischievous and irresponsible character, you might call them lower forms of intelligences* *existing in discarnate kind of manner. That's the objective explanation. Now the subjective explanation would imply that there is some kind of split in the personality of the person disturbed or the person of whom the phenomenon is centred. And there is a displacement of psychic energy which acts in a kind of explosive manner, throwing objects about the room. I myself, tend to lean towards the objective explanation because I don't think the subjective explanation does justice to all the facts".*

Narrator: That seemed to indicate to us that the service in the girl's bedroom was a form of exorcism. Certainly, there have been no manifestations since. What's the verdict? Well on the significance of what happened at Sauchie to Virginia Campbell, the Scope team is as divided for an opinion as any other group. Some of us take refuge in the usual open mind pointing out that when 90% of such cases are dismissed out of court, 10% still remain to baffle everyone, the same percentage hold course for Flying Saucers. Some of us accept the poltergeist possibility implicitly. One of us rejects out of hand and takes over the adolescent disturbance theory, stressing, that the girl was the youngest of a family of nine, the rest of whom had gone. That she was removed to a strange and possibly frightening environment, that the mention of the dog Toby and the friend Annie was significant, that the witnesses were predominately religious with an unconscious need to believe since as Wesley said to give up the Devil is to give up the Bible. And some of us line up with The Reverend Mr Lund when he says.

Reverend T.W. Lund States: *"It was a very humbling experience and I felt we were in the presence of forces hitherto almost unknown that we were just on the edge of a more or less uncharted ocean, that was my own feeling and I was feeling more or less lost in this quite new experience we sought help from the only power we thought could give us help".*

(*) Christian Shaw (Born in 1685 in Renfrewshire Scotland, Died 8th September 1737), Christian was a Scottish industrialist who is regarded by many, as the founder of the thread industry in Renfrewshire. As a child, she was instrumental in the Bargarran witch trials of 1697. (Source Wikipedia)

THE AUTHOR'S THOUGHTS ON THE
SCOPE PROGRAMME.

When I first heard this recording it simply blew me away. Here I was listening to the voices of the men who had first hand experiences in the Campbell home, men of integrity, who I'm sure were not given to exaggeration. They provided clear unemotional statements of what they saw, to say that they were solid and reliable witnesses would be an understatement. I guess without their exposure to the bizarre phenomena occurring in the Campbell household, they may not have believed it. But they were there, they were inches away from some astonishing events. Another thing that I took out of this programme, of which I almost missed and had to back track and hear it again, was a statement made by narrator who said,

*"There is a suggestion that the Sauchie poltergeist may have been **imported.*** (Author's italics in bold underline) *Their journey has been represented as a flight from the things that were already happening to Virginia, but this is not exactly clear"*

Oh, how I wish I could confirm this! I never for one-minute thought that they may had fled their farm in Moville County Donegal to move to Scotland simply because of poltergeist events occurring there! For me to listen to this 60 year old recording was just something else. Effectively, it's a time capsule of what, let's be honest, was a scary time in the life of young Virginia Campbell, part of which was recorded on audio tape as I say by men of integrity, pillars of the community. For me, this lends immense credibility to the case. The narrator came over slightly sceptical, but with an air of 'what if' in his voice. Of course, the Scope programme played but a few of those audio recordings, and one wonders where all the remaining recordings are? There must be more than this? Are

160

they lying something in a dark drawer, or tucked away at the back of a wardrobe, or indeed gathering dust in a loft somewhere? I guess we'll never know. Being 60 years old, they may have been thrown out. Who knows, maybe they will turn up one day like a long lost Lowrie painting! However, as we will see later, I did take steps to try and find these recordings (for a second time!)

Fellow Scottish UFO and Paranormal researcher Brian Allan also looked into the Sauchie case, and one interesting facet that I found coming out of Brian's research, was when he spoke about Dr. Logan. Brian managed to track down Dr. Logan, and in a conversation that he had with him, Dr. Logan stated that he was in no doubt, that the so called supernatural occurrences in the Campbell home could be explained in rational, physical, scientific terms. Dr. Logan went on to say that It is his opinion, whatever the mechanism was for these 'disturbances' to happen; then they could appear in anyone, at any given time. Of course, that logic takes us back to asking why! An interesting aspect that I found from Brian's re-investigation of this case was what Dr. Logan relayed to Brian. Dr. Logan stated that in his observations of Virginia and the sounds that he heard in her bedroom, he likened them to an MRI scanner *(Magnetic Resonance Imaging)* apparently when Dr. Logan had a scan in one of these machines, the noise it made was very similar, if not identical to the type of sounds heard in Virginia's bedroom. Brian is quoted as saying in his own article on his re-investigation.

"It is known that in suitable circumstances, when certain people interact with local magnetic fields, some truly extraordinary effects can and do occur. It is regrettable that there was not a co-ordinated scientific study carried out at the time; nowadays an occurrence such as this would produce some interesting findings"

Indeed. Brian also discovered that it was Dr. Nisbet that made the 8mm film of some of the phenomena that was a feature of the strange events in Virginia's bedroom. Brian

161

enquired if the film was still in existence, but he found out that as it was not the property of Dr. Logan, Brian believes that the family of Dr. Nisbet probably got rid of it.

ANOTHER SAUCHIE POLTERGEIST!
(The Maxwell Case)

Many years later in June 2000, when I lived in London, I received a telephone call at my work from one of my Scottish friends, ringing to tell me about a poltergeist case that was happening in a house in the same town of Sauchie near my old home town of Alloa in Clackmannanshire. This was too good to be true, I thought to myself, *"surely not"*. Not another poltergeist case in the same town surely! *(This would make it three! Park Crescent, Gartmorn Road and now another one in Park Crescent)* Generally speaking, poltergeist cases are usually short lived, as was the case in the famous 1960 incident previously mentioned. But for it to spring up and rear its ugly head again, in the 'SAME AREA' and close to where the other case happened, well it was something just short of incredible. Apparently, the local newspaper 'The Wee County News' was running with the story, so my first port of call was to contact them and find out more. This I did and they faxed through to me, the two page article on what was happening. The following are the basic facts from the Wee County News article on the incidents.

LIVING IN FEAR, *(Family say spook is forcing them out)*
{By Heidi Soholt} The Wee County News June 2000

A local family say that they are being hounded out of their home by a sinister presence believed to date back to the 1960s. The Maxwell's, from Park Crescent, Sauchie started hearing unexplainable noises, seeing household items moving and cupboards springing open soon after moving into their home a year ago. Mandy Maxwell (29) stated.

"Two weeks after we moved in strange things started happening. We could hear a baby crying and were lying asleep

162

one night when a cupboard flew open. The cupboard door had been secured with nails so there was no way it could have opened on its own".

Mandy went on to say, that she had also been pinned against a wall and thrown across a bedroom by an invisible force. The family were at first unaware of their home's strange history, and were horrified to learn that a recently published book, 'Ghost Hunters Guide To Britain' which features contributions from a range of authors, contained information on ghostly goings on at number 19 Park Crescent dating back to the 1960s, was this the Campbell's house! The book prompted a call from BBC Radio Scotland and the Maxwell's were interviewed about their experiences at number 30. Mandy's husband James (38) said that things have now escalated to the extent that the terrified family has had to move into one bedroom.

"Six of us are sleeping in the same room because of what's been happening in the other bedrooms. The weans, (Scottish term for children, author's italics in bold) are too scared to get up to go to the toilet at night. I've been onto the Paragon Housing about getting moved somewhere else, but they say there is nothing they can do. I've also been onto an estate agent about getting rented accommodation, but they've not got anything suitable for us. We've told Paragon that we would be prepared to take the kids out of school and move out of the district if it meant they would be safe".

Mandy said that she seemed to have been singled out by the ghost and still bore the bruises from being pushed down the stairs by it. She said she had caught glimpses of a dark shadowy figure described as 'semi-transparent' with water like ripples. *"No one will come to our house now"* said Mandy. In an attempt to keep the evil spirit at bay, James said that he has hung crucifixes on all of the bedroom doorframes. He said that he had also appealed to Father Kenneth McCaffrey from Alloa for help, but having discussed the matter with the Bishop, Father McCaffrey declined their request. James stated.

"We're seeing the poltergeist on a daily basis now and have been told that it has come back to the house because we've got a young family. If it gets any worse then I'll take a mattress and move my family into my car".

This then was the story that appeared (word for word) in the Wee County News. Now firstly I had to find out for sure, if indeed the house that was spoken about in Heidi's article was indeed the house which featured the famous case from 1960. I rang the newspaper up and offered my help as a researcher and someone who in point of fact did a re-appraisal of this famous case back in 1994 which was featured in their sister paper 'The Alloa Advertiser'. At this point I learned that my colleague Brian Allan from SPI Scotland had also notified the paper and offered his help. Knowing this, I then agreed for Brian Allan and SPI Scotland, (the research body that I founded back in 1979) to become officially involved with this case.

What we did find out, and this is vitally important that fellow researchers understand this. Is that the house in question in Park Crescent Sauchie which the above case refers to, is not, I repeat **'not'** the house that experienced those horrific poltergeist events of 1960. Somebody mentioned to the 'Wee County News' that this was the same house, and without any proper checking the 'Wee County News' ran with this piece of information, thereby unfortunately misleading its readers. This is an important fact, and one that you should be aware of because we don't want other authors writing things up for future books stating that the Sauchie Poltergeist re-surfaced in June 2000 after a 40 year absence. This won't do, so after all the 'hoo ha', this is just another independent poltergeist case from Sauchie. What I guess is quite unusual, is the fact that he original haunted house 'is in the same street' and is not too away from the current haunted house in question, but as I it is not the same house.

164

THE BRIAN ALLAN INVESTIGATION
OF THE MAXWELL CASE

In his own Investigation of this house, Brian Allan from Kincardine Central Scotland and his team comprising of Anne Marie Sneddon and Jim Lochead, uncovered that the six members of the Maxwell family had been subjected to strange noises and banging's coming from different parts of the house. Things really took a turn for the worse however, when Mrs Maxwell was thrown across her bedroom. Another strange thing that Brian uncovered in his investigation was the time when Mrs Maxwell heard a rustling sound which was coming from a carrier bag situated in the bedroom. Her initial thoughts were that a mouse had got into the bag, and not one who had a great fondness of mice; she woke her husband up from his sleep and asked him to take the mouse out of the bag. He took the bag out to the back garden, opened it up, and found. 'Nothing'! They then had problems with a bedroom cupboard door continually opening of its own accord, so much so that they decided to nail it shut, however, this did not stop the door from flying open, the door kept forcibly opening leaving the nails in place. Things were now getting so bad in the family home, that all family members decided to sleep in the same room. Thankfully, the only problems that they had in this room, was the sound of a baby crying, needless to say no baby was ever found.

The children were spooked by a dark shadowy outline moving about the hallway of which the youngest child chillingly called in *'the monster'*. Brian Allan also uncovered the fact that Mrs Maxwell simply refused to go upstairs on her own unless she was accompanied by others. Things got so bad that Mrs Maxwell started to spend her time at her mother's house. Brian and his team arranged with the family to spend the night where they would conduct their investigation. In Brian's report of the case he had this to say (in part)

"We sat quietly in darkness listening to the automatic systems in the house shutting down". "In the silence the ticking of the central heating pipes seemed very loud but eventually this too subsided". "The stillness was almost broken only by the sounds of the house 'talking', faint creaks from the woodwork and gurgles from the water pipes". "I thought I could detect the very faint, almost subliminal sound of voices, this proved to be emanating from the television in the sitting room". "We sat there for almost two hours but unfortunately nothing out of the ordinary occurred". "Just after midnight we went down to the sitting room to join the Maxwell's they had sensed nothing either"

"We remained in the house until 2 am and decided to call it off for the night." "We advised the young couple to tell their children, especially the two boys, that we had removed the 'monster' and taken it away with us." "We also explained that in our opinion, the children were affected by the fear of the adults, which was creating a vicious circle." "The mediums had already given us their opinion on the cause of the problem, so we gently suggested this to the Maxwell's." "I told them that it was quite probable that since there was no disturbance while the children were away from the house, then the unconscious stress of them being there was 'invoking' the presence." "Although they were unsure of this, they agreed that it could be possible, and decided to give it a few more weeks to see if the occurrences would cease". "We left a contact telephone number in case things took a turn for the worse, hopefully it will not be needed".

At the end of the day, Brian and his team believe that there wasn't any real ghostly phenomenon occurring in the Maxwell house, (nothing that convinced them anyway) still there was no denying, that the Maxwell family had been spooked by something, but was it all down to their own imagination or something else?

166

Through the Sauchie Legends Facebook page, I managed to track down Mandy who has since remarried. She confirmed the events at 30 Park Crescent and went on to say,

"I stayed in Park Crescent in Sauchie, not the same house, but I had things happen in there that I had to move out with my family. I was in the local newspaper the Alloa Advertiser, and also in ghost hunters guide to Scotland. The activity still continues to every house we move to which has been seen and heard by family and friends"

ALLOA ADVERTISER 2020

I presented some of the extracts from the local newspapers earlier in this book regarding the Sauchie case this was basically to set the scene for you the reader to see the depth of this fascinating case. During January 2020, I took the step of contacting the local newspaper to Sauchie, the Alloa Advertiser where I asked its readers if they could furnish me with any information regarding the Sauchie Poltergeist. I was looking obviously to hear from anyone who might have been in Virginia's class at that time. Moreover, I was looking to see if anyone had any photographs of Virginia including school class photographs. It drew a blank; I received no communications at all! Anyway, there were two local newspapers to Sauchie back in 1960, one was the Alloa Advertiser, which is still going strong today, and the other was the Alloa Journal, now long gone. The following that you are about to read, is the full text from both Alloa newspapers and how they covered these astonishing events back in 1960.

Title:	Ghost, Poltergeist, or what!
	(Strange Events Disturb Sauchie Household)
Newspaper:	Alloa Journal
Date:	Friday December 2nd, 1960

Virginia Campbell lived in a lonely house on the hills of Donegal in Ireland until two months ago. Eleven years old, she is the youngest of a large grown up family and her mother, Mrs

Anne Campbell, brought her to stay with a married son at 19 Park Crescent Sauchie. Just over a week ago, strange things began to happen to Virginia. Heavy pieces of furniture were seen to move when she entered a room, doors opened when she approached them and then were found difficult to shut.

Reliable Witnesses

Other and more unusual happenings occurred which have been witnessed by several responsible people. Virginia and her mother came from their home in Ireland two months ago to live with Virginia's married brother in Sauchie. Mrs Campbell found employment in a Dollar Academy boarding house and Virginia joined her niece Margaret and became a pupil at Sauchie School. But both little girls have had to be withdrawn from school temporarily because of the publicity and teasing which Virginia's unusual experiences have occasioned. Worried and anxious, Virginia's brother asked the Reverend T. W. Lund to try and help and also Doctor H. W. Nisbet of Tillicoultry, who attended the family, was called in.

Greatly Impressed

Both men have been greatly impressed with what they have been told and with what they themselves have seen. Their concern for the wellbeing of Virginia and their family has increased during the past week because of the effect which gossip, and publicity are having upon them. On Tuesday Mr Lund reported the whole matter to the Rev Horace Walker, Secretary of the Home Board of the Church of Scotland at their offices in Edinburgh, but a spokesman there, told the Journal yesterday that no action had as yet been decided upon. It is possible however at least one minister who is experienced in these matters may visit Virginia this weekend. Virginia is still being looked after by her friends and her physical health is still the responsibility of Dr. Nisbet. She is now staying with a cousin in Dollar, and yesterday it was reported that she was much quieter. But the testing time will come when she returns to the house in Park Crescent.

168

Lost Pet Dog

Before she came to Scotland, Virginia lost a pet dog of which she was very fond of and a little girlfriend died. Both occurrences upset her very much. One night when sitting on the edge of Virginia's bed, Mrs Campbell was roughly pushed off, and as she stood watching, she saw the blankets and sheets rising and falling above Virginia while the child made little moaning sounds like someone in pain. During the past week, the Rev T.W. Lund who has witnessed some of these happenings, has consistently refused to make any statements on what he has seen or to comment on his reasons for reporting the happenings to the Secretary of the Home Board. And, in view of inaccuracies of reporting his statements, Dr. Nisbet has refused to give information to the National Press since last Monday. The Rev, Dr T Crouther Gordon of Clackmannan who was the Presbytery's representative on a recent committee appointed by the General Assembly of the Church of Scotland to consider the subject of spiritual healing, said yesterday.

"I cannot possibly comment on what has been happening at Sauchie without first having an opportunity to examine carefully all the evidence".

Approached by the Journal, Mr James Henderson, Secretary of the Alloa Spiritualist Church, said,

"In my opinion this little girl has certain unusual psychic qualities and I am concerned that some person who has passed on is trying to communicate through her. I believe that a responsible medium should be taken to see the little girl for such a person could certainly help her. All that has been reported as happening in connection with her emphasises this necessity"

Bring Relief

"The medium might be able to take over from Virginia the pressure which is being put upon her from the other side and so bring relief to her. I am convinced that this little girl, if properly looked after spiritually, might be able to help many hundreds of people as the late Helen Duncan did"

Mr Henderson's understanding of the events surrounding Virginia was later endorsed by Mr James McNee, Scottish Secretary of the Spiritualist National Church. In an interview with a representative of the Journal last night, Mr McNee said,

"Happenings such as are taking place in connection with this little girl are not nearly so unusual as many people think, and contrary to much popular opinion, they are not necessarily evil in nature. Children are much more alive psychically than are adults and are often actually through unconsciously real mediums. If much of what is usually called their 'blethers' was seriously examined, they would be discovered to contain psychic communications from people who......" **(Author's note, I do not have the rest of this article unfortunately)**

Title: Doctor and Minister See Sauchie girl (The Strange Case of Virginia   Campbell)
Newspaper: Alloa Advertiser
Date: Friday December 2nd, 1960

Five doctors and two leading Church of Scotland Ministers have now seen 11-year-old Sauchie schoolgirl Virginia Campbell who is believed to be haunted by a poltergeist. Furniture moves and strange things happen in her presence. Dr. W.H. Nisbet, Tillicoultry stated in an interview, *"The child may have telekinetic powers"*. Dr. Nisbet has had to treat Virginia's family for hysteria. The child resides with her mother, married brother, and sister in law. The doctor, tired and worried said, *"Things have happened which I do not care to explain and they do not have a medical explanation"* The happenings occurred

170

in the girl's school, her teacher saw something, and in her home. Said Dr. Nisbet; *"Virginia does not control the happenings verbally, but I do not know whether she controls them from her mind"* Dr. Nisbet said he and the other doctors and ministers, had visited Virginia to satisfy themselves that things did happen, *"We confirmed that they did"*. Asked if he thought a leprechaun or poltergeist had invaded Virginia's life, he replied, *"I do not even know what a leprechaun is? A poltergeist! I looked up the meaning a few days ago and it may, or may not apply in this case"* At Sauchie School, the headmaster Mr Peter Hill said, *"I have never seen furniture shifting and we have not got any of our desks tied down. Things may have happened in the girl's home"*. Mr Hill suggested that the poltergeist may just be group hypnosis, but Dr. Nisbet turned down this theory. *"Group hypnosis does not apply in this case"* he said. At the Campbell's Council home understandably, they do not want to talk.

Church Attitude

Neighbours are guarded in talking about Virginia and her strange powers. They share the family's distress and do not wish to add to it by pandering to the sensation mongers and supplying them with further 'stories. In the question of poltergeists, the Church of Scotland is non-committal. Official pronouncements have been avoided by the General Assembly. At the Kirk's Headquarters in Edinburgh, an official said,

"The girl is entirely in the care of her doctor and minister. Her whole future and mental stability will depend on peace and quiet. This is entirely a personal thing"

The Rev. J.W. Stevenson, editor of the Kirk's magazine, 'Life and Work', recalled in an interview, an experience he had a year ago. He had been asked to visit the home of Baroness Kilbride at Fairmilehead, Edinburgh. In her house, doors had opened, strange noises were heard, articles moved mysteriously from room to room. Mr Stevenson and the Baroness prayed; the strange happenings completely stopped. Mr Stevenson

171

discussed it as a simple case of a minster praying with a person, and the prayer apparently being answered. But when asked about exorcism, Mr Stevenson replied, *"In the Church of Scotland we do not use that word, although other denominations do"*. But while Spiritualists and poltergeists are regarded with suspicion by most ministers, a few have become firmly convinced. One of the most outspoken is the Reverend Thomas Jeffrey, a former Alloa man and brother of Mr R.J. Jeffrey, and the Reverend George Jeffrey (an ex Moderator of the Church of Scotland) Now 81, Mr Jeffery has been a 'believer' in the spirit world for more than 50 years.

"People scoff about stories of ghosts and spooks, but they have not really studied the subject"

He said. *"In the case of this little girl, we have examples of well-known phenomena"*. Mr Jeffrey explained how John Wesley, the founder of Methodism, had had similar experiences in his father's home. Doors opened before one of Wesley's sisters. Mysterious noises shattered the peace of the house. Then one-night Wesley's mother prayed for her daughter to be relieved of her torment. The disturbances ceased said Mr Jeffery,

"But long before this, such phenomena were written in the Bible, when the boy Samuel heard the voices, the old priest Eli did not. But he knew that the boy had the gift from God"

Asked what could be done to help Virginia, Mr Jeffery explained,

"Some sympathetic person who knows about these things should go and speak to the spirit, say what they are doing and tell it to be quiet"

Rev. A. Rose Rankin, F.S.A. Minister of the Sauchie and Fishcross U.P. Church said,

172

"I have not taken much interest in the affair. Personally, I would like to contact the home and have a talk with the girl concerned. For unless I see the actual manifestations, I am afraid I can't accept the stories. To my mind it would be a great kindness to the home, if the people would leave it in peace"

A Debunker

Finally, a debunker, a Major Henry Douglas Home BBC man who has spent years investigating poltergeists many years ago he played a big part in exposing the story of Borley Rectory in Surrey, 'the most haunted house in England'. The Major said,

"Ninety out of a hundred cases can be explained no more mysterious than David Nixon on T.V. But the other ten cases, well some remain a mystery"

The following report from the Alloa Advertiser tells how the local church viewed the reporting of the Sauchie Poltergeist case. It was written by someone going under the simple name of the 'The Pilgrim' and each week he gave his own personal views to local news stories. As you will read, he was none too happy about certain elements of the Sauchie case. Some of the text from this article, which is not relevant to the Sauchie case, I have omitted.

Title: The Advertiser Feature. The Pilgrim Looks at Spooks
Newspaper: Alloa Advertiser
Date: Friday December 2nd, 1960

"Queer happenings these, up in Sauchie" I remarked to the Pilgrim when I met him in the middle of the week. "So, everybody says, but nobody seems to know much about what exactly is happening. The tale, as I've heard it, is that some sort of strange activity has focused round a young girl up there, furniture moved about and knocks are heard where there is no one to be seen, and I've heard it said too, that the lid of the desk

173

at school banged without good reason, (there must be something in that when the children were well warned not to discuss the matter out of school") "That's about all I've heard too, Pilgrim", I said. "But as far as the children are concerned, I've also heard that the bairns have been teasing the girl a lot which can't add to her peace of mind can it"? There was a long pause, then the Pilgrim said, "I wonder how much there is in all this? I wonder how much is rumour and how much is truth"? "I'm sorry you asked that Pilgrim!" "Why"? "Because I was going to ask you much the same questions!" "How should I know?" "Well I imagined that you might have very definite ideas about these things in general, if not in this case in particular". "It's not a subject that is very easy to be definite about, unless you've lived in the middle of such activities yourself, and I'm glad to say I haven't. I've never seen a ghost, and I've had more than a hint of second sight, such small hints that they might just be coincidence. And I suppose if you were determined to explain them away, the instance of telepathy I've experienced could be crossed off as coincidence too!" "But ghosts, you really don't believe in ghosts, do you"? To my surprise the Pilgrim was at a loss. "It's not a question I would like to answer a hundred per cent, "yes" or "no". Put it like this, when I hear and read of so many hundreds and hundreds of reputable people who say over a spell of hundreds of years that they've seen something of the kind, who am I to say, 'There's no such thing, your imagination was bothering you'. Supposing someone whose evidence would be trusted implacably in a court case, a senior police officer perhaps said to me, "You can laugh at me if you like, but I swear that on the stroke of midnight I saw two black horses pulling a black coach along Church Street and they vanished just as they reached the County Library, who am I to tell him that he is a liar"? "I see your point", I agreed. "But if anyone said they believed in ghosts; they'd still be laughed at". "Aye, and if anyone said there was something strange in Loch Ness they would be laughed at too, though mourners at a funeral quite clearly saw something in the loch the other day". He laughed. "What are you going to make of the kind of people who say, (as one teacher said up in Sauchie), I won't believe it until I see something happening right under my eyes, and then I'll phone Bellsdyke and ask them to come and take me away"? *(Author's note, Bellsdyke was a hospital several miles away that catered for mental illnesses)*

He shook his head. "We've a tremendous amount to learn about these things, and we won't learn it by behaving like the countryman gawking at the giraffe and saying, "There ain't no such critter"? "Have you ever been to a Spiritualist séance"? "Not me. I believe there are some things you're as well to leave alone"! "But how do you square that with what you've just said about finding out about these things"? "I can't square them, I just know there's a difference between trying to find out why a house has acquired a reputation for being haunted, and going to a séance and trying to conjure up the spirits of the dead. It may be unreasonable, but that's how I feel. And I'll tell you something else that may be unreasonable but is a fact, a lot of people have asked me whether I believe in ghosts, and they all use the same tone of voice as you, which says as clearly as words, 'I must admit, there's something in it but I'm ashamed to admit it straight out"

Title: Virginia On The Air
Newspaper: The Alloa Journal
Date: Friday December 16th, 1960?

Two Tillicoultry doctors used a tape recording of sound phenomena which had been heard during the recent psychic illness of little Virginia Campbell of Sauchie in the BBC Scottish Home Service programme 'Scope on Tuesday'

Lid Opened

The sounds in themselves, gently knocking sounds were not terrifying, but when a child's voice started screaming, *"Mummy, Mummy"*, that happened when Virginia saw the lid of the linen basket starting to open. The doctors explained it was then that listeners realised that something unusual was happening. Those taking part in the BBC programme besides

Dr. Nisbet and Dr. Logan, were the Rev. T.W. Lund of Sauchie and the Rev. Murdo Ewan Macdonald of St George's West Church Edinburgh. Mr MacDonald described the sounds and movements witnessed, and he considered that there were two possible explanations and he favoured the explanation that the phenomena were caused by some 'lower forms of intelligence'. The Presbytery of Stirling and Dunblane at its meeting on Tuesday, decided to ask the general Assembly's Church and Nation Committee to consider the conduct of a certain section of the National Press in the exploitation of such matters with a view to making representations to the Press Council.

Title: News of the Week. Virginia Back at School
Newspaper: The Alloa Journal
Date: Friday December 9th, 1960?

Virginia Campbell, the 11 year-old Irish girl who lives in Park Crescent Sauchie, was all set to return to school on Monday after her upsetting experiences of last week when she was troubled by strange phenomena.

Happy Child

When school time arrived however, so great was the battery of cameras and reporters outside the house that her parents decided to keep Virginia at home. They told our reporter that Virginia is now perfectly well and happy but they thought that Dr. H. W. Nisbet and their local minster would continue to keep a watchful eye on their child in case of a return of the disturbing happenings. Virginia has been attending school now since the middle of the week and is getting along happily in class and with her playmates.

Title: Virginia Is Now Returning to Normal. (Child had nothing to do with poltergeist, Dr. Nisbet)
Newspaper: The Alloa Advertiser.
Date: Friday 9th December 1960

Eleven year old Virginia Campbell the Sauchie girl who it is claimed, is being troubled by a poltergeist, and is expected to return to school this week, and there is every indication that her life may soon have returned to normal. Dr. William Nisbet, Tillicoultry, who has been treating Virginia, said at the weekend that the child had nothing to do with the poltergeist which had been plaguing her. Interviewed at his home in Stirling Street Tillicoultry, the doctor said,

"Virginia is not responsible for what has happened, the child is innocent. What has taken place was not conjured by the child herself, an outside agent is responsible"

Dr. Nisbet, father of three children then added,

"Believe me, something unfortunate has been going on in that house. I cannot give you an explanation. I have my own thoughts, but they are private for the moment. I hope to explain it fully, but that will be when I have had time to think about it more"

When the poltergeist was first reported, Virginia's mother, Mrs Annie Campbell, called in Dr. Nisbet, his partner Dr. Logan, and local Minister, Rev Thomas Lund. The three have already sent a report to the Church of Scotland.

The Dog

But last night Dr. Nisbet outlined what he thought was the CAUSE the EFFECT and the TREATMENT of the case.

"We have several theories about the cause" he said. *"The most important was the dog that the child left behind in Ireland. We thought that this was affecting her mind because it was her pet and she missed it terribly. Dr. Logan decided to bring his dog to the house to see if its presence would help, it didn't, the phenomena went on. It meant that either a dog was not the cause, or that her own dog was the only cure. The girl was hysterical all the time the phenomena were appearing. We*

177

decided then, to try sedation". Dr. Nisbet went on, *"Virginia was given mild tranquilisers to quieten her"*

Still There

"If the phenomena were being conjured by her own imagination they would no longer appear if her brain was dulled. But even though the brain was not working normally, the phenomena still appeared". Dr. Nisbet paused as his daughter burst into the room, collected some Christmas wrapping and left.

"The next thing we tried was a change of environment. Virginia was moved to a house in Dollar for two nights. The manifestations still appeared. She was brought back to Sauchie and we tried isolation. The child was put to bed and left on her own to get to sleep, but still the phenomena appeared and made itself heard from a room below. We could hear the child screaming and heard sawing and bouncing noises" Dr. Nisbet continued, *"Last Thursday three ministers were sent by the Church of Scotland. When Virginia went to bed, a short service was held at her bedside, we all prayed".* The doctor paused, *"Since that night nothing has happened. I believe the cure is now complete. In any case, we have on record by cine camera and tape recorder, what has happened, a moving linen box, the lid of the box opening and closing, rippling bedclothes, moving pillows, and bouncing noises".*

Its Over

"The tape and film will be available to any person who is interested in this case", said Dr. Nisbet. Virginia has been off school for more than a week, but these last three nights she has slept untroubled. On Sunday, the family went for a car drive. They chatted happily over tea at a wayside café, and they reassured each other 'the haunting is over'. Virginia, her cheeks flushed, came dancing into the house after the outing sucking an outsized cat's face lollipop. She sat giggling at the antics of Popeye on television. Said her mother, *"It's*

178

wonderful to see Virginia like her old self again, we want her to forget". Virginia smiled back at her mother, *"I'm happy now"* she said.

Title: Sauchie Ghost on The Air. (Ministers and Doctor sum up)
Newspaper: Alloa Advertiser
Date: Friday December 16th, 1960

The poltergeist of Sauchie made a public broadcast on Tuesday night. Thousands heard it on the B.B.C. Scottish Home Service programme 'Scope' There was nothing mysterious about the sounds themselves, they were only such mundane things as the noise of a hammer on wood and also a saw at work. These were the noises that plagued 11-year-old Irish girl Virginia Campbell after she came to live in her brother's home in Park Crescent Sauchie. They were recorded on tape by Dr. William Logan of Tillicoultry and in the broadcast they formed the background to a discussion on the poltergeist.

Screams

The noises themselves were not frightening. The knocking was like a hammer on wood, and certainly could not have been done by a child's hand. It was only when Virginia was heard screaming, *"Mummy, Mummy"* that the listener realised that something unusual was happening. Dr. Logan explained the screams by saying, *"That was when the lid of the linen box started to open"* Six independent people saw and heard the happenings at Sauchie, four Church of Scotland Ministers, Dr. Logan and Dr. William Nisbet of Tillicoultry. One of the ministers, the Rev, T.W. Lund of Sauchie Parish Church said, *"It was a very humbling experience"*. The Rev Murdo MacDonald said, *"We heard knockings and saw with our own eyes, the rippling of the bedclothes. We held a simple service at the girl's bedside and since then, the girl has not been disturbed"*

179

Spirits

Mr Macdonald summed up. *"These happenings have either a subjective or an objective explanation. The objective one is that the disturbances are caused by spirits, not necessarily evil, but of lower forms of intelligence. The subjective is that it is a displacement of psychic energy, an explosion. I lean to the objective explanation, the subjective does not measure up to the facts".*

Press Criticism

Stirling and Dunblane Presbytery on Tuesday night unanimously agreed to ask the General Assembly's Church and Nation Committee to consider the conduct of certain national newspapers in the poltergeist inquiry with a view to making representation to the Press Council.

Title: Poltergeist Probe.
Newspaper: Alloa Advertiser
Date: Friday December 23rd, 1960

When the Sauchie poltergeist story broke a few weeks ago, every effort was made by this newspaper to treat the matter with the greatest possible discretion to obviate any unnecessary distress to the parent of the girl who was the unfortunate objective of the visitation. In the first treatment of the story by our mid week contemporary, 'The Alloa Circular', the girl's name and address were not disclosed, but that very morning, the story was splashed in the National press and it became obvious that publicity could no longer be withheld, though the matter continued to be played down (and never up) in subsequent issues of the 'Advertiser'. Now we note that this whole question of press publicity with particular reference to the Sauchie Poltergeist has been the subject of some forthright comment by Tillicoultry minister Rev. P.D.G. Campbell, M.A. at last week's meeting of the Stirling and Dunblane Presbytery.

Of what help, asked Mr Campbell, were the swarms of reporters that descended on Sauchie, like one of the plagues of Egypt? Of what help to her were the banner headlines and the front page news? And he went on to expose to his Presbyterial colleagues some of the artifices and deceits employed by reporters to gain entry into this particular Sauchie home, and, once in, to photograph the householder secretly and against his express injunctions.

Well, as we have said, our own conscience in this matter is clear. Competition between the National newspapers is fierce, (conscience is one of the first casualties) and our playing down of the matter was not viewed as a mark of efficiency in certain quarters, but where the question of acting prejudicially to a young person's health is concerned, we have no regrets on erring on the safe side. Perhaps some of the professional men (not only in Journalism) involved in the Sauchie case may have cause to examine their own consciences in the matter. In one case at least, there was a strange switch from 'putting you on your honour' to using my own 'discretion' when it came to divulging information.

Title: A Plague of Pressmen at Sauchie. (Hillfoots Minister Condemns Poltergeists 'Visitation')
Newspaper: Alloa Advertiser
Date: Friday December 30th, 1960

After a strongly worded statement by the Reverend P.D. G. Campbell, M.A. Minister of St Serf's Church Tillicoultry, at a meeting of the Presbytery of Stirling and Dunblane in Allan Park Church Stirling last Tuesday night, it was decided to request the Assembly's Church and Nation Committee to consider the actions of representatives of some sections of the National Press in news gathering with a view to making representations to the Press Council. At one time, Mr Campbell referred to certain newspaper reporters as having descended like one of the plagues of Egypt in trying to get information about one incident in the area. He said that if he were to choose a text for his theme, it would be from Leviticus, 19, verse 16, *"Thou shalt not go up and down as a table bearer among thy*

181

people". His report concerned particularly the National Press, and certainly one section of it.

Many Capacities

Newspapers were essential parts of modern life they acted in many capacities, as safety values for people with a grievance, as guardians of liberty, and mouth pieces of pressure groups of varying parties as advertising media, and as disseminators of news. His concern was with papers in their primary function as 'news' papers. In the past few weeks, said Mr Campbell, various events within the Presbytery had hit the headlines. But he emphasised, he wanted before going further, to pay tribute to the local press for its consistently accurate, and where it merited, sympathetic treatment of all proceedings. They had never failed the Presbytery in their courtesy and co-oporation. It has been said that the Church was 'always against things', that it was negative in its outlook. Recently they had passed on the Assembly's injunction against raffles and had also commended the positive virtue of Christian Stewardship. In one paper the positive commendation was omitted the feelings of ordinary decency and common human sympathy. Parents were bereaved under tragic circumstances. Reporters descended upon the stricken household. Some made their enquiry and went on their way. Two others, seen by the father, wished to interview and photograph the mother. Their request was refused. Later, the same evening, they returned, and stated they had instructions to get an interview and photograph of the mother in order, they said, *"To bring home this tragedy to our readers".* 'Moderator continued, Mr Campbell, *"I dare say no more, lest my feelings so run away with me that I forget that the person who gave such an order, and the persons who tried to fulfil it are supposed to be men of integrity. Is any paper an organ of such high moral tone that it alone has such a mission of righteousness".*

182

False Pose

But the case that accorded the greatest publicity, said Mr Campbell, and has achieved the greatest notoriety, was that involving the strange happenings in Sauchie with banner headlines and front page news.

Sensational Presentation

There were two aspects of the case which he wanted members of the Presbytery to consider. The methods of presentation were one, and the other was the method by which reporters gathered their news. The presentation was sensational in the worst sense. It included unsubstantiated rumours in 'capitals. It included verbatim the text of a letter from the child's mother to the father. The propriety of printing such a letter, no matter how come by, was extremely doubtful. But the sensationalism of the whole business, must have been, and was, a grave handicap to those who were grappling with a difficult and distressing situation. Was it not deceitful when in another man's house to photograph him secretly and against his express injunctions? When the father of the Sauchie girl came to the house, he was accompanied by two men who claimed to be his friends. One of them at least claimed to be a contractor on the pretext of going to the bathroom. One went upstairs but he went to see and report.

Their Identity

Only after they were out of the house when arrangements were being made late at night for their accommodation, did they reveal they were not contractors, they were not from Northern Ireland, they had met the father for the first time that day. They were in fact reporters. Mr Campbell stressed that if the public knew that these were the methods employed to produce news stories, and if the public realised that they were liable to receive such treatment themselves, the same of newspapers relying on such methods would suffer a catastrophic decline. Without comment, the Presbytery agreed to Mr Campbell's request for

183

passing the matter to the Assembly Church and Nation Committee.

Title: Poltergeists
Newspaper: Alloa Advertiser
Date: Friday December 1960

Writing in the Glasgow Herald on the subject of poltergeists, well known Dollar Journalist W. Kersley Holmes, has these comments to make.

"Those who are interested in unusual happenings hope that there is more foundation for the Sauchie Poltergeist affair than for the tales of Borley Rectory (a haunted mansion of long ago) After the death of Mr Harry Price who might be called the compere of that sensation, 'the most haunted house in England' was thoroughly examined by the Psychical Research Society for a long time suspicious, and they proved the whole business a very clever hoax. Their findings were published. Still, queer things do happen in Clackmannanshire? Years ago a girl who had been out with a pram not very far from Sauchie, reported that the baby it contained had been attacked by an eagle which was not to be diverted even by the offer of a sweet biscuit. The tale was rather spoilt by the discovery that the eagle was in fact an escaped tame jackdaw"

STILL IN THE PRESS

Since the 1960's, there has been a number of references in the local Alloa newspapers about the Sauchie Poltergeist. As you will see, the following report comes from 2003.

SCARY STORIES FROM THE COUNTY

The Alloa Advertiser of Thursday 30th October 2003, (their Halloween edition) had a middle page spread entitled, *'Sauchie's Supernatural Experience'* which was all about the Sauchie Poltergeist. There was a further column on this middle page spread entitled, *'Scary Stories From The County'*, the

184

County of course was referring to the 'Wee County' the smallest county in Scotland located in Clackmannanshire. I won't reprint this 2003 article on the Sauchie Poltergeist, as it pretty much states much of what I have already written. But what I will note from that article is that it said that Virginia and her family moved away from the area and have refused to speak to anyone about the events of 1960. It went onto say that Virginia, now in her 50's, was happily married and living in the Sheffield area in the heart of England. What I will reprint however, is that interesting 'sub story' about those scary stories from the 'Wee County'. This piece was written by the Advertiser's Stuart Nicolson, he wrote.

Although 'Wee Hughie', the so called Sauchie Poltergeist is without doubt the most famous of the county's spooky residents, there are plenty others lurking in the shadows. Many of the best local scary stories focus on Alloa's Greenside Cemetery, with its imposing Gothic appearance being enough to send shivers down the spine even today. In June 1658, the cemetery was the centre of the Alloa Witch Trials, which saw five women convicted of being in league with the Devil for over 20 years, doing his bidding by murdering two other local women. While in the 1820's, the number of bodies being stolen by grave robbers, similar to Edinburgh's notorious Burke and Hare, led to the formation of a local society for the protection of the dead. And in 1909, the unfortunate occupants of a house bordering the cemetery were alarmed to hear loud tapping noises coupled with what sounded like people arguing in a foreign tongue. Like the story of Virginia Campbell some 58 years later, the 'Great Alloa Ghost Scare' became an overnight national sensation with an eminent Glasgow doctor turning up at the haunted house and bravely pledging to banish it back to the spirit world as reporters looked on. The doctor's exorcism attempt ended in failure, but the inhabitants of the house, didn't appear overly concerned as adverts immediately appeared in the local press encouraging people to come along and see the ghost, for a small fee of course. Nine years later, hundreds of people stopped in busy Mill Street to stare at a mysterious elderly woman of 'unearthly appearance' who was spotted peering out of an open attic window.

Spirits of Ships

When the authorities climbed the stairs to the attic, they found no trace of the old woman whatsoever, but for days afterwards, shoppers would walk down the opposite side of the street, casting covert glances up at the window which had caused the commotion. The spirits of a series of ships built in Alloa by Conrad Klovborg at the turn of the 19th century which all sank or simply disappeared were said to be haunting the town's docks. And in 1930, two women living in the huts, originally built as accommodation for people working at the Cauldron Aircraft Factory near Lime Tree Walk, collapsed after an apparition appeared before them, sparking a frantic all-night ghost hunt. However, rumours quickly began circulating that the 'ghost' had in fact been a novelist gathering material for a book.

Other towns in Clackmannanshire have had their fare share of ghostly goings on too, with a spectre said to be haunting Tait's Tomb, on the road between Tillicoultry and Dollar, plucking up enough courage to get on a passing bus during the First World War, before vanishing into thin air. While in 1875, a ghostly figure dressed all in white, spent several weeks wandering around the streets of Alva after dark. But our favourite story concerns a wicked Tillicoultry Laird, who struck one of the Monks at Cambuskenneth several hundred years ago and died shortly afterwards, apparently as a result of 'over eating'. Soon after burying him in the local graveyard, locals were somewhat perturbed to find the Laird's hand sticking out of the ground. He was reinterred on a number of occasions, but every time, the hand would reappear. A meeting was hastily held by the men of the town, who considered paying a sum of money to the Monks in return for a lifting of the curse, before deciding that sticking the biggest rock they could find on top of the grave, would probably be a cheaper option.

MY FILMING WITH THE B.B.C. ONE SHOW

Being at the forefront of UFO and Paranormal research, I often get contacted by members of the media to assist them with the makeup of television shows and documentaries. In early 2019, I filmed a piece for the B.B.C One Show, made by One Tribe T.V. on one of Scotland's most famous UFO Abductions cases, known as 'The A70 Incident'. This involved two Scottish men who claimed to have been abducted from their vehicle on the desolate (in part) stretch of road known as the A70 in Central Scotland. As I had worked with the One Show before, I received a call from Tom Parry, one of the producers at One Tribe T.V. who made that short piece for the One Show in 2019, and he asked if I had any more unusual and bizarre Investigations that I had worked on that they might consider as a piece for the B.B.C. One Show? I did, and plenty of them! I settled on two ideas for One Tribe T.V. the first one being, the Sauchie Poltergeist case which had never ever been seen on television as a news piece or docudrama, before. The only news to come out about the Sauchie Poltergeist was massive newspapers accounts from both local and National newspapers (and a few overseas) As well as newspapers, there was one major radio news piece about the Sauchie Poltergeist, and that was on B.B.C. Radio Scotland back in December 1960. After that piece, there were (as far as I know) no major media coverage on this famous case, certainly as I've stated, no television coverage. So, visually, the Sauchie Poltergeist had never been presented on television before. I've always said that this would make a great news piece or docudrama for television, and whilst a docudrama would be more befitting of this impressive case, a short five minute piece on National Television at Prime Time, would certainly suffice and do it justice. And, as we have read throughout this book, the town of Sauchie was very close to where I lived when I stayed in Scotland. The down side of all this, as far as providing witnesses to One Tribe T.V. the makers of this show, was of course that some of the classmates of Virginia Campbell had

187

either moved away from the area or had sadly passed on. I was sadly to learn whilst doing my third Investigation into the Sauchie Poltergeist (1984-1987-2020) that teacher Margaret Davidson (formally Margaret Stewart) who was one of the major witnesses in this case had passed away a few years ago. So, trying to obtain potential first hand witnesses would prove to be a struggle, 'as it certainly did'. I even placed a short piece in the Alloa Advertiser asking for any people who had been in Virginia Campbell's class at that time, to get in touch, 'nobody did' so clearly I had my work cut out trying to get some 'talking heads' for the lovely chaps at One Tribe T.V. Other than myself, One Tribe T.V. managed to track down Dr. William Logan's wife Sheila, also a doctor but now retired, who agreed to go on camera, but more of all this later.

The second piece that I spoke to One Tribe T.V. about was the Dechmont Woods UFO Incident of which forestry worker Robert Taylor encountered a hovering domed shaped object in some woods near Livingston Central Scotland and which was the focus of my seventh book, *'The Dechmont Woods UFO Incident', (An ordinary day, an extraordinary event)* available on lulu and Amazon. So, with those two suggested cases, they went away to speak to their bosses. The upshot was that the management at One Tribe T.V. loved the two cases I presented them with. They then pitched these two cases to the big wigs at the B.B.C and they loved it too. Both were commissioned, a budget was set, a presenter was sought (Matt Allwright from shows such as Rogue Traders and Watchdog) and a date in February 2020 was set for filming. The following is but a brief rundown of that weekend's filming.

TRAVELLING BACK TO SCOTLAND

I travelled back up to my homeland of Scotland on Friday 14th February 2020 during storm Dennis, and I can tell you that my take off from Gatwick Airport was a wee bit hairy to say the least, but thankfully those lovely pilots of Easy Jet made sure that I arrived safely in Edinburgh. From there I was met by producer and director Tom Parry, where we proceeded to jump into the One Tribe T.V. van and drove across to the town of

188

Deans near Livingston where our air B&B was situated. As there were no filming that day, Tom, and the other One Tribe T.V. people Cameron Howells (Researcher) Sonny Mackay (Camera Operator) and Joe Hufford (Camera Operator) all went out for a lovely Nando's meal in nearby Livingston.

Saturday 15th February 2020

After collecting presenter Matt Allwright at his hotel, our first port of call on Saturday the 15th of February, was to do some filming on part of the Ochil Hills near the town of Dollar. It had been arranged by the team, that a local farmer would take them up one of the hills in order for the team to get some good commanding shots of the Forth Valley looking over to the town of Sauchie. Driving over to Dollar the weather had been pretty poor with driving rain which thankfully stopped when we reached the farmhouse near Dollar. With filming complete, it was then a short drive over to the town of Sauchie where Virginia Campbell and her family had lived back in 1960. All this countryside was very familiar to me, simply because, this was my old home turf. I used to live in Sauchie before I moved to England, so to be filming here in Sauchie was a bonus, considering we could have been filming anywhere else in the whole of Scotland, but here we were on my old home turf. Our next filming location was the Mansfield Pub in Sauchie which pretty much backs onto the Campbell's former back garden. The Mansfield was a pub that I had also frequented during my time in Sauchie and many a lovely meal was had in there, especially at Christmas. We arrived just after 09:30am and the manager of the Mansfield along with his son, had opened up early for us and provided us with hot tea and coffees along with bacon rolls, which I can tell you, were demolished very quickly by the chaps at One Tribe. We set up the cameras in the lounge and Matt and I were sat in front of a small but roaring log fire and proceeded to get right down to talking what I knew about the Sauchie Poltergeist. With my piece done, I asked Tom the producer if I had some time to pop round and see my mother Ellen who lived just around the corner at Braeside and whose house faces onto the Sauchie Poltergeist house albeit, a short distance up (some coincidence eh!) Tom happily said that I had, so I rushed out into the pouring Scottish rain and within a matter of minutes was in my mother's front room enjoying a cup of tea. Whilst at my mother's, I looked out of her front living room window to see the chaps at One Tribe T.V. filming a piece near the Sauchie Poltergeist house. It was absolutely chucking it down, and good use of the golf umbrellas placed above the expensive cameras, ensured that no water damage crept into the cameras themselves. Storm Dennis sure was making its presence felt! After chatting with my mother for 10 to 15 minutes, I went out into the rain and met back up with the team where after filing a few more minutes in the rain with Matt doing his piece to camera, we jumped back into the van and drove off to Edinburgh to film retired police detective Ian Wark for the Dechmont Woods UFO programme. I won't mention too much about this filming here, as the nature of this book is of course on the Sauchie Poltergeist, all I will say is that Ian Wark did a marvellous job in presenting the facts to One Tribe T.V. on his role in the Dechmont Woods Incident. After filming in Edinburgh, we drove back to Sauchie in the hope that the rain might ease off when we got there and we could do some more filming, it didn't, well not really, but during a break in the rain where it was not so heavy, One Tribe did manage to get some more footage, ah the good old Scottish weather!

After filming on the street at Park Crescent, we once more jumped in the van and headed back to the nearby town of Dollar where our next interviewee was waiting, Sheila Logan, the wife of Dr. William Logan who was witness to many of the Sauchie poltergeist events and who recorded their sounds. Sadly Dr. Logan is no longer with us, but his wife, who herself was a doctor, was more than willing to share what she saw with us. I must admit, I was really looking forward to hearing what she had to say. I personally had never interviewed her and just to hear that One Tribe T.V. had managed to track her down was terrific. After getting slightly lost in the Dollar countryside, we eventually found her house which was off the beaten track and, after taking our shoes off, we were ushered into her lovely home. She had a friend called Brian who was visiting, who, we later found out, didn't know that Sheila was part and parcel of the Sauchie Poltergeist story, Sheila never brought it up with him, so he too, was hearing about it for the first time. After setting up the cameras, Matt Allwright got down to interviewing Sheila about her role in the case. I ensured that I used the voice recorder on my phone to capture this interview of which the full transcript you will read shortly. After this interview, we headed back to Livingston where we dropped presented Matt Allwright off at his hotel after which we headed to our air B&B. We all met up later where we had a lovely meal at the Tony Macaroni restaurant.

The following day, Sunday 16th February, after a hearty breakfast made by Cameron and Joe, we drove over to Dechmont Woods near Livingston to film my part as a researcher on one of Scotland's biggest UFO mysteries, which was the traumatic events that occurred to forestry worker Robert (Bob) Taylor when he encountered what he believed to have been a UFO in Dechmont Woods. Thankfully there was a lull in storm Dennis, and we had blue skies to film under, a big change from the previous day. All in all, my piece to camera went out and it was aired to the British public on the B.B.C. One Show a few weeks later. I must admit, it was great to be back in Scotland, and to film in my old home town was just great. Matt Allwright who interviewed me, was a true professional, and his well thought out questions were a joy to answer (although some were tongue in cheek!) Of course, on both shoots I said so much more, way more than what was presented when it came out on television. I'm sure Tom Parry the One Tribe T.V. producer/director had a very hard job trying to cut and paste all the best bits from the interviews as well as the reconstructions etc. I'm sure that so much good 'stuff' was left on the cutting room floor simply because of the time constraints of the piece, just five minutes long. This was my third B.B.C One Show, with the A70 case in 2019, and these two cases Sauchie and Dechmont, in 2020.

So, with both subjects covered, it was time to head back to Edinburgh Airport to catch my flight back to London Gatwick.

The flight was due to take off at 5:55pm, it didn't, and it eventually took off at 7:45pm. My train leaving Gatwick Airport to Hastings was also late and I eventually arrived back in Hastings England at five minutes past midnight, tired but extremely happy that the British public had the opportunity to learn about two of Scotland's biggest mysteries. It had been great fun working with the lovely guys of One Tribe T.V. and I wish them continued success with their future filming projects.

As mentioned above, I left my audio recorder on my phone recording the interview with Sheila Logan.   Here is the transcript of that interview.

Interview with retired doctor Sheila Logan at her home near Dollar Clackmannanshire, Central Scotland.
(15th February 2020)
Interviewer, Matt Allwright.

What follows, is word for word on what former doctor Sheila Logan had to say about her role in the Sauchie Poltergeist case. Dr. Sheila Logan came along to the Campbell household on the request of her husband Dr. William Logan. William, as we have read elsewhere, had already visited the Campbell house on a few occasions, and in this interview, retired doctor, Sheila Logan, gives her recollections about what happened when she visited the family home.

Abbreviations
(MA)   Matt Allwright
(SL)   Sheila Logan

(MA) *"Dr. Logan, tell me how you became involved in the Sauchie haunting"?*

(SL) *"Well I became involved in it because my husband, Dr. William Logan was a G.P. in Tillicoultry and was the G.P. of the girl who was involved in this particular episode He told me a lot about it, I was interested to see for myself and as I am not a particular believer in the paranormal, I really wanted to see what was happening. I was very sceptical about the whole* affair and he suggested that I come along one day to see for myself."

(MA) *"I mean you are a woman of science you were a doctor is that fair to say that, would you consider yourself a woman of science"?*

(SL) *"Yes"*

(MA) *"Would that be why you were sceptical about it?"*

(SL) *"No, not entirely, but it was partly because I'm just more of a believer in what can be measured and explained rather than, theories".*

(MA) *"So when somebody reported to you and your husband, your husband said, "Well this is something that I am going to have to deal with". What were you thinking, what was your reaction?"*

(SL) *"I was thinking that somebody was involved in setting this up, that it wasn't anything beyond the bounds of possibility".*

(MA) *"So a prank or a hoax, would that describe it"?*

(SL) *"Something like that yes"*

(MA) *"So what happened then, did your husband attend, did you attend, how did it play out"?*

(SL) *"This whole episode had been going on for about two weeks before I got involved. The girl was moved from Sauchie to Dollar to another house thinking that perhaps her episodes were due to the house rather than her but in fact it continued when she came to Dollar. And it was at that point that I went along one afternoon".*

(MA) *"What were you hearing about what was happening"?*

(SL) *"I was hearing what people had seen that furniture had moved by itself. There had been knocking noises of various kinds. There had been a disturbance at school. And various ministers had become involved and had tried a service of intercession in an attempt to clear this matter up. And I was very curious to see for myself what was going on".*

(MA) *"Did you think to yourself well, there has to be a solution, and maybe I am the person that can point it out or discover it"?*

(SL) *"No, I didn't think that, I was just interested to see what was happening"*

(MA) *"OK, so we have several weeks, or a number of weeks leading up to the point where you get the chance to see with your own eyes and hear with your own ears what's happening"?*

(SL) *"Yes"*

(MA) *"OK then how did you approach that then"?*

(SL) *"With an open mind. I went to see what was happening and go away and think about it and try and make sense of it"*

(MA) *"OK, so describe to me what happened when you approached the house"*

(SL) *"The girl was lying in bed; she wasn't disturbed in any way she was a perfectly normal 11 year old. But there was a series of knockings, both the sound of a ball bouncing down the staircase and rappings in the room which could become agitated or calmed down, they varied in intensity and the counterpane of the bed (**Counterpane is another word for**

194

bedspread/quilt, author's italics in bold) *which she was not near, rippled.* *It was in the days when a silk type of counterpane was on a bed instead of downies,* **(Author's italics.** **Duvet is another word for Downies)** *and it rippled".*

(MA) *"The girl is in the bed at this stage"?*

(SL) *"The girl was in the bed, and of course I looked hard to see if she was doing any rippling, but I couldn't see that she was".*

(MA) *"Is it the sort of thing that you could simulate somehow, that you could make happen with perhaps something underneath the surface..."?*

(SL) *"I think that's possible, if you were determined to deceive someone, I think you could. Somebody could have been outside bouncing a ball down; I had no way of telling that. I can only tell you what I saw; I can't tell you why it happened"*

(MA) *"So you see these phenomena, you hear the sounds, then what did you do next. Did you investigate anymore? Was it just the fact that you were witnessing it that it was enough?"*

(SL) *"I looked to see if there was anybody outside the door doing anything to the stairs. But by this time I knew very well of what everyone else had seen, it wasn't a surprise to me that these things happened, because they had been witnessed by ministers and various doctors"*

(MA) *"I'm really interested to know, I mean, you were there, you are there to add your testimony your witness to it as well. How did you feel, did you feel frustrated and annoyed that you couldn't do anymore"?*

(SL) *"There was absolutely no feeling of any eeriness or anything that would make me feel uncomfortable. I certainly was sorry that I couldn't add anything to it, but I didn't feel* *that there was any inclination that I had that anybody else didn't have".*

(MA) *"Your husband also spent time with Virginia, was this in Sauchie and also in Dollar"?*

(SL) *"Yes, mostly in Sauchie".*

(MA) *"OK, and what were the reports that he brought back from the house?"*

(SL) *"Sometimes the girl could become quite hysterical and hit out at people and didn't seem to remember the next day that this had happened. He had seen evidence of that. He had taken a dog along to see if the dog had any particular sensitivities. And this had tended to upset her, as it reminded her of the dog she'd left in Ireland. He found that on one occasion when she had been quite hysterical and upset, that her pulse was absolutely steady and normal, he thought that this was unusual in somebody who had been so agitated".*

(MA) *"Did he draw any conclusions from that"?*

(SL) *"No, no, neither of us knew the answer to this, we just knew what we saw".*

(MA) *"You are faced with a puzzle"*

(SL) *"Yes"*

(MA) *"Was that infuriating in any way?"*

(SL) *"It's always been very interesting, and I've always been interested in to see what evidence other people have come up with, or theories that other people have come up with, but so far I don't think that there have been anyone who has been able to explain it"*

(MA) *"What was it you were witnessing; what do you think you saw?"*

(SL) *"I don't know. Some sort of force that the girl was able, perhaps unconsciously to make things move. Now I know that sounds very odd, but there are a whole lot of things that can't be explained but are quite rational".*

(MA) *"It sounds like you are talking about some form of kinetic energy or Psychokinesis is that........"*

(SL) *"Well I can't put a name to it, but I think that it is possible that a very disturbed person can produce this sort of phenomenon".*

(MA) *"Are you familiar with the film 'Carrie' have you ever seen that?"*

(SL) *"No"*

(MA) *"It concerns a very disturbed woman who makes things happen with her mind, very bad things actually. From what you are saying, that sounds like the best explanation that you can have, for what you saw is some kind of psychic kinetic action of some sort"?*

(SL) *"Yes, it always seems to happen to people who are very disturbed for one reason or another".*

(MA) *"Does that jar at all with you in anyway? I mean, you are a woman of science, a doctor, does that feel that that is at odds with that in any way?"*

(SL) *"No I don't think so, I think that there are a lot of forces that have not yet been discovered or investigated in any way, perhaps in time we will learn what causes this"*

(MA) *"I'm interested in that your husband would have come home and would have had his conclusions. Can you tell* *me a little about the conversations that you had with each other about what to make of it all"?*

(SL) *"He's certainly told me of what he'd seen, and we did discuss what could possibly have been the cause of it, but we didn't come up with an answer".*

(MA) *"Really, and the time that you had together, a mystery that you had, a puzzle that you couldn't really resolve, that's kind of great* (Both laugh) *These things don't tend to happen to people during the course of their lives. To both witness something together. As people of science, you know the people who are tasked with coming up with answers for us all, but you still both have this mystery between you"*

(SL) *"Well we both knew that we didn't know everything"*

(MA) *"OK, tell me what I've missed in this story, because there are bound to be things, you know, a life time of wondering about this, and things that have cropped up that maybe I haven't asked you about"*

(SL) *"No, I can't think of anything that has any bearing on this subject at all"*

(MA) *"Do you know how the story ended, because there is so much interest in this at the time and really since?"*

(SL) *"Well it was investigated by a paper, and they apparently tracked down the girl, five years later and found that she was a perfectly normal teenager with very little memory of what had happened and not disturbed in any way"*

(MA) *"So she couldn't really remember it"?*

(SL) *"So she could remember it but wasn't terribly interested in it. She saw this as an episode in her past and was getting on with her being a teenager"*

(MA) *"So whatever it was, it was a phase"!*

(SL) *"It was a phase very definitely with her"*

(MA) *"When you tell this story to people that you were involved with this over the years, what do they make of it, how do they react"?*

(SL) *"It isn't anything that I have discussed very much actually".*

(MA) *"Because the fascination about it is clearly out there"*

(SL) *"Yes. I can't say that I have conversations about it. In fact Brian here knew nothing about it till last night"*

(MA) *"Really this is your friend"* (Points to Brian in the room)

(SL) *"Yes a friend of mine who is visiting"*

(MA) *"So you have close friends who never knew that you were a part of it at all"?*

(SL) *"Yes"*

(MA) *"How curious. I mean it is a curious thing to carry for all those years"*

(SL) *"Well it is a long time in the past you know, and life goes on"*

(MA) *"It's the sort of thing that I think I would really remember"*

(SL) *"Well I remember it, but I don't feel that I have to discuss it with other people much. Partly because I can't give any answers".*

(MA) *"So it's one of those open ended mysteries"?*

(SL) *"As far as I'm concerned yes"*

(MA) *"Would you love to know what it was all about"?*

(SL) *"Oh I would"?*

(MA) *"I can't give you any answers"* (Both laugh) *"I can't offer anything at all only more questions, of which are of no help to you"*

NB: At this point, Tom Parry, the producer of this piece, cut in and asked Sheila if she would be so kind as to go back a bit, and talk more about the time when she first went into the house where Virginia lived, and to describe her feelings as she walked into the house.

(SL) *"Well actually it was all very normal, there wasn't that many other people there, there wasn't a particular atmosphere. As G.P.'s we were constantly walking into other people's houses it was just like any other visit that I might have made".*

(MA) *"What was it like walking up to the steps of that house knowing the reports that your husband and other people had been making about what was going on"?*

(SL) *"Well I was feeling intense interest in what I might see, but when I reached the house, the house was perfectly normal in every way. There was no particular atmosphere to be concerned about and it was really just like any other G.P visit that I might have made"*

(MA) *"It was another house visit for you"*

(SL) *"Yes"*

(MA) *"But with symptoms that you have never really recognised before with anybody else"?*

200

(SL) *"That's right"*

(MA) *"Now when your husband first reported what was happening. How did he tell you about it"?*

(SL) *"You do realise that this is 60 years ago,* (Both laugh)

(MA) *"I do".*

(SL) *"I don't remember how he told me about it"*

(MA) *"You know that bit where your partner comes home from work or somewhere else and they say, "You'll never guess what happened at work today, was there a moment like that"?*

(SL) *"Well I suppose that was the case, but I can't say that I really remember it, I'm sorry"*

(MA) *"You and your husband are clearly very matter fact"*

(SL) *"Yes I'm afraid so"* (Laughs)

NB: At this point producer Tom Parry stepped in to ask both Sheila and Matt to discuss the press cuttings and other letters that were spread about a table in front of them.

(MA) *"The doctor that is mentioned in this one"* (points to document) *"is Dr Owen".* (Matt begins to read part of the document out) *"The Doctor said that I've always believed that there is an explanation for everything, but in this case there seems to be no answer"* (Matt then poses the question to Sheila). *"Responsible and sensible citizens are responding in a way that they have no answers. Would you put yourself in that group as well"?*

(SL) *"Yes I would. We saw things happening that we can't explain"*

(MA) *"Other people put the name of this like a Poltergeist, or ghost"*

(SL) *"Uh huh"*

(MA) *"Does that make sense to you; would you go that far"?*

(SL) *"No I wouldn't. I don't think that in any way she was involved with mischievous spirits or spirits of any kind. I think that there will be a matter of fact answer to it which we do not yet know"*

(MA) *"But, at the same time, within, those answers, you're prepared to accept the idea that somebody can make things happen with their mind if they are in an extreme emotional state".*

(SL) *"Yes, certainly"*

(MA) *"So to that, a lot of people would be extreme, would be outside of what they would already understand"*

(SL) *"A lot of people would have thought about the causation of these sorts of things, but if they are involved in it, they have to try and come up with some sort of answer, and that was mine"*

(MA) *"So it's very Sherlock Holmes, in the absence of anything that you can evidence, then the most likely thing is, the one that you most likely have to accept"?*

(SL) *"Yes"*

NB: Matt backtracked here and again asked the question about the terminology of the word poltergeist and how people would react to it.

(MA) *"Why do you think then that people will use those terms, things like poltergeist to describe what is happening here"*

(SL) *"I think this belonged to a more credulous age when people did believe in spirits. In fact, apparently two women were burned as witches who got involved in a poltergeist situation. But I think we have moved on from that sort of idea now".*

(MA) *"So we were still seeing the tail end if you like, of ghosts, folklore"*

(SL) *"Yes"*

(MA) *"And it was a term hanging over from that time to describe what we were seeing"?*

(SL) *"Yes"*

(MA) *"Is there another term that we could use for it then that's more descriptive"?*

(SL) (Sheila laughs) *"If there is, I don't know it"*

(MA) *"Mrs Logan, many thanks for speaking with me today about your involvement in the Sauchie Poltergeist"*

(SL) *"Your welcome"*

One thing that I needed clearing up, was the question of 'what bedroom' in the Campbell household these strange occurrences took place. So, I telephoned Mrs Logan to ask her this question, knowing that is was after all, 60 years ago and she might not recollect. However, surprisingly she did, and told me that it was the front bedroom and when I asked if she was sure, she said yes, as she could hear the street sounds outside the window, cars, people etc. Whilst I attended Sheila Logan's house that night with One Tribe T.V. she made me aware of some letters from various people that I found most interesting none more so that the letter from one Helen Cooke from the now defunct London Weekend Television (LWT) Here is that letter in its entirety.

LETTER FROM LONDON WEEKEND TELEVISION TO DR. LOGAN

Monday 03 July 2000

Dear Dr. Logan,

"My name is Helen Cooke and I am an associate producer working for London Weekend TV".

*"I am writing in the hope that you can give me a ring. I am working on a programme for ITV that looks into people's experiences of hauntings and ghosts and we are planning to possibly feature Virginia Campbell's story. I have spoken to some of the surviving people who remember the events in Sauchie. I also understand you and your partner Dr. Nisbet filmed on film, and tape recorded some events in Virginia's room at the time she was ill. I would just like to explain what it is we are doing and hopefully speak to you about your experience. Please give me a call and I will ring you right back". "My numbers are **** Let me stress again that this is just a chat and there is no obligation, it's just a chance for us to have a talk about what happened".*

"I look forward to hearing from you".
Yours Sincerely
Helen Cooke.

LOST BUT NOT FOUND!

Sheila told in that she had sent the audio tape to London Weekend Television and that they never got it back! Needless to say, I found this most shocking. Here we have the Logan's sending L.W.T. their prized possession and the people at

London Weekend Television never had the decency to send it back. Admittedly this has happened to me too whilst working with the media, I've given them photographs and other items, and sometimes never receiving them back. Now whilst here in 2020, London Weekend Television are no longer operating, I believed they merged with Carlton T.V. and later Granada. To check this, I looked up Wikipedia and here is what I found.

Carlton Television and LWT are now run as a single entity (ITV London), with a single management team appointed to both companies. Both continue to have a separate legal existence however, and still have separate licences, although this is now just a formality.

So, I decided to see if I could track down this missing 60 year old tape sent by Sheila to London Weekend Television in 'good faith'. I knew that it would be extremely difficult but thought I would give it a try anyway. I spoke to someone at I.T.V. (Independent Television Network) who could see my dilemma (once I had explained it all to him). He suggested that I e-mail I.T.V.'s archive department which I did, here is my request which was sent on the 21st of February 2020.

Dear Sir/Madam,

"I'm hoping that you can help me with this old archive request".

"20 years ago, LWT (London Weekend Television) requested an audio tape from a Dr. William Logan. This tape was requested by one Helen Cooke, an associate producer working at the time for LWT. The reason why LWT wanted this audio tape, was to feature its recordings of a poltergeist? Yes, that's correct, a poltergeist. It is one of Scotland's biggest poltergeist cases and I am currently writing a book about it. The case itself occurred in 1960, if you Google it you will get more info about it".

"Anyway, the tape was sent down to London and the doctor never got it back. 20 years have passed (I'm only now picking up on this as I've just heard where the tape went to) LWT as we know merged with Carlton Television, and I was told that I.T.V. now retain a lot of property and archive material from LWT and Carlton. I don't know if the LWT programme eventually aired, if it did, we are looking at anything from July through to December 2000. I'm not necessarily looking for a copy of the show, but if you have a copy then yes that would be great. I'm more looking for the return of the audio tape of the Sauchie Poltergeist".

"PLEASE NOTE: I have attached a copy of the letter from LWT asking for the tape (which was sent) I hope 'you' can help, or at the very least, point me in the right direction".
"I look forward to your reply".
Yours Sincerely,
Malcolm Robinson.

I received the generic reply of.

Dear Viewer,

"Thanks for your e-mail". "We're currently experiencing a high volume of enquiries for archive requests so please allow 14 days for a response".
Regards, Robin Bray, Programme Copy Sales.

And lo and behold, I did receive a response, although not one that made me smile! It said.
Requests. Viewers. viewers.requests@itv.com
To: Malcolm Robinson
Friday 28 Feb at 16:08

Dear Malcolm Robinson,

"Thanks for your enquiry and apologies for the delay in replying.

It looks like this letter from Helen Cooke was research for the programme 'Britain's Most Terrifying Ghost Stories' that was transmitted on 23 November 2001. However, the library database entry doesn't include enough detail to indicate whether the Sauchie story was featured. I've also checked the archive assets held for the title and only the transmission master tapes for the completed programme have been retained".

Regards, Robin Bray Programme Copy Sales, ITV plc

So, they didn't find it. If this audio tape has not been thrown out, then it sits somewhere within the confines of a desk drawer or box, stored away waiting for someone to re-discover it.

Another interesting letter that Sheila showed me when we visited her house was a letter from the also defunct Sunday Mirror. This 55 year old letter, held a piece of information that I've been looking for, for years! Here is that letter in its entirety addressed to Dr. William Logan.

SUNDAY MIRROR LETTER.
May 19th, 1965

Dear Dr. Logan,

"Please find enclosed a rough draft of the first article on the Sauchie Poltergeist, which has already been approved by Dr. Owen. It is in the second article that we expect to use the names of the investigators in the book. Perhaps you would be kind enough to approve the enclosed or make any necessary amendments".

"The credit which was promised for the photograph will very soon be on the way to the person we agreed upon. Since meeting you, I have concluded a contract with Virginia's parents in Bedford, and I have also met the young lady herself. Every word of the article is with their full approval, and Dr.

Owen is helping us with the preparation of the next instalment.
So nice to have met you and your charming wife".
Yours Sincerely, Victor Simms.

THE SEARCH FOR VIRGINIA CAMPBELL!

Wow, here for the first time we have a reference to where Virginia Campbell and her family moved to after their time spent in Scotland. Bedford is a town in the burgh of Bedfordshire England and is roughly just under three hours drive from my home in Hastings East Sussex. Now admittedly this was a long shot, (a very long shot) but I decided to give it a try anyway and write to some Bedfordshire newspapers in an attempt to see if anyone knew the Campbell's current whereabouts. Of course, they may have moved away again, but it had to be tried. Here is the letter that I wrote to those Bedfordshire newspapers.

Titled: For Letters Page or small piece in newspaper.

Dear Sir/Madam,

"I wonder if you would be so kind as to find a small space in your newspaper for this request?"

"I'm currently searching for information regarding a family that moved to Bedford during the 1960's, possibly 1965. This is for a family tree I'm working on. The family name is Campbell who initially came from Donegal in Ireland, then settled in Sauchie Scotland, and, I believe, somewhere in Bedford during the 1960's. Their names are Annie and James Campbell and their daughter Virginia. Virginia would be around 15 or 16 at the time of the move to Bedford. If anyone has any information about this family, could they either contact me on ***** or e-mail me at malckyspi@yahoo.com"

Thank you. Malcolm Robinson.

Well staff writer Erica Roffe from the Bedford Independent newspaper e-mailed me back to ask if perhaps I had a photograph of the Campbell family to place in the newspaper to go along with the story. I had to tell her that I hadn't, and that I only had a photograph of young Virginia, which I sent her. About half an hour after I had sent Erica that photo, she sent me the link for the newspaper which showed my request for people to come forward, this is that link, https://www.bedfordindependent.co.uk/letters-searching-for-the-campbell-family/ Well I received one telephone call and one e-mail, both from people who had the Campbell name from Bedford who felt they could help. Sadly, what they had to tell me didn't match anything that I already had or could help further. There was no link to the Campbell family that I was so keen to discover. And then, later on, dynamite!

COULD THIS REALLY BE VIRGINIA CAMPBELL?

It was February 2020 and I was sitting at home watching television when my mobile phone rang, I normally don't take calls in the evening but I know that because of my news paper request looking for information about the whereabouts of Virginia Campbell, I just might get some calls from the Bedfordshire area, so I answered the call and spoke to a Daisy Watson (pseudonym), an 85 year old lady from Bedford in England who proceeded to firstly ask me about my search for Virginia and the Campbell family, whereupon she then proceeded to give me the following information. She said that she knew a Campbell family that had moved from Scotland to Bedford back in the 1960's, but she only really knew three sisters at that time, Vera, Beryl and Irene. She went on to say that the youngest of the family was called Virginia, but she didn't know the names of the parents, and went on to say that sadly both parents had died a few years previously in Bedford. And then came the bombshell, she matter of fact said to me,

"Yes, Virginia had a terrible time with a poltergeist, it was in all the papers you know, did you know about that Mr Robinson"?

I was almost on the floor when she said this, now how many Campbell families have moved from Ireland to Scotland and then to Bedford in England with the youngest member of the family being called Virginia who had a poltergeist, what are the odds on that I ask you! I replied that yes, I had heard about this. And then came the second bombshell, she said something along the lines of.

"Yes, it followed her to Bedford, she had a terrible time with it, and then it just suddenly stopped"

Did I hear her correctly; did she really just say this? She went on to tell me that she more or less knew Vera from the Campbell family, who herself had sadly passed away due to an aneurism, and went on to talk about how they used to pal about and go places together when she was alive. When I asked if she knew where in Bedford Virginia was now staying, she replied that she was now actually living in Kempston, which is a small town adjacent to Bedford. Sadly, she didn't know where, and rarely saw her, the last time being in the street a year or so ago. She also lost contact with Virginia's other sisters, and at 85, she very rarely went out the house, so she was really in no position to make house calls so to speak. After chatting some more where I tried not to make it too obvious that I was more interested in Virginia's poltergeist, I thanked her for the information and said that I would probably be back in touch soon. Putting the phone down, I thought I had struck gold, had I really traced the whereabouts of Virginia Campbell? Certainly, all the signs were there that I had. And what about the poltergeist following Virginia down to Bedford, again wow. We know that when Virginia was moved from the house in Sauchie to another house in nearby Dollar, the poltergeist followed her there, and now here we have a lady telling me that she was aware that Virginia had the poltergeist in Scotland, and that it followed her to Bedford! Sadly, as this telephone call came early in the evening whilst I was watching T.V. I hadn't time to set up a recording of that call which I had been doing with other potential witnesses, so this call went unrecorded.

210

However, I knew that I would have to call her again and get her repeating this on tape as proof of what she was saying. So, a few days later, Sunday 1st March 2020, I called Daisy again, only this time, I was ready to ask more pertinent questions. The following, in part, is how that call went.

PHONE CALL TO DAISY WATSON
Abbreviations

(MR)   Malcolm Robinson
(DW)   Daisy Watson

(MR) *"Hi, is that Daisy?"*

(DW) *"Yes"*

(MR) *"Hi its Malcolm Robinson, we spoke on Friday night about the Campbells".*

(DW) *"Yes"*

(MR) *"I've just got a few very quick questions that I would like to ask you, is that OK, or would you prefer me to call you back"?*

(DW) *"Yes, that's OK"*

(MR) *"Was Beryl, Irene and Vera, sisters of Virginia or relatives of Virginia"?*

(DW) *"They are sisters"*

(MR) *"I thought that, but I just wanted to make sure"*

(DW) *"Four sisters' yes, and four brothers. Virginia was the youngest and Vera was the oldest. Have you had any more contacts to your request"?*

(MR) *"Not since your call, but I've had a few people before your call"*

(DW) *"Oh did you"*

(MR) *"Yes, but it looks like they were a different Campbell family. Do you still see Beryl"?*

(DW) *"I don't. If I saw her in town I would stop and talk to her yes. I would like to see her, but I don't know where she lives; only that she lives in town. Yes, I would like to be in contact with her but as the years go by, I don't get out as much as I used to, I'm not likely to see her"*

(MR) *"Yes, but if you do come across her, do pass on my details to her if you have them with you"*

(DW) *"You haven't heard from her yet, Beryl"?*

(MR) *"No, not at all unfortunately"*

(DW) *"And have you heard from Virginia"?*

(MR) *"No, not at all"*

(DW) *"They might yet. They might read in the paper you know, a bit later"*

(MR) *"Yes. Possibly, that may well be. Do you know the names of Virginia's mother and father"?*

(DW) *"No I didn't know their names; I didn't ever meet them. I know they both died in Bedford. They lived there some years. I wouldn't know how long but I know Vera was pleased that they were in Bedford. It was sad when they both died".*

(MR) *"Now you mentioned on Friday night that there was a story about Virginia with a poltergeist, tell me more about that"?*

212

(DW) *"Well when mum and dad came over, they brought Virginia with them who was a little girl then, I don't know how old, 10 or 12 or something like that, or 14, a young girl. And funny things happened in their flat. I think they were in the flat then. It would be a council flat. Well I mean, it got to be in the Daily Mirror, I think it was in the Mirror, I don't take the Mirror, but I know that there was a big spread in the paper about her. But I think it just died a death and nobody ever did anything else about it".*

(MR) *"Now do you mean that the poltergeist was with Virginia in Scotland or in Bedford"?*

(DW) *"It was happening in Bedford yes"*

(MR) *"And now Virginia is staying in Kempston not Bedford"?*

(DW) *"Yes. Kempston joins up with Bedford and Virginia lives in Kempston yes, with her second husband".*

(MR) *"Ah I see. Ah all right she's got a second husband now yes"*

(DW) *"Yes. The first marriage didn't last very long. I think she had a son with him"*

(MR) *"OK. So, when the poltergeist followed her to Bedford, how long did it last for, just a few weeks or less or a month"?*

(DW) *"Well it seemed to go on for a month or two. It died a sudden death. I don't know how it was cured or what they did or anything, but it was worrying at the time."*

(MR) *"And did Beryl tell you about this"?*

(DW) *"No Vera. Vera was my friend, she did nursing training with me"*

(MR) *"So Virginia is still around"?*

(DW) *"Yes Virginia is still around. She is able bodied, because I have seen her in the distance last year, she was able bodied, and she seemed OK. But she didn't see me, so I didn't speak to her"*

(MR) *"Well I do think in regards to what you have been saying, is that this could well be the family that I've been looking for"*

(DW) *"I'm sure it is. Yes, Vera used to tell me that they had a little small holding in Ireland, a farm she called it, but it was not very big, and they all lived there. But the boys came to England before she did, I think, they were older. And they did come to Vera's funeral, I saw them at the funeral"*

(MR) *"So they were eight in the family"*

(DW) *"They were a lovely family yes, mum and dad and the children, and they weren't Catholic. Vera married a local chap and had three children"*

(MR) *"And Virginia is on her second husband now"?*

(DW) *"Yes. For some time now she has been with this one"*

(MR) *"And she has had a son with the first husband"*

(DW) *"With the first husband yes. I hope you get some more answers, but there won't be that many people that know that name. They probably remember the poltergeist thing happening, but it wouldn't register who they were if you didn't have any contact with them would it"*

(MR) *"Yes"*

(DW) *"I don't think people would know that their name was Campbell"*

(MR) *"Now Virginia will of course have a married name now"?*

(DW) *"Yes, I don't know what that is"*

(MR) *"OK, no that's fine"*

(DW) *"I haven't got anything else really that I can tell you. I hope you can find out what you want to know"*

(MR) *"Well you have been very helpful Daisy. My next step is now to try and find Virginia and any members of the family. I will let you get back and enjoy your Sunday evening. If you feel you want to call me anytime, please do"*

(DW) *"Yes that's fine, bye bye"*

I have edited some of the conversation out of the above call but what I have left in, clearly shows her response to my question, which again was.

(MR) *"Now do you mean that the poltergeist was with Virginia in Scotland or in Bedford"?*

(DW) *"It was happening in Bedford yes"*

BEDFORD AND KEMPSTON FACEBOOK SITES

Another avenue that I tracked down in trying to trace Virginia Campbell was using the wonderful World Wide Web and the power of Facebook. And in the early part of March 2020, I sent a request to a number of Facebook sites based in Bedford and Kempston. These were a combination of the Kempston Community Facebook page, We Are Bedford, Facebook page. I used to Live In Kempston, Facebook page, and Bedford Memories, Facebook page. Sadly, nothing came of that.

CONTACTING DONEGAL NEWSPAPERS.

In point of fact, before I wrote off to the Bedfordshire newspapers, as mentioned earlier, and before I got that dynamite information that Virginia and her family had moved to Bedford, I felt that I should also try and see if perhaps anyone remembered the Campbell family in the Moville, Donegal area, so I sent an e-mail to a number of newspapers in Donegal. In this e-mail I was asking for anyone who knew the whereabouts of the Campbell family. I explained that they moved to Scotland in 1960, but I was interested to learn if, after they re-located to Scotland, that they might have come back and relocated in County Donegal, again, I drew another blank.

Whilst doing research on this book, I also found out that some of the large sand stones that were used to build the old Sauchie School that Virginia attended were used on one wall of the new build of houses when the Sauchie School was demolished. Indeed, I was told that Virginia's classroom was the last to be demolished. I regret not ever asking permission to get into this School prior to it being demolished. See the photographic section which shows the photograph showing how some of those old original sand stones were built into the new gable end of one of the houses, re-named Ballie Court.

You read the interview that was conducted by Matt Allwright of the B.B.C. One Show earlier in the book, and a lot of ground was covered in that interview, but at the back of my mind, there were still a few questions that I felt that I had to go back and ask retired doctor Sheila Logan about. This I did, and the following interview transcript that you are about to read, was conducted over the phone during the corona virus lockdown of Great Britain, where Prime Minister Boris Johnstone had asked the British people not to leave their house due to the ongoing virus that was affecting the world. After a

216

brief chat about how this horrible virus was affecting the world, I got down to asking some questions. Here is what transpired.

Phone Interview with retired doctor Sheila Logan
(29th February 2020)

Abbreviations

(MR) Malcolm Robinson
(SL) Sheila Logan

(MR) *"What year did you start your practice, and what year did you retire?"*

(SL) *"You mean the practice in Dollar"?*

(MR) *"Yes"*

(SL) *"72, and I retired in 92"*

(MR) *"As you stated to me, LWT (London Weekend Television) asked for the audio tape that your husband made of the poltergeist sounds and that you never got it back".*

(SL) *"No, we never got it back, and we tried to get it back and they said that they couldn't find it".*

(MR) *"Yes that's pretty bad that. I've asked them myself and they have tried to locate it, but they still can't find it"*

(SL) *"No"*

(MR) *"Now your husband also took the audio of the poltergeist sounds, was it William, your husband, who also took the cine footage, or was that footage taken by someone else"?*

(SL) *"I don't know definitely. If he did, I wouldn't know where it was. I mean it won't exist"*

217

(MR) *"Do you think it was your husband that took the film footage of it"?*

(SL) *"I think it's very likely, but I don't know definitely"*

(MR) *"But you wouldn't know where that was no"?*

(SL) *"We moved here 16 years ago, and a lot of things didn't move with us"*

(MR) *"OK. Was that in storage or did things go to somebody else?"*

(SL) *"It might have got thrown out. My daughter helped me to move as my husband wasn't well at that time, and it's quite possible that some things got put in the bin"*

(MR) *"Ah well, it's one of these things, it happens with house moves unfortunately"*

(SL) *"Yes"*

(MR) *"You mentioned in your interview with the B.B.C. One Show, that young Virginia moved for a brief spell to the town of Dollar".*

(SL) *"Yes she did".*

(MR) *"Do you know where in Dollar, that house was Sheila, what street it was?"*

(SL) *"I was trying to remember but I can't remember definitely"*

(MR) *"Do you know how many times you visited the Campbell House Sheila"?*

(SL) *"I only went once"*

218

(MR) *"Just the once!"*

(SL) *"Yes"*

(MR) *"And we spoke about what you heard at that property. Were the strange events in the front or back bedroom, can you remember?"*

(SL) *"Front bedroom"*

(MR) *"Definitely the front bedroom yeah"?*

(SL) *"Yes, because I looked out the window to see if there were any reason that there should be knocking sounds in the room"*

(MR) *"Uh huh. And the audio tape that your husband used to record the sounds of the poltergeist, was that a reel to reel tape, those big reels, or was it just a small cassette"?*

(SL) *"Difficult to say, because he had both bits of apparatus and the reel to reel was a bit big to carry around and I really don't know what he used at that particular time, whatever was current at that date"*

(MR) *"OK. And did you or your husband take any photographs of the house or of Virginia"?*

(SL) *"No"*

(MR) *"No* (laughs), *OK, that's fine"*

(SL) *"(Laughs) it's a pity that my husband isn't alive, because he was the prime mover but there you are"*

(MR) *"OK. Well many thanks again Sheila, you stay safe"*

(SL) *"I'm doing my best* (laughs)"

219

(MR) *"All the very best to you"*

(SL) *"Bye"*

IT'S A TOUGH ONE! (Do you have a poltergeist?)

I have been asked many times by different people over the years if the current tenants of that haunted house in Sauchie have experienced any strange phenomenon? It's a tough one this, not just for the Sauchie house, but I guess for any major poltergeist affected house. I mean do you just go up to that house, knock on the door and say to the new tenants,

"Hi, your house used to be haunted by a poltergeist and I was wondering if you or your family have experienced anything"?

Those new tenants might not know that their house was previously haunted, (some might, and some not) and if they were not aware of this, then this could come as a big shock, and one in which you, coming to their door with this information, might not fare so well! I personally (until research for the Sauchie case) have never ever knocked on a previously haunted house and asked the new occupants if they have experienced anything bizarre (much as I would like to!) I just feel that it's not right, maybe it's time to move on and not create any unnecessary ill feeling or upset. Now, for this book, I did write a letter to the current tenants of the Sauchie Poltergeist house, this is what I wrote.

Dear Householder,
"I guess this letter may come as a surprise and I was in two minds as to whether to send it, but here goes. I am writing on two counts".

Firstly
"I investigate claims pertaining to ghosts, poltergeists and many other weird and wonderful events. You may, or may not,

be aware that you live in a very special and famous house. Your house is known throughout the paranormal world as being one of the locations of the famous Sauchie Poltergeist from December 1960. The events also followed young Virginia Campbell who lived in your house to a local school. Anyway, I am writing a book about the Sauchie Poltergeist and I wonder if you would be so kind as to answer the questions below? I have enclosed a stamped address envelope for the return of your answers of feel free to e-mail me at malckyspi@yahoo.com"

Questions

1. "Did you know that when you moved into this house that it had the reputation as Scotland's most famous poltergeist case?"

2. "The events in your house stopped in early January 1961 (some say March) but they did stop. Have you ever experienced anything of a paranormal nature in your house?"

3. "Has anyone ever told you, or have you ever spoken to, anyone who was associated with this case, ie, former class mates of Virginia Campbell or friends of the Campbells?"

4. "What are your beliefs or opinions about ghosts and poltergeists?"

Secondly

"I am currently working with One Tribe T.V. who are making a short documentary on the famous Sauchie Poltergeist case and they have asked me if they could kindly interview any member of the family who live in your house. They have also asked if it's OK to film outside your house. The piece for the One Show only lasts 5 minutes so my interview, and anyone else, would be cut short to 40 seconds or so, maybe a little bit longer. Let me know if you would like to participate or would rather not, we will respect your decision either way".

221

"I look forward to your reply. (I have enclosed some further information about who I am) I am ex Tullibody/Alloa and moved to live in England in 1998".

With very best wishes.

Malcolm Robinson

And did I hear anything from the current tenants? No, I never did. I must respect their decision not to get in touch with me. I have since been told that it's a Polish family that occupies the house. Some things are maybe left best alone, I'm sure they felt so too.

MALCOLM'S SUMMING UP ON THE SAUCHIE POLTERGEIST

So, there we have it. We have taken a look at the Sauchie poltergeist and also a couple of other poltergeist cases from the town of Sauchie. To date, (for me) the Sauchie case hasn't been equalled, and to think that it occurred just a few miles away from where I lived at that time, was quite amazing. This case only lasted a few months, and everything eventually died down and things got back to normal. Years later the family moved out of the house and it's reported that they moved to the town of Bedford then Kempston in England, after which, the trail went cold. Oh, how it would be great to track Virginia down for an interview. Not just Virginia, I would have loved to have interviewed Virginia's cousin Margaret who shared the same room as Virginia at that time, and sometimes the same bed. She too was witness to the strange goings on. I would also have loved to have tracked down and spoken to the occupants of the house in the nearby town of Dollar where Virginia was sent to in the hopes that things may settle down, as we know, they didn't, and the paranormal events occurred there too, of which soon afterwards she was sent back to Sauchie. I would have loved to have gathered the thoughts of Doctor Nisbet, who also was witness to all the strange events. It would also have been great to speak to some more of Virginia's classmates and get their recollections of what they saw, but as we know, some have sadly since passed away, and others are untraceable. I would have liked to have spoken to Virginia's main headmaster, Mr. Peter Hill for his thoughts and of course the main principle researcher of the case, Mr A.R.G. Owen, thankfully we have his record of testimony throughout this book.

As I've stated elsewhere, I certainly don't subscribe to the views held by some of my other paranormal researchers, who state that it's all down to children of a certain age going through puberty, and that there is some sort of powerful external force that exudes from their body which propels chairs and the like across a room. I mean, let's be realistic here, there are literally thousands of teenage kids going through puberty right now, so, if this theory is the answer, then surely it goes without saying that there must be thousands of poltergeist cases occurring right now across the British isles. I don't subscribe to that theory. My belief, not just for the Sauchie case, but for all other poltergeist cases, is that we are dealing with a discarnate entity that has passed on, and has not moved forward and is trying to draw attention to themselves by hanging around the earth plane causing mischief and havoc. My view may not sit well with my fellow researchers and that's fine, but at the end of the day, it's what I believe. I am reminded at this point, of some very interesting comments made by UFO and Paranormal researcher Jenny Randles, when she said,

"It is perfectly possible that children have more paranormal experiences, not because they are gullible and have yet to learn what they should properly believe, but rather because they are open minded and perceptive and have yet to be taught what they must 'disbelieve"
Jenny Randles (Author Mind Monsters 1990)

Although some of the events were filmed and audio recorded, one can but imagine, that if this case had been around today, you can bet your bottom dollar that somebody would have recorded more of it on their I-Phone, but sadly, I-Phones were not around in 1960. At the end of the day, the Sauchie

Poltergeist is still talked about in the towns and villages all around Clackmannanshire, as I am sure it will be for many years to come. Whatever you the reader believe happened in that house in Park Crescent, and Sauchie Primary School, one thing you cannot deny, is that these events of a large linen chest moving across the floor with its lid flapping up and down, or of Virginia's pillow turning around 60 degrees underneath her head, or of her desk lid at school fluttering up and down, and of Virginia's teacher Margaret Stewart's own desk rising up into the air, and turning around 90 degrees, they happened. That was not imagination. That was not someone fooling around. No matter where you hang your hat, one thing you do have to concede, is that all this was witnessed by numerous people, who themselves I dare say, found it hard to accept what they were seeing. This either happened as stated, or everyone is delusional. I for one will never accept that all witnesses were delusional. I'm sure you will agree with me dear reader, that the world is indeed, a far more stranger place than we can ever imagine.

Virginia Campbell. 11 years old at the time of the
poltergeist events.

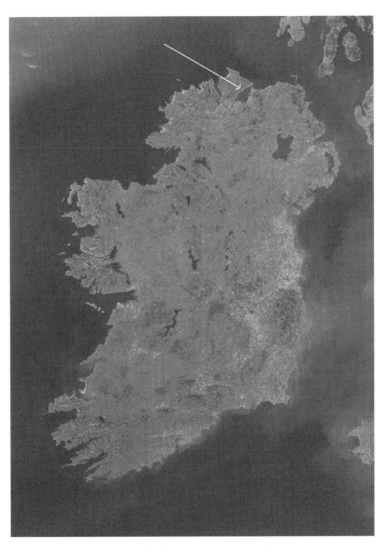

White Arrow points to the village of Moville, County Donegal, where the Campbell's had their farm before moving to Sauchie, Central Scotland.

The Sauchie Poltergeist House (on the left)

Toby. Virginia's Dog that was left behind in Ireland.

Reverend T.W. Lund. Witnessed the strange events.

Reverend Ewan Murdo MacDonald. Also witnessed the
strange events.

A.R.G. Owen. The principle investigator of the Sauchie Poltergeist at the time.

A.R.G. Owen playing the Sauchie Poltergeist sounds.

Doctors Sheila and William Logan. Both witness to the poltergeist events.

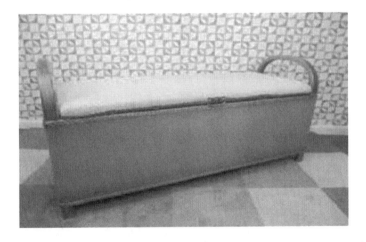

A 1960 Linen chest, similar to that which moved of its own accord in the Sauchie case with its lid flapping up and down as it moved.

Sauchie Primary School. Scene of some of the poltergeist events. (c) Raymond Fyfe

A Typical 1960's School Desk.

231

Arrow points to Virginia's classroom.
(c) Drummond Grieve

Arrow points to Virginia's Classroom. Sauchie School
(c) Frank Love

Typical 1960's school. (Not Sauchie)

Sauchie Primary School. (c) Drummond Grieve.

Sauchie Primary School from the road (c)
Drummond Grieve.

Where is that reel to reel tape now?

Peter Johnstone age 12, was in Virginia's class and was witness to the poltergeist events.

Arrow shows the area before Park Crescent was built.
circa late 1930's early 1940's.

2nd DECEMBER 1960

GHOST - POLTERGEIST - OR WHAT!

Strange Events Disturb Sauchie Household

VIRGINIA CAMPBELL lived in a lonely house on the hills of Donegal in Ireland until two months ago. Eleven years old, she is the youngest of a large grown-up family, and her mother, Mrs Anne Campbell, brought her to stay with a married son at 19 Park Crescent, Sauchie.

Just over a week ago strange things began to happen to Virginia. Heavy pieces of furniture were seen to move when she entered a room, doors opened when she approached them and then were found difficult to shut.

Reliable Witnesses

Other and more unusual happenings occurred which have been witnessed by several responsible local people.

Virginia and her mother came from their home in Ireland two months ago to live with Virginia's married brother in Sauchie. Mrs Campbell found employment in a Dollar Academy boarding-house and Virginia joined her niece Margaret and became a pupil at Sauchie School. But both little girls have had to be withdrawn from school temporarily because of the publicity and teasing which Virginia's unusual experiences have occasioned.

Worried and anxious, Virginia's brother asked the Rev. T. W. Lund to try to help, and Dr H. W. Nisbet of Tillicoultry who attends the family, was called in.

GREATLY IMPRESSED

Both men have been greatly impressed with what they have seen and with what they themselves have seen. Their concern for the well-being of Virginia and her family has increased during the past week because of the effect which gossip and publicity are having upon them.

On Tuesday Mr Lund reported the whole matter to the Rev. Horace Walker, Secretary of the Home Board of the Church of Scotland, at their offices in Edinburgh, but a spokesman there told the "Journal" yesterday that no action had as yet been decided upon. It is possible, however, that at least one minister who is experienced in these matters may visit Virginia this weekend.

Virginia is still being looked after by her friends and her physical health is still the responsibility of Dr Nisbet.

She is now staying with a cousin in Dollar and yesterday it was reported that she was much quieter, but the testing time will come when she returns to the house in Park Crescent.

Lost Pet Dog

Before she came to Scotland Virginia lost a pet dog of which she was very fond and a little girl friend died. Both of these occurrences upset her very much.

One night when sitting on the edge of Virginia's bed Mrs Campbell was roughly pushed off and as she stood watching she saw the blankets and sheets rising and falling above Virginia, while the child made little moaning sounds like someone in pain.

During the past week the Rev. T. W. Lund, who has witnessed some of these happenings, has consistently refused to make any statement on what he has seen or to comment on his reasons for reporting the happenings to the secretary of the Home Board. And in view of inaccuracies in reporting his statements Dr Nisbet has refused to give information to the national press since last Monday.

GREENFIELD BURGLARY

Two Men Sought

DESCRIPTIONS of two men seen entering the grounds of Greenfield House on Saturday night before a safe was blown in the Council Chambers and £455 stolen were issued by Alloa police yesterday.

Appeal

The C.I.D. are appealing to anyone who saw men answering the descriptions near Greenfield House or about the bus station or railway station on that night to come forward.

The descriptions of the two men are as follow:

No. 1.—Age twenty-five to thirty, about 5ft. 11in., slim build, wearing dark soft hat, medium grey suit, soft footwear, leather gloves, carrying a brief-case.

No. 2.—Age twenty to twenty-five, about 5ft. 6in., slim build, brown hair, wearing dark woollen jerkin tight at waist and wrists, soft footwear.

The burglars, who broke into Greenfield House late on Saturday night or early on Sunday morning did a neat, professional job of safeblowing.

The said safe planned with skill and, although the burglars must have been acquainted with the layout of the buildings and grounds it is thought that it was the work of experts from outside the county—perhaps from Glasgow.

Morning Rounds

The burglary was discovered by Council Officer Walter Dick when he made his rounds of the buildings early on Sunday morning.

The two money departments the offices of the Burgh Chamberlain and Burgh Factor were both...

Doctor and Minister see Sauchie girl

THE STRANGE CASE OF VIRGINIA CAMPBELL

FIVE doctors and two leading Church of Scotland ministers have now seen 11-year-old Sauchie schoolgirl Virginia Campbell who is believed to be haunted by a poltergeist. Furniture moves and strange things happen in her presence.

Dr W. H. Nisbet, Tillicoultry, stated in an interview: "The child may have telekinetic powers." Dr Nisbet has had to treat Virginia's family—the child resides with her mother, married brother and sister-in-law—for hysteria.

The doctor—tired and worried —said: "Things have happened which I do not care to explain— but they do not have any medical explanation.

"The happenings occurred in the girls' school — her teacher saw something—and in her home."

Said Dr Nisbet: "Virginia does not control the happenings verbally, but I do not know whether she controls them from her mind."

Dr Nisbet said he and the other doctors and ministers had visited Virginia to satisfy themselves that things did happen. "We confirmed that they did."

Asked if he thought a leprechaun or poltergeist had invaded Virginia's life replied: "I do not even know what a leprechaun is. A poltergeist?—I looked up the meaning a few days ago and it may or may not apply in this case."

At Sauchie School, the headmaster Mr Peter Hill said: "I have never seen furniture shifting, and we have not got any of our desks tied down. Things may have happened in the girl's home."

Mr Hill suggested that the poltergeist may just be group hypnosis. But Dr Nisbet turned down this theory. "Group hypnosis does not apply in this case," he said.

At the Campbells' council home understandably they do not want to talk.

CHURCH ATTITUDE

Neighbours are guarded in talking about Virginia and her strange powers. They share the family's distress and do not wish to add to it by pandering to the sensation mongers and supplying them with further "stories".

On the question of poltergeists the Church of Scotland is non-committal. Official pronouncements have been avoided by the General Assembly.

At the Kirk's headquarters in Edinburgh an official said: "The girl is entirely in the case of doctor and minister. Her whole future and mental stability will depend on peace and quiet. This is entirely a personal thing."

The Rev. J. W. Stevenson, editor of the kirk's magazine "Life and Work", recalled in an interview an experience he had a year ago. He had been asked to visit the home of Baroness Kilbride at Fairmilehead, Edinburgh. In her house doors had opened, strange noises were heard, articles moved mysteriously from room to room.

ALVA CHILD FOUND IN TROUGH

A tragic accident took place at the Boll Farm near Alva on Sunday forenoon resulting in the death of 18-month-old Douglas Beatson, infant son of Mr and Mrs James Beatson, who reside at the farm.

The child was found to be missing by his mother around noon and Mrs Beatson went to contact her husband who was working at a hen-house in an adjoining field.

The two went in search of the child who was found in a trough containing about a foot of water about thirty yards from the house.

Medical aid was summoned and Dr Faulkner applied artificial respiration but life was found to be extinct.

Much sympathy will be felt for Mr and Mrs Beatson and also the child's grandparents in the tragic loss they have sustained. The couple have one other child aged four years.

Mr Stevenson and the baroness prayed. The strange happenings completely stopped.

Mr Stevenson discussed it as a simple case of a minister praying with a person, and the prayer apparently being answered.

"But when asked about exorcism," Mr Stevenson remarked: "In the Church of Scotland we do not use that word, although other denominations do."

But while spiritualists and poltergeists are regarded with suspicion by most ministers, a few have become firmly convinced.

One of the most outspoken is the Rev. Thomas Jeffrey, former Alloa man and brother of Mr R. J. Jeffrey and the Rev. George Jeffrey (an ex-Moderator of the Church of Scotland). Now 81, Mr Jeffrey has been a believer in the spirit world for more than fifty years.

"People scoff about stories of ghosts and spooks, but they have not really studied the subject," he said.

"In the case of this little girl we have examples of well-known phenomena."

Mr Jeffrey explained how John Wesley, the founder of Methodism, had had similar experiences in his father's home. Doors opened before one of Wesley's sisters. Mysterious noises shattered the peace of the house.

Then one night Wesley's mother prayed for her daughter to be relieved of the torment. The disturbances ceased.

Said Mr Jeffrey: "But long before this, such phenomena were written in the Bible. When the boy Samuel heard the voices, the old priest Eli did not, but he knew the boy had the gift from God."

Asked what could be done to help Virginia, Mr Jeffrey explained: "Some sympathetic person who knows about these things should go and speak to the spirit, say what they are doing and tell it to be quiet."

Rev. A. Rose Rankin, F.S.A., minister of the Sauchie and Fishcross U.F. Church said: "I have not taken much interest in the affair. Personally I would like to contact the home and have a talk with the girl concerned.

"For unless I see the actual manifestations, I am afraid I can't accept the stories. To my mind it would be a great kindness to the home if the people would leave it in peace."

A DEBUNKER

Finally a debunker — Major Henry Douglas-Home, B.B.C. Bird Man, who has spent years investigating poltergeists. Many years ago he played a big part in exposing the story of Borley

The brid wedding, in Mr Georg Mains. Co shire, and Sharp. Sol Dollar.

Bridesma Sharp and was Miss M A. G. Dow

ALVA C

BOYS'

Questic

Whether—an they shoul to a youth was a m the attem Council at ing on W particular Councillor duction is to the Boy Queen Sc

Noting fro mittee minut had been

Alloa Advertiser December 1960.
Doctor and Minister see Sauchie Girl.

Mr Simpson then audience in his and witty manner ; recitations, One, tising piece was "Funeral." At an ing the service of -n went around the e members renew- nances. Mr Simp- vnd the afternoon later stage in the one joined in sing- a Jolly Good

received a most thanks. afternoon. Commit- ts Goodman, at the r Simpson, most ered a solo which ived.

se members were gates to Branch als Mrs Menzies eron to Tullibody; and Mrs Fraser to Irs Williamson and Falkirk, being held 9th December and spectively. Mrs sered on the Old re monthly Com—

ease note tickets Social will be given eeting.

CH TEAS

SE £82

auspices of the Board of St. rch, a most suc- on took place in Hall on Tuesday f Church funds. In inclement weather, any of ladies pat- fternoon Teas, and accommodation was scity. The catering were in the cap- perienced hands of Ils and Mrs Hugh fine band of assis- were kept busy all rving teas and suc- ie Cake and Candy A. C. Brand and ard, and their help- ually busy at the which brought in a Mrs A. Yates, at Gift and Book fo the total, which over £82.

Virginia is now returning to normal

"CHILD HAD NOTHING TO DO WITH POLTERGEIST" — DR NISBET

ELEVEN-YEAR-OLD VIRGINIA CAMPBELL, the Sauchie girl who, it is claimed, is being troubled by a poltergeist, is expected to return to school this week, and there is every indication that her life may soon have returned to normal.

Dr William Nisbet, Tillicoultry, who has been treating Virginia, said at the week-end that the child had nothing to do with the poltergeist which has been plaguing her.

Interviewed at his home, "Hillden," in Stirling Street, Tillicoultry, the doctor said: "Virginia is not responsible for what has happened. The child is innocent.

"What has taken place was not conjured by the child herself an outside agent is responsible."

Dr. Nisbet, father of three children, then added: "Believe me, something unfortunate has been going on in that house.

"I cannot give you an explana- tion. I have my own thoughts, but they are private for the mo- ment.

"I hope to explain it all fully. But that will be when I have had time to think about it more."

When the poltergeist was first reported Virginia's mother, Mrs Annie Campbell, called in Dr Nisbet, her partner, Dr William Logan and local minister, Rev. Thomas Lund.

The three have already sent a report to the Church of Scotland.

THE DOG

But last night, Dr Nisbet out- lined what he thought was the CAUSE, the EFFECT and the TREATMENT of the case.

"We have several theories about the cause," he said.

"The most important was the dog that the child left behind in Ireland.

"We thought that this was af- fecting her mind because it was her pet and she missed it terribly.

"Dr Logan decided to bring his dog to the house to see if its presence would help. It didn't.

"The phenomena went on. It meant that either a dog was not the cause or that her own dog was the only cure.

"The girl was hysterical all the time the phenomena were appear- ing. We decided then to try sedation."

Dr Nisbet went on: "Virginia was given mild tranquillisers to quieten her.

STILL THERE

"If the phenomena were being conjured by her own imagination they would no longer appear if her brain was dulled."

"But even though the brain was not working normally the pheno- mena still appeared."

Dr Nisbet paused as his daugh- ter burst into the room, collected some Christmas wrapping and left.

"The next thing we tried was a change of environment.

"Virginia was moved to a house in Dollar for two nights. The manifestations still appeared. She

was brought back to Sauchie and we tried isolation.

"The child was put to bed and left on her own to get to sleep."

"But still the phenomena ap- peared—and made itself heard. From a room below, we could hear the child screaming and mov- ing and bouncing noises."

Dr Nisbet continued: "Last Thursday three ministers were sent by the Church of Scotland.

"When Virginia went to bed a short service was held at her bed- side. We all prayed."

The doctor paused . . . "Since that night nothing has happened. I believe the cure is now complete.

"In any case, we have on record by one camera and tape recorder, what has happened — a moving jeep box, the lid of the box open- ing and closing, rippling bedclothes, moving pillows and bouncing noises.

IT'S OVER

"The tape and film will be available to any person who is interested in this case," said Dr Nisbet.

Virginia has been off school for more than a week. But these last three nights she has slept un- troubled.

On Sunday the family went for a car drive.

They chatted happily over tea at a wayside cafe. And they re- assured each other: "The haunt- ing is over."

Virginia, her cheeks flushed, came dancing into the house after the outing sucking an outsized car's face lollipop.

She sat giggling at the antics of Popeye on television.

Said her mother: "It's wonder- ful to see Virginia like her old self again. We want her to for- get."

Virginia smiled back at her mother. "I'm happy now," she

A MILLGROVE GUEST OCCASION

On Friday afternoon, Mill- grove Old People's Club had as guests 20 fellow pensioners from Tillicoultry O.A.P. Association, comprising both ladies and gents, and a most enjoyable after- noon was spent.

The Club President, Mrs Miller, welcomed everyone and hoped they would have a plea- sant afternoon.

Friendly games of whist and dominoes were engaged in, 14 tables being fully occupied. The following were the winners:— Dominoes—1, Mrs Munro; 2, Mrs Thrash; Gents.—1, Mr Brotherton; 2, Mr Grass. Whist —1, Mrs Harrill; 2, Mr Milne,

le Pilgrim and the Inquiry

straight up to the Pil- said "What do you the . . ." and w he answered "It's ice!" ict?" ndy ice." ire you talking about quiry into the packing

"I don't think that will hap- pen, whatever else!" I assured him. "I should imagine that learned counsel would soon sug- gest any such tendency and tell the person concerned that it would be the height of bad manners to let either a sudden conversion or a desperate attack of boredom come between Her Majesty's Commissioner and

worried when he looked over in that direction. I thought to myself that he was just trying mentally to grade the spectators into curious housewives, inter- ested lawyers, indignant former pupils stolid business-men, fel- low-headmasters, and so forth." I laughed and added "He would have a job—most of the cate- gories merge into each other

Alloa Advertiser 9th December 1960.
Virginia is now returning to normal.

239

NEWS OF THE WEEK

SUDDEN DEATH OF MR LANCE

When Miss Morgan, housekeeper to Mr Alfred Lance, of 17 Alexandra Drive, Alloa, returned home late on Wednesday evening she found her employer in a state of collapse. A doctor was summoned, but Mr Lance was found to be dead.

Sad Year

By this sudden death a whole household has been wiped out this year. Mr Lance's mother died on 7th January and his father on 14th May.

Mr Lance, who succeeded his father in his radio, television and electrician's business in Mar Place, was only forty-three years of age. He is survived by an only sister, Mrs Wallace, whose home is in Glasgow.

Alfred Lance was a shy and reserved man who was greatly respected for his sterling personal qualities. He was an active member of the Round Table and of Moncrieff Church, where he attended Holy Communion last Sunday.

Y.M. AT HOME TO VISITORS

The Alloa Headquarters of the Y.M.C.A. in Mar Street were brightly illuminated this week for the Association's centenary celebrations.

A five-day programme, during which the Y.M.C.A. is "At Home" to the general public and is demonstrating its many activities, began on Wednesday night with an entertainment to a party of old age pensioners. It took the form of a combined film show and concert, and a tea donated by Bailie A. Nicol.

The guests were welcomed by Mr W. Jarvis, the club treasurer, who touched in a short talk on the hundred-year history of the club.

At the conclusion of the entertainment an old-age pensioner spokesman thanked the club, the artistes and the willing helpers.

New County Savings Drive

The Wee County may soon have its own small-scale "Ernie" scheme.

This suggestion for boosting savings in Clackmannanshire was enthusiastically received at a special meeting of the County Savings Committee held in Greenfield House on Wednesday night.

Alloa Area of the National Coal Board, which has many savings groups inside and outside the county, has indicated its willingness to co-operate with such a scheme and other large employers in the area are also expected to take part.

The Scheme

Details have not yet been worked out, but the idea might be to start with an area, bring it down to a firm, then a group within a firm, and finally an individual who would be winner of a small prize, to the value of, say, £25.

The meeting was called to consider the national campaign to increase savings which is being launched with the message "Be a shareholder in Britain."

Firms which already run savings organisations in the district but do not link up with the savings stamps scheme are to be asked to do so.

Those having stamp schemes find that almost half of the savings invested by their workers are in the form of savings stamps.

Up To Parents

Schoolteachers are no longer taking part in the organising of school savings groups and the alternative way of encouraging savings among children is to persuade parents through the works and factories to buy stamps for them.

One of the most important aspects of national savings is the organising of street savings groups and a renewed effort is being made in this direction.

Tullibody has already given a ...

VIRGINIA BACK AT SCHOOL

Virginia Campbell, the 11-year-old Irish girl who lives at 19 Park Crescent, Sauchie, was all set to return to school on Monday after her upsetting experiences of last week when she was troubled by strange phenomena.

Happy Child

When school-time arrived, however, so great was the battery of cameras and reporters outside the house that her parents decided to keep Virginia at home.

They told our reporter that Virginia is now perfectly well and happy, but they thought that Dr R. W. Nisbet and their local minister would continue to keep a watchful eye on their child in case of a return of the disturbing happenings.

Virginia has been attending school now since the middle of the week and is getting along happily in class and with her playmates.

Road Collision Sequel

When a lorry collided with a motor-car while reversing in Lower Mill Street, Tillicoultry, on October 26 the incident gave rise to three charges against three different people.

The driver of the lorry, Thomas Hamilton, 9 Scarre Terrace, Glasgow, was fined £4 or sixteen days at Alloa Sheriff Court on Wednesday for careless driving.

George McDonald, a miner of 55 Stalker Avenue, Tillicoultry, was charged at the same Court with driving the motor-car without having a licence and was fined £2 or fifteen days. He admitted a previous conviction for the same offence.

Catherine Montgomery or McDonald or Gillespie ...

COMMUNION SERVICES
11.3[?] a.m. and 6.30 p.m.
Ref. J. Rose Rankin
Kirk Session to meet at 11 a.m.
Retiring Offerings for Church
Assembly Schemes
Members who have changed their
address within recent weeks
please intimate same on Sunday.

ST JOHN'S EPISCOPAL CHURCH
BROAD STREET, ALLOA

Rector:
Rev. J. M. C. Hannah, M.A.
8.30—Holy Communion
11.15 a.m.
First Sundays—Holy Communion
Other Sundays—Mattins
11.15—Sunday School.
12.30—Bible Class
6.30—Evensong.

CHRISTIAN SCIENCE SOCIETY

Branch of the Mother Church, The
First Church of Christ, Scientist,
in Boston, Massachusetts
PARK AVENUE, STIRLING
(at Clarendon Place)
Sunday Service—11.15 a.m.
Testimony Meeting—
Every Wednesday at 7.30 p.m.
Reading Room Open Monday and
Thursday from 3 to 5 p.m. and
Tuesday from 7 to 9 p.m.

CHRISTIAN SPIRITUALIST CHURCH

SCOTTISH NATIONAL PARTY
ROOMS
Whins Road, Alloa
Speaker and Demonstrator
Mr G. Innes
(Glasgow)
Service starts at 6 p.m.
A cordial welcome is extended to all

EBENEZER HALL
PARKHEAD ROAD, SAUCHIE

Meeting Hours:
11.30—Breaking of Bread
1.15—Sunday School and
Bible Class
3.15—Ministry
6.30—Gospel Meeting
Speaker:
Mr J. Gillespie
(Alloa)
A Hearty Welcome
is Extended to All

Guildswomen Confer

The quarterly conference of Section VII District of the Co-opera-
tive Women's Guilds took place in
Clackmannan Town Hall on Saturday under the auspices of the
Clackmannan branch.
Mrs A Flynn, President of the
Clackmannan Guild, extended a
welcome to delegates from thirty-
five branches in the area.
Mrs Muir, Larbert, President of

KNOCKING SOUNDS HEARD

VIRGINIA ON THE AIR

Two Tillicoultry doctors
used a tape-recording of
sound phenomena which had
been heard during the recent
psychic illness of little
Virginia Campbell of Sauchie
in the B.B.C. Scottish Home
Service programme "Scope"
on Tuesday.

Lid Opened

The sounds in themselves,
gentle knocking sounds were not
terrifying but when a child's voice
started screaming "Mummy!
Mummy!"—that happened when
Virginia saw the lid of the linen
basket starting to open, the doctors explained—it was then that
listeners realised that something
unusual was happening.
Those taking part in the B.B.C.
programme besides Drs Nisbet and
Logan were the Rev. T. W. Lund
of Sauchie and the Rev. Murdo
Ewan MacDonald, of St George's
West Church, Edinburgh.
Mr MacDonald described the
sounds and movements witnessed,
and he considered that there were
two possible explanations and he
favoured the explanation that the
phenomena were caused by some
"lower forms of intelligence."
The Presbytery of Stirling and
Dunblane at its meeting on Tuesday decided to ask the General
Assembly's Church and Nation
Committee to consider the conduct of a certain section of the
national press in the exploitation
of such matters with a view to
making representation to the
Press Council.

THE MESSIAH

A choir and soloists from Alloa
Amateur Operatic Society are to
give a Christmas selection from
Handel's "Messiah" in the West
Church on Sunday night.
Thirty-four of the fifty-six num-
bers of this immortal work will be
given.
The performance will be con-
ducted by Mr Arthur Muddiman,
and the soloists will be Soprano,
Mrs E. McClement; and Miss J.
Muir; tenor, Mr D. Dewar and
Mr E. McDonald; bass, Mr J. Sloan
and Mr R. M. Sloan.
Accompanists will be Mr Robert
Younger at the organ and Mrs
Dorothy Allan at the piano.
Admission programmes can be
obtained from Mr G. P. Horne,
dental surgeon, Mar Place, or Mr
Mr David Dewar at the Co-opera-
tive Central Grocery, High Street

Brevities

If brevity is the soul of wit the
public meeting of Alloa Town
Council on Monday was a scin-
tillating one. It lasted exactly
eight minutes.

The Education Committee has
accepted the resignation of Mrs L.
B. Stewart of St Serf's School,
Tullibody, as from January 3.

* * *

Miss Janet Higham is to resign
from the teaching staff of Sauchie
School on January 3.

The residents of Inglewood
Eventide Home are having their
Christmas dinner and party on
Tuesday first at five o'clock.

Tenders for the erection of two
houses on a "gap site" at Whins
Road have been approved by the
Department of Health. They will
be single-storey cottages of two
apartments.

County Councillors and Alloa
Town Councillors are to have a
joint-outing to Kirkcaldy on July
18. They are to be the guests of
Wimpey for an inspection of
housing projects in the linoleum
burgh.

* * *

Mr Joseph Hislop, of the Works
Department of Alloa Town Council, reaches the retiring age of
sixty-five next week, but he is to
continue his services for another
year.

Alloa Town Council has decided
against the use of "diatomaceous
earth" for the filtration of water
at Alloa Public Baths. The old-
established method of sand-
filtration is to be introduced at
the pond.

A CHRISTMAS GESTURE

A Christmas present of
£100 with an expression of
the hope that their plans for
improvements will prosper
has been received by the
committee of Sauchie Public
Hall from Samuel Jones and
Company of Tillicoultry.

The gift was announced at a
meeting of the committee on
Wednesday night when official
instructions were issued for the
preparation of plans and estimates
for alterations to the main Public
Hall. Plans will include enlarging
the hall and providing new cloak-
rooms and kitchen facilities.
Alterations to the club premises
including the provision of a bar
were agreed upon several months

Alloa Journal 16 Dec 1960

ALL
[?]

After [?]
lided wit[h]
motor-car
fermline
Home Fa
Friday, A
Keown, a
Argyll St
without s[?]

Sev[?]

The occu[p]
George Hu
for Clackm[?]
severely inj
hospital.
against Per[?]
his team
Championsh[?]
At Alloa [?]
nesday McK
failing to s[?]
and was fin
native of
ment.
He plead
further ch[?]
his lorry w
attention. A
Sheriff Mur
not proven

Alloa
M

Old folk[s]
members de[?]
and treasu[re]
Old-Age Pen
of the year
noon.
Mrs John[?]
the opening
was observ[ed]
George Rob[?]
Delegation
branch socia[l]
and Mrs P[?]
December [?]
Mrs Russell
way and M[?]
ford, both of
Miss McG[?]
the area me[?]
on December
A hamper
were receiv[ed]
from Frances
Pond. The [?]
held on Jan[?]

Wom[?]
Fu[?]

seen billowing
smey, of an un-
d condemned two
in Forth Street,
Tuesday in Nov-

e in the neigh-
t to investigate,
were in the gar-
They climbed over
den walls and dis-
sight. They again
when they made
time. it was dis-
hey had left be-
containing 45 lbs.
copper,
had been newly
was noticed that
been entered by
ndow. A wood
urning in an up-
d this had been
the insulation off

es led to Alex-
. fisherman, 26
Allou, and he de-
edge of the theft.
that he had been
the time. but was
at an identifica-

were revealed by
al V. E. Cuthbert
f Court on Wed-
urns had admitted
ge.
s convictions were
urns and the Fis-
the value of the
which was 15s.
vered.
ay imposed a fine
alternative of 24
ment. Four weeks
r payment.

Poltergeist Probe

WHEN the Sauchie polter-
geist story broke a few
weeks ago, every effort was
made by this newspaper to treat
the matter with the greatest
possible discretion to obviate
any unnecessary distress to the
parents of the girl who was the
unfortunate objective of the
visitation.

In the first treatment of the
story by our mid-week contemporary "The Alloa Circular", the
the girl's name and address were
not disclosed, but that very
morning the story was splashed
in the national press and it became obvious that publicity
could no longer be withheld—
though the matter continued to
be played down (and never up)
in subsequent issues of the
"Advertiser."

New we note that this whole
question of press publicity—
with particular reference to the
Sauchie poltergeist—has been
the subject of some forthright
comment by Tillicoultry minister Rev. P. D. G. Campbell,
M.A. at last week's meeting of
the Stirling and Dunblane Presbytery.

Of what help, asked Mr
Campbell, were the swarms of
reporters that descended (on
Sauchie) like one of the plagues
of Egypt? Of what help to her
were the banner headlines and
the front page news?

And he went on to expose
to his Presbyterial colleagues

some of the artifices and deceits
employed by reporters to gain
entry to this particular Sauchie
home and (once in) to photograph the householder secretly
and against his express injunctions.

Well. as we have said, our
own conscience in this matter is
clear. Competition between the
national newspapers is fierce
(conscience is one of the first
casualties) and our playing
down of the matter was not
viewed as a mark of efficiency
in certain quarters—but where
the question of acting prejudi-
cally to a young person's health
is concerned we have no regrets
in erring on the safe side.

Perhaps some of the professional men (not only in journalism) involved in "the Sauchie
case" may have cause to examine their own consciences in
the matter. In one case at least
there was a strange switch from
"putting you on your honour"
to "using my own discretion"
when it came to divulging information.

Ernie's Xmas

ERNIE continues to view the
Wee County with a parsi-
monious eye—if one can imagine the optical organ being so
afflicted!

In the December edition of
the Premium Savings Bond
draw Clackmannanshire's share
is one £50 prize and eleven
£25's.

The quota certainly shows a
step-up from the November
distribution but it is far from
munificent—particularly at this
festive season—though incidentally we note that Stirlingshire
(a far larger community of
savers) also fails to break the
£50 barrier: two £50's and fifty-
six £25's are her portion.

For the record the organisers
state that five bond-holders won
£1,000, five won £500, nine won
£250 and twelve £100, so here's
hoping that one of the bigger
prizes may come this way in the
New Year.

Vintage Vista

AND now for a story appro-
priate to this festive period
of the year and which rather
amused us the other day. Perhaps we're telling it in a rather
different form.

A man was standing outside
a licensed grocer's shop admiring the sparkling array of vin-

motorists failed to reali
there was such an acute
at the Clackmannan ce
corner and Mr T. R.
thought that a larger w
sign should be erected
the Alloa side.

When the dangerous corn
discussed the County Roa
veyor stated that accordi
information received fron
police, there had been fou
dents during the past three
—the fourth one occurre
week-end when a car c
through the cemetery wall

Mr Ross stated that two
accidents were caused by
failing to stop at the hal
and another car had a bur
at the bend.

However, Mr George Gr
agreed with these figures. H
that since the present officer
to Clackmannan there had
six accidents. The week pr
the officer taking up duty
County town there had bee
other accident. These figur
not take into account the
dents that were not report

Chairman J. Stephens ren
that it looked as if the Cc
tee would require to get
reports in writing in futur
also stated that motorists
inclined to think that the f
field road was the main
and they were often too f
realising that they had a t
make.

The Clackmannan cemetei
ner arose during a discussior
the question of having i
white lines on the road be
Kilbagie and Blackgrange i
was under consideration.

STOP WATCH

Members were informed
the Road Surveyor had no
tained a stop watch to carr
a survey of the speed of vi
at corners, but a start coul
be made at the moment d
the recent frosty weather.

It was agreed to continu
matter until the result of the
test was made and that ob
tions be made about the (
mannan cemetery corner ar
Mary Bridge.

SPEED LIMIT AT KENNET

The Scottish Home Depar
have informed the Roads Co
tee that they will be prepar
upgrade the 30 mile an hour
limit within the present area
are not prepared to exten
signposts at either end of K
village.

Lord Mar, who was see
by Mr C. Eccles, moved that
cation be made to the Hom
partment to have the speed

ALLOA
ADVERTISER
23rd DECEMBER
1960

TA IN!

DAY

WILL BE IN HIS

Alloa Advertiser 23rd December 1960. Poltergeist Probe.

A plague of pressmen at Sauchie

HILLFOOTS MINISTER CONDEMNS POLTERGEIST "VISITATION"

AFTER a strongly worded statement by the Rev. P. D. G. Campbell, M.A., minister of St. Serf's Church, Tillicoultry, at a meeting of the Presbytery of Stirling and Dunblane in Allan Park Church, Stirling last Tuesday night, it was decided to request the Assembly's Church and Nation Committee to consider the actions of representatives of some sections of the National Press in news gathering with a view to making representations to the Press Council.

At one time Mr Campbell referred to certain newspaper reporters as having "descended like one of the plagues of Egypt" in trying to get information about one incident in the area.

He said that if he were to choose a text for his theme it would be from Leviticus 19, verse 16: "Thou shalt not go up and down as a talebearer among thy people." His report concerned particularly the National Press, and certainly one section of it.

MANY CAPACITIES

Newspapers were essential parts of modern life. They acted in many capacities — as safety valves for people with a grievance, as guardians of liberty, as mouthpieces of pressure groups of varying parties, as advertising media, and as disseminators of news. His concern was with papers in their primary function as 'news' papers.

In the past few weeks, said Mr Campbell, various events within the Presbytery had hit the headlines. But, he emphasised, he wanted, before going further, to pay tribute to the local press for its consistently accurate and, where it merited, sympathetic treatment of all proceedings. They had never failed the Presbytery in their courtesy and co-operation.

It had been said that the Church was always 'against things'; that it was negative in its outlook. Recently, they had passed on the Assembly's injunction against raffles, and had also commended the positive virtue of Christian stewardship.

In one paper the positive commendation was omitted. The purely negative prohibition of

the feelings of ordinary decency and common human sympathy. Parents were bereaved under tragic circumstances. Reporters descended upon the stricken household. Some made their enquiry and went their way.

Two others, seen by the father, wished to interview and photograph the mother. Their request was refused.

Later the same evening they returned, and stated they had instructions to get an interview and photograph of the mother in order, they said, "to bring home this tragedy to our readers."

"Moderator," continued Mr Campbell, "I dare say no more lest my feelings so run away with me that I forget that the person who gave such an order and the persons who tried to fulfil it are supposed to be men. Is any moral gone that it alone has such a mission of righteousness?"

FALSE POSE

Last week-end, he continued, there was a fatal accident at Dunblane. The man killed had, earlier, achieved some notoriety. His companion at the time of the crash was injured and admitted to Stirling Royal Infirmary.

The following day the telephone hardly stopped ringing. Reporters, dissatisfied with the official statement issued, went to considerable lengths, even to the extent of posing as brother and sister of the injured person, to secure news. This was not reporting. It was persecution.

But the case that was accorded the greatest publicity, said Mr Campbell, and has achieved the greatest notoriety was that involving the strange happenings in

help to her were the banner headlines and the front page news?

SENSATIONAL PRESENTATION

There were two aspects of the case which he wanted members of the Presbytery to consider. The method of presentation was one, and the other was the method by which reporters gathered their news.

The presentation was sensational in the worst sense. It included unsubstantiated rumours in capitals. It included verbatim the text of a letter from the child's mother to the father.

The propriety of printing such a letter, no matter how come by, was extremely doubtful. But the sensationalism of the whole business must have been, and was, a grave handicap to those who were grappling with a difficult and distressing situation.

Then there was the method by which the news was come by. When the United States exposed the wiles of Russia in planting listening devices around the Embassy in Moscow, everyone was horrified.

Horrified, they were, because the idea of eavesdropping was repugnant to most people. Ability to eavesdrop was apparently an advantage for certain reporters.

Was it not eavesdropping to report what was overheard of a telephone conversation between two other people as though you had been one of them?

Further, was it not deceitful when, in another man's house, to photograph him secretly, and against his express injunctions? When the father of the Sauchie girl came to the house he was accompanied by two men who claimed to be his friends.

One of them, at least, claimed to be a contractor. On the pretext of going to the bathroom, one went upstairs, but he went to see and report.

THEIR IDENTITY

Only after they were out of the house, when arrangements were being made late at night for their accommodation, did they reveal they were not contractors; they were not from Northern Ireland; they had met the father for the first time that day; they were, in fact, reporters.

Mr Campbell stressed that if the public knew that these were

Part of the Sunday Mirror article on the Sauchie
Poltergeist. 1965

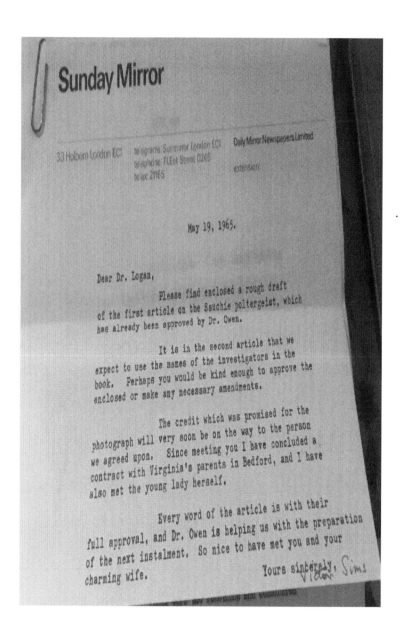

Sunday Mirror

33 Holborn London EC1   telegrams: Sunmirror London EC1   Daily Mirror Newspapers Limited
telephone: FLEet Street 0246
telex: 21165   extension

May 19, 1965.

Dear Dr. Logan,

Please find enclosed a rough draft of the first article on the Sauchie poltergeist, which has already been approved by Dr. Owen.

It is in the second article that we expect to use the names of the investigators in the book. Perhaps you would be kind enough to approve the enclosed or make any necessary amendments.

The credit which was promised for the photograph will very soon be on the way to the person we agreed upon. Since meeting you I have concluded a contract with Virginia's parents in Bedford, and I have also met the young lady herself.

Every word of the article is with their full approval, and Dr. Owen is helping us with the preparation of the next instalment. So nice to have met you and your charming wife.

Yours sincerely, Sims

Sunday Mirror Letter 1965 stating that the Campbell's had relocated to the English town of Bedford.

The author's write up on the Sauchie Poltergeist from the Alloa Advertiser April 13th 1994

London Weekend Television Limited
The London Television Centre
Upper Ground
London SE1 9LT
Telephone 020 7620 1620

William and Sheila Logan.

Monday, 03 July 2000

Dear Dr. Logan,

My name is Helen Cooke and I am an associate producer working for London Weekend TV.

I am writing in the hope that you can give me a ring. I am working on a programme for ITV that looks into people's experiences of hauntings and ghosts and we are planning to possibly feature Virginia Campbell's story. I have spoken to some of the surviving people who remember the events in Sauchie.

I also understand you and your partner Dr. Nesbit filmed on film and tape recorded some events in Virginia's room at the time she was ill.

I would just like to explain what it is we are doing and hopefully speak to you about your experience. Please give me a call and I will ring you right back.

My numbers are (work) 0207 261 3243 – let me stress again that this is just a chat and there is no obligation, its just a chance for us to have a talk about what happened.

I look forward to hearing from you.

Yours sincerely,

H. Cooke

Helen Cooke

LWT Letter June 2000. Do they still have the main Sauchie Poltergeist recordings?

Filming in the rain near Park Crescent Sauchie. For the BBC One Show. Presenter Matt Allwright speaks to the camera. February 2020
(c) Malcolm Robinson

Matt Allwright presenter for the Sauchie Poltergeist piece for the BBC One Show, with author Malcolm Robinson. The Mansfield pub Sauchie. February 2020

One Tribe TV filming at the Sauchie Mansfield pub for a sequence for the BBC One Show on the Sauchie Poltergeist. February 2020 © Malcolm Robinson.

Sheila Logan being interviewed by Matt Allwright for the BBC One Show. February 2020 (c) Malcolm Robinson

The author with Sheila Logan, who witnessed some of the poltergeist phenomenon herself. (c) Malcolm Robinson

The white buildings on the right, now occupy where the
Sauchie Primary School once stood.
Photo May 2020
(c) Garry McKenzie

The Sauchie Poltergeist house today. May 2020.
(c) Garry McKenzie

253

Some of the old stone from the demolished Sauchie Primary School, was used in the gable end of one of the houses that now occupy the location of the old Sauchie Primary School. May 2020.

(c) Garry McKenzie

Paranormal investigator looking for clues on Sauchie Poltergeist

By Jack Stanners
Reporter
jstanners@alloaadvertiser.co.uk

A PARANORMAL investigator is looking to hear from Wee County residents with information about the infamous Sauchie Poltergeist.

Former Tullibody resident Malcolm Robinson, 62, is researching rumours of the supernatural being, which is said to have plagued the town in late 1960.

The poltergeist was said to have focused its attention on an 11-year-old girl called Virginia Campbell between November-December of that year.

It was claimed the poltergeist moved a wooden chest in her bedroom and even lifted her desk while she was at school.

There was also an occasion where her pillow apparently rotated 60 degrees while her head was lying on it.

According to paranormal

Malcolm Robinson wants to hear from locals about the Sauchie Poltergeist

website PSI Encyclopedia, some of the occurrences were observed by multiple independent witnesses, including a local vicar and a doctor.

Now Malcolm, who founded the Strange Phenomena Investigations group back in 1979, is on the case.

He wants to talk to former classmates of Virginia Campbell, and is also looking for pictures of her, and testimony from any Clacks residents who have had paranormal experiences.

Malcolm hopes to use any material he can gather in his upcoming book, 'The Sauchie Poltergeist and other Scottish Ghostly Tales'.

His other works include 'The Monsters of Loch Ness' and 'The Dechmont Woods UFO Incident', and he has lectured widely across Scotland and England.

Malcolm can be contacted by emailing malckyspi@yahoo.com, or by calling him directly, using 07949 178 855.

All contact will be dealt with in the strictest confidence, and identities can be changed if required.

My quest to find former classmates of Virginia Campbell from the readers of the Alloa Advertiser, 15th January 2020 was of little success.

255

Virginia Campbell at15 years old. Three years after the
disturbing events at Park Crescent Sauchie.

CHAPTER FIVE

SO, WHAT IS A POLTERGEIST?

"In my opinion the Sauchie case must be regarded as establishing beyond all reasonable doubt the objective reality of some poltergeist phenomena".

Dr. A.R.G. Owen, Mathematician and Psychical Researcher

There are many weird and wonderful explanations put forward to try and explain the poltergeist, and in this chapter, we shall try and present but a few. Some would say that the answer lies with any number of upcoming explanations, whilst others would say that none of the upcoming theories will help to explain the poltergeist. The vast majority of people would assume that the poltergeist is a deceased individual who is not happy that they have passed on, and as such, revert to mischievous pranks, the throwing around of objects, causing fires, creating pools of water in the family home and a whole lot more. However, there is also the case that the poltergeist has nothing at all to do with a deceased individual, and that there is a more prosaic explanation which has nothing to do with the supernatural. Certain parapsychologists are coming around to the idea that the poltergeist is in effect, generated by a 'living' individual, mostly unintentional. The bizarre and often frightening nature of the poltergeist effects, the movement of objects etc, is done by a troubled mind, a mind that is more often than not, under physical and emotional stress, largely due to going through puberty, an aspect we will come back to shortly. The late great parapsychologist William G. Roll firmly believed that the poltergeist was all down to a 'living person' and had nothing to do with the paranormal.

In the Fife poltergeist case mentioned earlier in this book, which was investigated by both Tricia Robertson and Professor Archie Roy both from the Scottish Society of Psychical Research, Tricia Robertson gave her feelings as to what could lie behind the poltergeist phenomenon, more so with cases of young pubescent children, she wrote,

*"The phenomena involved with this type of case (**The Fife case, author's italics in bold**) are fascinating, as are the resolutions. It would appear that no one fully understands the power of the human psyche but we can only poorly estimate the latent abilities we may possess, which under certain circumstances seem to externalise themselves in some kind of physical phenomena. People sometimes ask me why everyone under stress does not manifest poltergeist phenomena. My answer is, 'I don't know'. Some people have nervous breakdowns, others do not. It would therefore appear that incarnate, and discarnate, personalities can produce similar 'poltergeist type events. This should give us pause for thought in each case as a discarnate survival hypothesis is not always required, but sometimes it is the most parsimonious and 'best' explanation"*

"As stated above, all kinds of smells can enter your house from the outside, even from a passing car, so such scents might not necessarily mean poltergeist.

Such scents and odours can also be a sign of ghost activity, as they might be associated with a spirit or with a residual haunting.

Ghosts and Poltergeists. What is the Difference?

It goes without saying that there is a marked difference between what a ghost is and what a poltergeist is. By reading this book you will know that the poltergeist can be extremely destructive. This tends to set them aside from your normal haunting. That said, hauntings themselves are equally different! Ghosts are like batteries, they don't always last that long. We may look at it like those old VHS video tapes, which after many times being re-recorded over and over, the colour and sound deteriorates. Are ghosts some kind of energy that only lasts for a certain period of time, after which that energy dissipates never to be seen again? Well as far as 'some' ghosts go, I certainly think so. At this point I'd like to tell you that ghosts are not always what they seem! We have a number of different variations of ghostly phenomena, for instance.

- **Ghosts of the recently deceased.** (These may be seen moments after death by family or friends who are psychically aware to perceive such visions)

- **Animal Ghosts.** Yes, even your pets have been seen coming back from the grave by grieving owners.

- **Ghosts that are aware of you?** Incredibly, we have a few ghosts who seem to want to strike up a conversation with you. They have been seen to speak, but no words come out of their mouths, then, as if disappointed, they just disappear.

- **Ghosts that are unaware of you!** These are your typical ghosts, seen but for a fleeting moment and move by you as if you were just not there.

- **Transparent Ghosts.** Again, another typical ghost, those that you can see through, there is no solidity to them.

- **Solid Appearing Ghosts.** Quite the reverse. Some people have seen the spirit of someone who has passed over, either in the street or in their home, appearing completely solid, whereupon they just disappear!

- **Ghosts that navigate past furniture.** Yes, very strange, how can this be, they are ghosts/spirits after all, surely, they don't need to navigate past furniture, they could surely pass through it. But we have on record, some cases where this is so.

- **Ghosts of the living?** This is something that is most perplexing. A doppelganger, in other words, people are seeing 'YOU' in another part of the country, or, on some occasions, another part of the world! Research has shown that the 'real you' is back at home. Now whilst this could just be a 'look a like,' the person who has seen what they thought was you, state, that the person they saw, was wearing the same clothes as you! In my research, I have not come across anyone who has spoken to this so called 'double', and if so, what transpired next.

- **Stone Tape Ghosts?** Basically, these are not sightings of ghosts as such; in point of fact it's the very fabric of the building that seems to store, over time, various sounds that have impregnated themselves into the walls, usually stone walls. These type of 'stone tape ghosts', are usually found in old buildings the very fabric of the stone, being conducive to allowing this to happen. Again, just like an old VHS Video Recorder storing sound and vision, under certain conditions, an old building can replay to those perceptive of it, let's say a vicious argument of old, the clinking of glasses, the sounds of laughter and merriment etc. A good case in point is a pub in Kenfig Mid Glamorgan called the Prince of Wales, check it out on Google.

- **Crisis Ghosts.** Like ghosts of the living, a crisis ghost is essentially someone who is at death's door, they may be shipwrecked in the ocean flaying about knowing that death was very near, as was the case to a lady who I spoke to many years ago. She related a story to me that during the Second World War, she was knitting at her home in North London, when all of a sudden she saw just a few yards in front of her, a vision something akin to a television set which showed her son desperately trying to stay afloat in the sea. Seconds later, he disappeared beneath the waves. A few weeks later she received a telegram from the Admiralty saying that sadly her son's ship was torpedoed in the North Atlantic and that he was lost at sea. Now this is where it gets interesting, for the telegram gave the exact time and date that the mother was witnessing this same scene back at her home in North London. There are similar crisis ghost tales such as this.

• **Anniversary Ghosts.** Put simply, these are ghosts that appear on say the 22nd of November of every year, (or any notable given date) and who may walk the corridors of say a stately home or castle. Again, the literature is riddled with claims such as this. It has always been my intention to test this one out and set up equipment where one of these anniversary ghosts walk and see if we can capture it. This, I haven't done as yet, but look forward to doing in due course.

The Poltergeist

We won't go into what a poltergeist is here, as it has been covered elsewhere throughout this book, suffice it to say, that after consultation with a family who have reported such an occurrence, it is up to the investigator to ascertain what in point of fact is occurring in the home, needless to say, it would soon become apparent to any researcher worth his or her salt that there would be a major difference, that said, it still begs the question, what is behind these disturbances? The poltergeist is usually short lived, and should dissipate after a short period of time, that said, some poltergeist reports have gone on for months, thankfully, they too eventually fade away. So, this brings us to what is a poltergeist, well, needless to say, it's not so cut and dried as you may think. We will now take a look at some theories to explain the poltergeist of which the answer may lie in either one or none of the following theories.

THEORIES (So what could a poltergeist be?)

The following are but some of what a number of paranormal researchers have put down to be the root cause of the poltergeist. They are.

1) RSPK. (Recurrent Spontaneous Psychokinesis)
2) Ley Lines/ Earth Energies/Ultrasound.
3) Hallucinations people on drugs.

4) Hoaxes.
5) Attention seeking, fame and fortune.
6) Misinterpretation.
7) Sexual energy.
8) Schizophrenia.
9) The Hutchinson Effect.
10) A Spirit of a deceased person.

So, let us take a look at the above suggestions a little bit more closely.

THEORY ONE: RSPK
(Recurrent Spontaneous Psychokinesis)

It was paranormal researcher William G Roll's belief, that the root cause of the poltergeist phenomenon was an energy coming from an individual, and he gave it the name of, Recurrent Spontaneous Psychokinesis, or (RSPK) for short. What he couldn't determine, was how that mechanism operated, what caused it to start? Was it to do with the human brain? It goes without saying that we know so little about the human brain, but science admittedly is 'catching up' and many studies of the brain from various scientists are now slowly detecting certain things, that many years ago would have seemed ridiculous. Let us not forget that the human brain is an incredible organ, an organ that can be fooled fairly easily, and I refer to someone who can be put under hypnosis, and whilst under hypnosis, the hypnotist will touch the person on say the back of his hand telling him that it was a lighted match that was touching his hand, and the individual would react as if he was being burned. Indeed, under hypnosis people have eaten an onion whilst being told that it was an apple! So, the brain can be fooled into thinking things differently whilst under certain conditions. What I am referring to is, under duress or stressful conditions, can the human brain be fooled into seeing and feeling certain conditions which in point of fact, are not what they seem! And if so, can some sort of manifestations arise from an individual to affect household objects to move of their own accord? Is it the same or similar type of energy that Uri

Geller and others, use to bend spoons etc? It's fair to say, that there are many parapsychologists who are leaning towards this unconscious P.K. angle. The well know psychoanalyst Nandor Fodor, described P.K. as, *"a bundle of projected repressions."* She may not be too far off the mark! Doing research for this book, I came across some interesting comments from Uri Geller's web site. It stated, and I quote.

"There are even more direct links between poltergeists and certain types of psychological strain, one of the more interesting being evidenced in the case of an Englishwoman, Miss H. Power, who lived during the late 1800s. According to her detailed testimony, it happened while she was sitting in her living room one day, boiling inwardly because a book she was reading was rubbing against the grain of her profoundest religious beliefs. Suddenly, while in her frenzied emotional state, her handbag went flying under an end table, rapping and ticking sounds broke out around the room, and a drawing board fell over, all in rapid sequence. In some way her emotions appeared to have externalised PK energy".

It has been said that there are far more historical reports surrounding females than males and we could ask ourselves why? Is it truly the changes going on in the female body and if so why, there are equally hormonal changes occurring in the male body? The noted English parapsychologist Hereward Carrington was quoted as saying.

"An energy seems to be radiated from the body in such cases, which induces these phenomena, when the sex energies are blossoming into maturity within the body, It would almost seem as if these energies, instead of taking their normal course, were externalised beyond the limits of the body." [H. Carrington, The Story of Psychic Science, (London, 1930), pp. 145-146.]

When we look at the division of opinions between those who believe that it is a spirit that is causing destruction and mayhem in a family home, to those who believe that all these effects are nothing but some kind of 'energy' coming from the unfortunate victim, then we have to ask why? Could it be as Uri Geller speculates, that, and I quote.

"The poltergeist focus can be looked on as an energized person whose newfound powers have opened a hole in our reality and let through entities from other planes".

Uri considers the possibility that the subconscious, in certain circumstances, is under a lot of emotional stress, and this emotional stress, in some cases (not all) can, to a degree, cause a form of dissociation, which as he states, splits the person's energy body into 'entities' that function separately, each of whom have some kind of role to play in the mayhem that follows. Uri goes on to say that perhaps our world is composed of different levels and densities of PSI energy, and that maybe when all these different types of energy are brought together in this form of dissociation, some kind of 'thought form' or externalised 'effect' is brought to bear as seen by the poltergeist effects. This idea has been called the 'psychic crystallization theory,' and as stated, this might' be the result of the human mind blending with a PSI substratum. Could, under certain circumstances, our unconscious thoughts or psychic energy somehow affect another person's auric field of which the spin off from this could be the poltergeist effect? This thought of course gives us more questions than answers, and whilst all theories should be looked at when trying to answer the poltergeist enigma, we have to be careful we don't push that boat out too far and lose sight of the shore! Reading Uri's web site regarding the poltergeist effect was truly fascinating, more so when I learned that Samuel Lentine, who is a physicist at the Rensselaer Polytechnical Institute, a private research University based in Troy, New York, has been fascinated by 'thought forms' and set out to see if he could 'create them'! Samuel believes that these 'thought forms' can be created by mixing PSI energies much in the same way as you can create certain chemicals by mixing other chemicals. Samuel has since stopped experimenting with meditation, which was his way of entering this strange arena as he found that 'human created entities' could appear and exist for short periods of time. He was quoted as saying.

"It's not exactly the safest of experiments, the forms sometimes leave your control and, like anything else, can have negative effects. For that reason, I've more or less stopped working with them and am not sure one should get into it until we have more knowledge."

THEORY TWO
(Earth Energies – Electromagnetic Fields - Ley Lines Infra Sound)

In some respects, we are back to the human brain and what it perceives to be real or not. With this theory we know that there are indeed conditions coming up through the Earth's surface which can, and 'does', affect the human brain. So, does this theory have any merit when it comes to solving the poltergeist phenomenon? Earth energies come in different groups. First up we will take a look at Ley Lines and see if this might have a bearing on poltergeist events.

Ley Lines

Ley lines effectively are straight lines underneath the ground which connect various human structures and landmarks, the likes of churches, earth mounds, and historic sites. Back in the day before the building of roads, ancient man just had the lay of the land, he still had to get from A to B in the quickest way possible. So, by looking across the land at various structures etc, that was his road, that straight line, from structure to structure, building to building. But was there something more to it that this? Is this just too simple an answer? There are those who would state that whilst the above is of course credible, there is more to it, and that there are these invisible energies underneath the Earth which certain people can tap into as an alternative way to get from A to B. History tells us that the concept of Ley Lines was suggested by Englishman Alfred

Watkins back in the 1924. His theory on Ley Lines came out in his bestselling book, 'The Old Straight Track'. This one book caught the imagination of many people, and a whole arena was built up through people reading this book who also attributed it to having connotations to other such mysteries namely route tracks for alien spacecraft which this author thinks extremely ludicrous. Needless to say, scientists and archaeologists look upon ley lines as nothing but pseudo-archaeology and pseudo-science. Scientists will tell you that ley lines cannot be detected by any device such as a magnetometer, and that it is only the so called 'New Age' community that can feel and detect this energy. One of the ways that the 'New Agers' will tell you how to detect these ley lines, is by the act of dowsing, using either a divining rod or a pendulum. Archaeologist Tom C. Lethbridge was of the opinion that the human body is some kind of antenna, and that this antenna is somehow attuned to the very fabric of the land. Tom started to use his dowsing rod and soon detected underground streams, coins, and other lost objects. He soon found out, that if he asked in his mind that he wanted to find a certain item which could be a coin or whatever, his dowsing rods eventually found that what he requested in his mind and pointed to the ground beneath his feet. Tom also found what he claimed were these Ley Lines, or Energy Lines which criss crossed the earth. But where does the Ley Line theory come into play regarding the poltergeist? Well some researchers speculate that it could be, that when some Ley Lines criss cross the earth, that crossing point has created some kind of 'black' or 'dark energy' which can affect any given house that rests above it. Now admittedly this sounds quite ridiculous and extremely speculative more so as we don't know what type of 'energy' is allegedly generated at these crossing points (if any energy is generated at all!) And even if some kind of dark energy does erupt for want of a better word, what allows it to do so, and when does it do so, and for how long does it do so? All questions which desire an answer. For me, I don't think that a Ley Line 'crossing point' with its dark energy is the answer to the poltergeist mystery, I could be wrong, but I don't think so.

Atmospheric Conditions.

Can certain atmospheric conditions play a part in the poltergeist effect? Studies have shown that differences in air pressure can have quite a noticeable effect on the human body. Some people experience these changes more than others. For those who are frequent flyers, we have all had our ears popping during a flight as your ear equalizes due to the changing of pressure. Some people prior to a thunderstorm approaching start to get headaches or get a stiffening of their joints, so there clearly is a change with the human body with certain atmospheric conditions. But again, can these atmospheric conditions play any role in the poltergeist effect? For me no, they can't. Other than headaches and joint pain, I don't believe that atmospheric conditions, changes in air pressure etc, can make household objects move of their own accord or cause people to see things which are not there. Climatic weather conditions, changes in air pressure etc, can cover a large amount of land and if this had a bearing on what we see in poltergeist cases, then surely whole towns would be under a poltergeist attack, so again, not for me.

Seismic effects in the Sauchie Area 1960?

Fellow Scottish researcher Brian Allan wrote an interesting piece in his article *'Legacy of the Sauchie Poltergeist'* written in 2000, Brian brings to bear the possibility of magnetic fields and seismic effects which might have had a bearing on the Sauchie poltergeist, (the main thrust of this book) He stated, and I quote;

"One particular set of events discounted at the time was an outbreak of earth tremors in the vicinity of Sauchie and Dollar, interestingly, both these villages are situated close by the Ochil Hills. The involvement of vibrations created by earth quakes was discounted because of the consideration that the type and

magnitude of vibrations required to cause heavy items to move around, would have caused structural damage to the houses, this is probably correct, but other factors has been forgotten; (A) the incidence of strong magnetic fields created by these seismic disturbances, and (B) a phenomenon called sonic levitation. In the case of scenario, (A), modern thinking and research suggests that when someone suffers from a condition known as 'Electrical Hypersensitivity' (E.H.), then it is possible for the strange manifestations to be explained within the realms of physics. An E.H. person can interact with either local geo-magnetic field or fields created by electrical equipment and cause it to be re-radiated and focussed. This in turn creates magnetic eddy currents and vortices that can and do cause highly unusual local phenomena, viz. items move around, noises and bangs, even levitation. Scenario (B) draws on the fact that under certain circumstances sound alone is sufficient to render items weightless".

"This explanation has been proffered as one of the methods by which the ancient Egyptians manoeuvred huge stone blocks used in the construction of the pyramids into position. An American researcher Tom Danley and two colleagues instigated this type of technology and filed a US patent, No. 5036944 based on their research. Based on their findings, An acoustic levitator includes a pair of opposed sound sources which have interfering sound waves producing acoustic energy wells in which an object may be levitated. The phase of one sound source may be changed relative to the other in order to move the object along an axis between the sound sources. This type of technology was allegedly discovered, or perhaps that should be re-discovered, over 70 years ago by Charles Worral Keeley the obscure cult inventor of 'free energy' machines and other assorted esoterica. In the case of Keeley, his device was allegedly activated by the expedient of blowing a trumpet, which induced sympathetic resonance in the device thereby rendering it weightless. While this explanation may appear as incredible as the poltergeist phenomenon itself, it should not be totally ruled out because the frequency of natural acoustic energy released during earthquakes cannot be discounted,

268

(earthquakes were measured in the vicinity during the poltergeist activity)"

Brian does raise some very interesting points in his article but freely admits that this seismic and magnetic theory is only that, a theory, but it should be considered, I guess not just for the Sauchie case, but for potentially other major poltergeist cases as well.

Infrasound and Dr Richard Wiseman.

There has been a lot of debate recently as to the possibility that many ghost sightings can be put down to infrasound. So, what is infrasound? Well Wikipedia tells us that Infrasound is a low-frequency sound, with a frequency below the lower limit of audibility (generally 20 Hz). The hearing process will gradually diminish and become less sensitive as the frequency decreases. The ear is of course the main organ for sensing infrasound, but various parts of the body can detect infra sound if it is of a higher intensity. In Diana Brown's article in the science blog, 'How Things Work' May 30th, 2017 titled, 'Infrasound and Paranormal Activity, Are They Connected?' she stated, and I quote;

"It was engineer Vic Tandy in 1980 that discovered infrasound could be responsible for perceived 'hauntings'. In his paper 'Ghost in the Machine', Tandy describes working in a laboratory that had a reputation for being eerie. People complained of feeling anxious and uncomfortable there. Tandy himself thought he saw an apparition. One day, a fencing foil clamped in a vice started vibrating for no reason. He found a fan emitting noise at a frequency of 19 Hz, and when it was turned off, the noise and the feelings of discomfort disappeared. Tandy found that these low-frequency vibrations caused blurred vision, dizziness, and feelings of fear in humans. He repeated his experiment at several locations reputed to be haunted."

One gentleman who has done an incredible amount of work on infra sound and its 'ghostly aspects', is Professor Richard

Wiseman who is a psychologist based at the University of Hertfordshire. Richard has appeared on many television documentaries relating to ghosts and the paranormal giving his sceptical feelings about the subject. He is on record as saying.

"Ghosts have been around for many hundreds if not thousands of years. They've been with us for a long time and understanding why, that's the case, whether it's because there's evidence for their existence, or because we have a need to believe in ghosts. I tend towards the latter explanation it doesn't seem to be going away any time soon. It's a topic that most scientists steer clear of but actually I think there's some interesting science to be done there".

Richard has worked in many so called haunted locations and using his infra sound machines has detected that low frequency sound can cause people to have paranormal and unusual experiences. These people will be in an environment where they themselves cannot detect these low frequency sounds, but as Richard Wiseman has shown, his machines when in the same area, can detect these low frequencies where people are saying that they are feeling frightened, or have been touched by an invisible entity. In Richard's on line blog, The Ghost in the Brain, https://richardwiseman.wordpress.com/2009/01/06/the-ghost-in-the-brain/ he had this to say;

"Some scientists have suggested that this level of sound may be present at some allegedly haunted sites and so cause people to have odd sensations that they attribute to a ghost, our findings support these ideas. I have conducted quite a few joint studies into the psychology of so called haunted locations, including Hampton Court Palace in London, and a set of underground vaults in Edinburgh. This work has examined various 'normal' explanations for people's experiences, including suggestion, expectation, infrasound, and electromagnetic fields. As is so often the case with research into the paranormal, the work has proved controversial, with some arguing that 'ghostly' phenomena are due to spirits. However, a remarkable new study provides perhaps the strongest

evidence to date that ghostly experiences are due to neural, rather than spiritual, activity"

In an article in the Scotsman newspaper of 9th March 2009 entitled, *'A Spirited Experiment: The Science of Ghosts'*. Wiseman stated that he has been interested in the psychology aspect of the paranormal for 25 years, and admits to being sceptical, but not, he hastened to add, an armchair sceptic. He stated.

"There's a case for engaging with the evidence but I don't pretend that there's some part of me that believes in the afterlife because I don't."

One of Richard Wiseman's biggest experiments, certainly when it comes to research on Scottish soil, occurred back in 2001, when his team descended down into the famous Edinburgh Vaults. He surprisingly found people to go down with him who apparently had no prior knowledge of how spooky this place was, (really!) This was done with a view to monitor their reactions; needless to say, the results he got were encouraging. He stated to the Scotsman newspaper.

"We had certain places that had a reputation for being haunted and when we took people into those places even when they didn't know the history, they had weird experiences. That suggests there is something about that location which is creating those ghostly experiences, whether it's the size, or the look, or the lighting levels. There's something there to be explained. That surprised me because I thought it was all in the mind, in that you just get some people who are easily scared, who believe in the paranormal, and when you take them into a place that's allegedly haunted, they scare themselves into having an experience. What we showed in the Vaults investigation is actually that location matters. There were some places that made people a lot more scared and more likely to have these experiences than others. That was a nice surprise because it means there's more science to be done."

271

So, whilst I will accept that infra sound can indeed cause some people to experience strange effects of what some would say are of a paranormal aspect, where does infra sound come into the poltergeist equation? Again, if there are certain locations of which low level infra sound can be felt, then can that also move furniture and objects around? Certain sounds at a high frequency as we know, can, to a small degree, misplace objects, but with the poltergeist we are looking at fires starting, pools of water appearing, and on rare occasions, attacks on people! So, for me, I would tend to rule infra sound out of the poltergeist effect, but not rule it out on some ghost locations. I do believe that infra sound can and does affect people in certain ways in making them feel, sense and taste, things which they falsely attribute to spirits of the dead.

THEORY THREE
(Drugs - Hallucinations)

I make no apology for bringing drugs into the equation in looking at answers to explain the poltergeist enigma. My research group always has to ask the tricky question whether or not, the occupants of a haunted house are taking any medication/drugs for any problematic ailment that they might be having. It's not a question we like asking, but we have to, as needless to say the sceptics of this world would ask, *"Why didn't we ask this question"*. Of course not all drugs will have you hallucinating, more so the official prescribed over the counter drugs (unless of course taken in large doses) As we know, there are many drugs out there that can, and do, make people hallucinate some of these drugs are of course amphetamines, cocaine, LSD, ecstasy, heavy alcohol abuse and certain types of mushrooms. They see a whole range of weird and wonderful things, majestic colours, strange beings, weird shapes and a whole lot more. These things, we are told, are 'not real' there is no substance to them, they are mind projections like a night time dream has escaped into a day reality and is masquerading in front of the drug taker. These drug induced effects simply alter the drug taker's perception of the world around them. Most, if not 'all' people who have experienced

272

poltergeist effects (as far as I know) have not been on drugs whilst claiming poltergeist effects, if you the reader know of any, then do please write to me at the address at the end of the book. Hallucinations do not just happen when people are on drugs, there are a number of other areas where people can suffer hallucinations into thinking that they are looking at something supernatural. Some people have reported due to extreme tiredness or sleep deprivation, that they start seeing weird things. Then of course we have the often frightening sleep states of hypnagogic imagery, this is the state just before falling asleep when again, some people see strange visions or the hypnopompic state where people are just starting to wake up, again weird hallucinogenic imagery is reported. These can be quite frightening to people who are experiencing this for the first time. They may see people that they don't know suddenly appear, or objects moving around the room. These bizarre sleep states are more common with people who suffer from narcolepsy. Fever can also cause hallucinations. There is something called the Charles Bonnet syndrome which affects certain older people who are losing their sight. Wikipedia tells us, and I quote.

'These hallucinations usually last for about 12 to 18 months and can take the form of simple, repeated patterns or complex images of people, objects or landscapes. In the UK, around 100,000 people are thought to be affected by Charles Bonnet syndrome. Hallucinations can sometimes occur in frail older people who are ill. The hallucinations may start before other signs that the person is unwell. They may be caused by a chest infection or urine infection, for example"

So, the bottom line with this theory is of course, are people who report poltergeist events on drugs, and as I stated earlier, as far as I know, they are not. So, are they suffering from a medical condition which brings these visions on? Yes possibly. So how can we explain the displaced furniture in the poltergeist home, the attacks on individuals etc? Is this also attributable to drugs? Well to a degree yes, people on drugs may harm themselves, they are not in full control of their body and mind

273

and may bump into things and knock things over, scratching themselves in the process, that would be the only alternative to 'some' but not all, alleged poltergeist cases.

THEORY FOUR
(Hoaxes, an attempt to get a better house!)

It is human nature that people can and will construct hoaxes. It may be for a laugh at the expense of a friend or someone who they don't like. It could be a revenge thing, or it could be, when it comes to the poltergeist angle, an attempt by a family to get out of a property, that's not haunted. The family might be well down the council list for a house, and this might be the last resort to try and get better housing. Thankfully, I've never worked on an investigation where this has been the case. It's up to the researchers to determine the truth of the matter. Diligent research must be undertaken to ensure that the wool is not being pulled over one's eyes. The adage is, *'always be on your guard'.*

THEORY FIVE
(Fame & Fortune. Attention Seeking. Histrionic personality disorder).

Again, it is human nature to seek fame and fortune we would all love to be rich and famous. It is of course feasible that some people make want to make up a false poltergeist claim in the hopes that they will make a lot of money from it, either through the media, or through charging paranormal investigators to come to the home and see for themselves. Again, we can't rule out this theory, but as stated before, it's up to the investigators to rule out this angle.

There is something called Histrionic personality disorder, or (HPD) for short. This has been classed by the American Psychiatric Association as a personality disorder. Apparently, it begins in early adulthood and these people seek excessive attention and a longing for appreciation and a need, if not desire, for people to like them. They exaggerate and claim things which seem preposterous, but again this is all linked for the need for recognition to be the centre of attention. Could those people who suffer from this (HPD) make up false poltergeist claims for this recognition? Again, it's a possibility and one of which the investigators have to explore.

THEORY SIX
(Misinterpretation)

There are so many people who see and hear things differently from the rest of us. There are those who know that as a house cools down during the night from a hot day, the house is settling down, noises will start to happen. The floorboards creak due to the change of temperature, yet there are those people who will misconstrue these sounds, and who will believe that these noises are spirits up to mischief. Admittedly these types of people are the ones who may well have a strong belief in the supernatural and life after death. What one hears as a house settling down, the other hears as a ghost doing its rounds. The human brain is hard wired to make sense out of nonsense, but as I have stated earlier, the human brain can be fooled. Whilst some may see a white fluffy cloud in the sky, others will see the shape of a face. We humans have the capacity to make something out of nothing, and in the paranormal world, that takes some investigating. So, things are not always what they seem. If you take a friend and tell him you are taking him into a haunted house, needless to say his expectations will be up, and his heart beat may be racing. The expectation of perhaps seeing a ghost will be there. And whilst during the night, shadows may take on a human form, and if that person fled out of that non haunted house, he may well go on to tell others that he saw a ghost and then suddenly we have a mythology that would be garnished on that property. (I'm sure you see what I mean)

THEORY SEVEN
(Repressed Sexual Energy)

Now this is a theory of which the vast majority of paranormal researchers will tell you in the answer to the poltergeist mystery. Its job done; let's all go home. Really! Not for me it's not, and I will tell you why in a moment. For now, though, let's take a look at why this theory is so favoured by some of my colleagues and peers. The belief is, that the poltergeist is in fact a person focused enigma, by that I mean, that most poltergeists cases centre around young children, mostly females as they are going through puberty, the changes of their body, more so the hormonal changes, can, my peers believe, produce poltergeist activity. There could also be great emotional turmoil with that individual which coupled together, might create some kind of psychokinetic event to transpire!

I have said it many times before, that the theory that poltergeists are the result of children going through puberty, is, for me, totally and utterly preposterous. I mean, when we look at the state of the U.K. right now and the breakdown in family values in the Inner City towns, one would expect that we would be swamped off our feet with thousands of poltergeist cases on a daily basis. No, not for me I'm afraid, I'm not buying it. Whatever you may think poltergeists are, I personally don't think it's down to repressed sexually energy.

In the web site Occult World, they had a piece on the Sauchie Poltergeist, they stated, and I quote.

"The most likely cause was Virginia herself. Her rapid pubescence may have generated the energy to create poltergeist forces. These forces also may have been exacerbated by repressed homesickness, shyness and feelings of alienation. She may have been extremely self conscious about her physical changes, which may explain the violent eruption of knockings on the occasion when Margaret was instructed to get back into bed with her the 'trances' which were not comparable to

276

mediumistic trances, did give evidence of emotional upset. Finally, the entire episode may have been in part an attention getting device".

Well I would tend to disagree with that. I don't believe that being away from Ireland, coming to a new country that she didn't know, and going through puberty and seeking attention, was the cause of the Sauchie Poltergeist. People of course have a right to their opinions, as I do, its facts, not speculations that give validity to cases such as this. I don't as yet see, any scientific evidence to back up the repressed sexual energy coming from teenage girls to cause such havoc.

There is of course a similar theory to the one above, and that is what's known as, Spontaneous Recurring Psychokinesis. Basically, there are some individuals who may be going through some extremely stressful situations. It could be the fear of losing one's home, the breakup of a marriage or the death of a loved one. Some claim that the build up of stress would be so strong, that some kind of 'energy' would be released from that person which would move around furniture and displace ornaments etc. That individual may not be aware that he or she is the root cause of all this destruction, and would no doubt think that he had a poltergeist in the home. Again, like the repressed sexual energy theory above, I don't hold out too much merit on this one. I could be wrong, stranger things have happened!

THEORY EIGHT
(Schizophrenia)

The following theory is Schizophrenia which means someone who has a 'split personality'. My research showed me that this condition (a mental illness) affects 1 in 100 people. The symptoms associated with this illness are very similar to what one would experience with poltergeist effects, namely the person who has this condition may hear voices and see visual hallucinations of things, people who are not there, not in the 'real' world anyway! Admittedly there are a number of

277

different types of schizophrenia and not all are the same! Some forms of schizophrenia, however, are similar when we look at parallels to the poltergeist case. Probably the hearing of voices is the biggest aspect of this condition, and whilst the hearing of voices in poltergeist cases are not so prevalent, we should at least bring this aspect to bear when we look at the overall poltergeist phenomenon. I mentioned above that there are various forms of schizophrenia, well I learned from the web site, *'Re Think Mental Illness'* of a number of variations (I won't go into them all here, but will mention a few) needless to say that paranoid schizophrenia is the most common form of schizophrenia of which the individual will suffer prominent hallucinations and/or delusions. Then we have 'Hebephrenic schizophrenia' of which the web site tells us that there is disorganised behaviour without purpose. Disorganised thoughts, of which 'other people' may find it difficult to understand the individual with this medical condition. Furthermore, with this aspect of the condition, they would play pranks, but thankfully this type of schizophrenia is short lasting but the condition does sadly come with delusions and hallucinations, and interestingly, in so far as the principle of the poltergeist attentions, this form of schizophrenia can develop between 15 and 25 years old, which, as we have learned throughout this book, is the age span of when we usually get the poltergeist events. Then we have what's called, 'Cenesthopathic schizophrenia'. With this condition, people suffer from unusual bodily sensations. Could some of these bodily sensations be similar to what individuals experience when it comes to the poltergeist? And I refer to scratches appearing on the body, uncomfortable feelings on the body as if being touched by an invisible person!

So, what causes schizophrenia? Well from the *'Rethink Mental Illness'* web site I take the following quote.

"Nobody knows exactly what causes schizophrenia; it is likely to be the result of several factors. For example: brain chemistry, genetics and birth complications can cause schizophrenia. Some people can develop the illness as a result

278

of a stressful event, such as the death of a loved one or the loss of a job. Experiences like growing up in a town or city, stressful life events and moving to a new town or country can also trigger symptoms of psychosis and schizophrenia. There is a strong link between the use of strong cannabis and the development of schizophrenia".

So, is schizophrenia a candidate for the poltergeist effect? Well maybe in some cases yes as far as some of the effects goes. But what we have to remember is the fact that other people have seen strange things near and around the poltergeist victim, so unless schizophrenia can affect those people too, (which I very much doubt) then schizophrenia for me, is not a candidate to explain the poltergeist.

THEORY NINE
(The Hutchinson Effect)

Then we have what is known as the Hutchinson Effect. There is a Canadian chap called John Hutchinson, who is an Inventor, and his work in his laboratory is nothing short of miraculous. His laboratory is crammed full of equipment, from oscilloscopes to various other electronic machines. Some people say that he was the new Nikola Tesla, or at the very least, trying to outdo him with his own experiments. So, what's so special about John and his experiments, experiments which I might add can be found on the internet, (Type in the Hutchinson Effect on You Tube) well simply put, it can make metals dissolve, and other objects float up into the air, and a whole lot more. In Tasha Shayne's fantastic piece on John Hutchinson, (The Hutchison Effect; Nikola Tesla Inspires A Bizarre Discovery). Featured on the Gaia web site, (January 1st, 2020) she writes.

"The Hutchison Effect was discovered in 1979, while John Hutchison was attempting to recreate Tesla's experiments. Upon activating Tesla coils, a static electricity generator, and other equipment, Hutchison felt something hit him in the

279

shoulder. He discovered it was a piece of metal and didn't necessarily think twice about it. Picking the object up from where it had landed, he tossed it back to where he believed he'd previously placed it. Again, it hit him, sparking the curiosity that would eventually lead him to the discovery that fundamental frequencies can deprive various materials of their gravity. Upon replication of this process, Hutchison claims that activation of these materials created a complex electromagnetic field, causing heavy metals to defy gravity, sail up to the ceiling, and even shred into pieces. According to the Hutchison Effect website, it was the Canadian government that coined the phenomenon the "Hutchison-Effect" after a thorough investigation".

I have seen some of John Hutchinson's videos on the internet, and I must say they are most unusual. The thing is, John himself can't really say for sure what is going on with his experiments; he is quoted as saying.

"As with much of the new energy field, no one can say for sure. Some theorists think the effect is the result of opposing electromagnetic fields cancelling each other out, creating a powerful flow of space energy. The Canadian government also reported invisible samples phasing in and out of existence"

The reason I have brought the Hutchinson effect into play regarding our theories concerning the poltergeist effect, is simply that, some of the effects that we see on John Hutchinson's videos, are strikingly similar to the effects that we see in some poltergeist houses, and I refer to the levitation of objects.

As stated in Tasha's article, the Hutchinson effect does not just levitate objects, (which includes ice cream)? But turns metal into dust and causes different materials to 'fuse together'. However, I must point out that whilst John Hutchinson's videos are visually incredible, there is a lot of scepticism attached to how he goes about his experiments. Indeed, he can't replicate his 'effects' when he has other observers in the room with him. His sceptical commentators' state that John's effects, are all caused by hidden magnets and filming certain experiments upside down creating the visual stunning effect of things floating out of jars etc. Furthermore, John himself has even admitted to faking one of his experiments. Tasha Shayne in her article on John Hutchinson goes on to say.

"The U.S. Military and a team of scientists from Los Alamos National Laboratories paid Hutchison a visit in 1983 and filmed his experiments. Three years later, the Canadian Security Intelligence Service told him that his work was 'a matter of National Security' and that its defence contractor had his technology and was developing it. This and the numerous government raids made on Hutchison's laboratory provide ample evidence that the government cared enough about the inventor's activities to closely monitor his actions and confiscate his materials and it's still not clear why. No attempt to replicate Hutchison's experiments by a third party has so far been successful. Many agencies, including NASA, have attempted to recreate the Hutchison Effect".

So, as we can see dear reader, although under a cloud of suspicion as to how John created his spectacular videos, there were a number of Government and NASA officials who all felt that John had 'something'. Again, could these strange effects that John manage to achieve in his laboratory, happen in the Sauchie Poltergeist house? Well evidently 'not'. There was no high-tech equipment in the Campbell household back in 1960, for me, the Sauchie case is completely different to what John managed to achieve in his laboratory. Yes, there were some similarities, but John had all the equipment, the Campbell's did not.

THEORY TEN
(A Spirit of a Deceased Person)

This theory, to many people, is probably the theory that would explain the poltergeist, but is it? Can it really be people who have passed on who just want to hang around the Earth plane and wreak havoc? Well as with the above theories, let's take a look at this one.

First and foremost, there is some kind of intelligence behind the poltergeist effects, but is that in itself evidence that there is a disembodied human soul behind it? To cause physical harm to people sets the poltergeist aside from your normal haunting. The destructive aspect of the poltergeist sets it aside, and as far as I know, there has not been any recorded deaths associated with a poltergeist outbreak, (if this is incorrect, please contact me with the address at the end of this book) But why! Why does the poltergeist throw heavy objects at people, objects which can consist of heavy wardrobes, all of which, miss people by a matter of inches? Why is this? If the poltergeist is out to cause harm, then surely a bodily strike would be in its interest, but apparently not! Yes it has left deep and red scratches on people's bodies, (The South Shields poltergeist being a case in point) is the poltergeist capable of evil, does it have a set purpose, and that purpose is solely to destroy and alarm members of a household? Is it a trapped earthbound spirit? In other words, someone who has passed to the other side and can't accept the fact that they have moved on, so tend to hang around the earth plane, and the only way in which they can make themselves known, is to cause mischief, mayhem and destruction? Is it just pure frustration, again, they can't accept that they have passed on? They find themselves in a condition, a twilight world if you like with no semblance of getting out. If this is the case, what would you do! Would you try and move and throw things around to ensure that someone recognises that you are there? This of course is presuming that there is a 'life after death' and I make no apologies to the reader in saying that due to my 40 odd years of research on this topic, I for one, am firmly convinced that this is so, that we all survive the grave and live, albeit, in another wondrous condition.

We have all heard stories and read in other books, about people who have passed to spirit, and in the first few seconds, they find themselves enveloped in a warm tunnel of light, of which at the end of it, they suddenly see figures, and as the figures get closer, they see that it is family or friends who have passed to spirit before them. But do these stories have any basis in fact? Could it not be oxygen starvation to the dying brain that somehow brings forth what could be a hallucination? Or, on the other side of the coin, is it the 'real deal' ie, it is your relatives that have gone before you and are coming to greet you? Its either one of the other, the sceptic will say it's the oxygen starvation to the brain or some other medical condition, whilst the believer will say spirit. We however, in this book, are looking for an answer to the poltergeist enigma, and in this theory, we look to solve/discuss the earthbound spirit hypothesis.

Now we have looked at some theories above and it's fair to say that the answer to the poltergeist phenomenon may not even be in this short list, it could be something entirely different, something so, 'out of the box,' that we haven't even considered it! I keep going back to the fact that the poltergeist effects have been seen, heard and felt, by not just the one person, but by others too, so it can't surely be a medical condition unless that medical condition can externalise itself and affect others. At the end of the day, I think that the poltergeist is indeed 'spirit based'. It is not a pleasant spirit and not someone you would welcome to any party. But is it an individual or the energy left behind by an individual, who sees him or herself in an entirely new environment and this 'burst of changeable energy at death, thrusts itself on the very fabric of a house or building? Now that's as maybe, but then we have to consider that the poltergeist is not a 'one off event', in other words, it can last for up to several months or as little as a few weeks, (depending on which case you believe is real!) So if some kind of spirit energy is being released, it might not be from a person who has died in that house, it may be from someone next door, or indeed someone in the same street or another town, or it's known to the harassed individual, and if so, that in itself is quite something! Why would a person dying in another street/town, affect a specific house in another town? This is all speculation by me, I always try to 'think out the box' and provide possible answers no matter how outlandish they may seem, to try and explain a specific case or event. Then we have to consider that if our family members who have 'gone before us' are not there to meet us in death, then what do we resort to? Spiritual violence! Surely those who have gone before would want to come and greet us at death, and wouldn't waste any time in doing so, and this is the one thing for me as a researcher that I struggle with. I would like to believe that when our time comes, we will all be met by our family and friends who have gone before us. Not to be met by family and friends at the point of death, is a sobering thought, and one which as a believer in the afterlife does not make any sense. But we are here, trying to answer what causes the poltergeist effect and I still believe that the poltergeist effect is spirit, it's not, (for me) young children going through puberty of which some form of psychic sexual energy is casting off from them to cause these events, I'll never accept that. I could be wrong of course, as I've said above, there might be something else to explain the poltergeist effects that we haven't thought of. But until I see strong evidence to suggest otherwise, I believe that what we are dealing with here is a trapped 'earthbound spirit' on a wrecking spree for attention, and is perhaps, looking for help in 'moving on'.

I BELIEVE A POLTERGEIST IS!
(The thoughts of my paranormal colleagues).

When I am writing a book about a certain subject, I always like to ask the opinions of my fellow paranormal researchers as to what 'they' think a certain paranormal or UFO event might be, and this book is no different. It is always nice to hear what other researchers think could be the cause behind a poltergeist manifestation. So, here we go, here are the thoughts of but some of my fellow researchers.

DARREN W. RITSON 'The Nature' of the Poltergeist'.

"I'm often asked about my thoughts in regards to what a poltergeist really is and truth be told, it has to be said; I have no idea whatsoever, nobody has. Maurice Grosse, the lead investigator of the Enfield Poltergeist case once said

"No one knows what they are, and anyone that says they know is a charlatan",

"I would tend to agree with him on that, for as it stands today, we still don't have the answer. That doesn't mean to say that we will never know what the poltergeist is; on the contrary, I really believe one day down the line we will have an understanding of their fundamental nature; this I am convinced. In the meanwhile, however, we most plod on slowly documenting what cases we can, when we can, studying the effects and the bewildering array of phenomena that they produce in an often spectacular but terrifying fashion. But what are the theories behind the nature of the poltergeist? There are a number of thoughts that have been forthcoming by researchers. In the old days, a poltergeist was seen as a 'noisy ghost', indeed, the word poltergeist is an old German word meaning just that; a disruptive spirit that seems to be hell bent on causing mayhem and misery by banging loudly, throwing things around, smashing objects, overturning furniture and even in some cases, pulling people out of their beds. Poltergeists, much to the relief of its victims, have a relatively short shelf life as they tend to peter out after a few months or so or even weeks, if you are lucky. Sometimes, it is though, that poltergeists produce only a handful of affects prior to its cessation, and in some instances producing only one single isolated incident. This of course, can make them extremely difficult to document and investigate as they are over before they even begin. However, it must be stressed that in some extreme cases, poltergeists can last up to over a year". (Enfield, 1977-1978, South Shields 2005-2006)

"Another theory in regards to the poltergeist phenomenon, is known as Recurrent Spontaneous Psychokinesis (RSPK) which was first coined by William G Roll in 1958 while writing a paper detailing an investigation into the Seaford Poltergeist, in Long Island, New York, USA. RSPK is, in a nutshell, the alleged ability to manipulate inanimate objects subconsciously with the power of the mind throwing them around; this could be

285

anything as small as a coin, to something as big as a bed; and in some cases, people! It is thought by some that those that produce PK effects (usually pubescent children, but this is not always the case) are frustrated or troubled in some way and bottle up their emotions and anger until it is released and externalised in the form of RSPK. I often refer to RSPK as a psychic temper tantrum. One thing I have noticed is that the characteristics of being evil, malicious, spiteful, sadistic, unkind, vindictive, and creating abject misery for others whether its conscious or subconscious, are idiosyncrasies to which both human being and the poltergeist most certainly share; maybe this suggests in some way that the poltergeist comes from within a person after all? and not as some suggest; a discarnate entity from another realm. All people, every last one of us regardless of how good we may seem, are more than capable of doing unscrupulous things; we all have a dark side whether we like it or even know it; and we all have bad thoughts. Some sadly act upon their urges and desires for no good reason. Perhaps 'we' are that mischievous spirit after all? Is this why the poltergeist is always destructive? They always seem to carry out malicious acts, and not acts of kindness. Why don't you ever hear of a poltergeist tidying up your house, doing your dishes or even depositing money into your bank account? Because if they wanted to, they could! Perhaps the destruction and misery is just our 'true nature' manifesting? This is only one tenuous link however, but I feel it's a parallel worth taking note of. If the RSPK theory becomes accepted as its cause, then the poltergeist's paranormal repertoire may one day become normal, or better understood as it may indeed be the case that it is occurring/operating within our physical world as opposed to an 'otherworld'. Then, I dare say our current laws of physics will ultimately have to change. I dread to think however, what will happen when RSPK is understood and then potentially harnessed. Would it be used to our advantage, for the good of mankind, or would it be used as a weapon against fellow man? It's an interesting thought. The jury is still out of course as to what the true nature of the poltergeist is, some cases suggest a rudimentary intelligence at work independent of a host or focus, yet other cases indicate the possibility of

RSPK and a human agent. Some cases I am sad to say, are nothing more than pranksters larking about, misinterpretation and blatant hoaxing ".

Who is Darren W. Ritson?

Darren W. Ritson is a good friend of mine and has written numerous books on the paranormal. He has been interested in the supernatural all his life and has had his own strange experiences as a child, and latterly as an adult whilst investigating haunted houses. He is a Civil Servant who lives in North Tyneside, England.

ANHONY NORTH 'Poltergeist Reality'

"We are told that the usual poltergeist infests a house. This is incorrect. It affects a household, phenomena usually centres around a child. Some theorists argue that the initial prompter is some form of psychological trauma the child has experienced. Effects can begin with disruptive behaviour. This disturbs the 'culture' of the household and a fear becomes prevalent. The child feeds on this and begins to display typical, but involuntary, mediumistic tendencies. This intensifies the fear and an alternative culture develops. Unconscious information can attach to the fears and phenomena will begin to break out in a communal hallucinatory way, aping any locally known phenomena and classic poltergeist activity. In effect, a communal psychodrama is being enacted based upon the sum total of the minds involved. This is why a sceptical researcher never sees phenomena, and why an exorcism can sometimes work. An additional mind has joined the production to ease the drama. I'm convinced a poltergeist can be answered in this way. However, I want to take this 'psychodrama' idea out into the normal world. In effect, I am saying that a 'culture' can so easily develop, in which behaviour can become conditioned by the culture itself. A classic case is a cult, where a guru seems to totally dominate the very psyche of his disciples. The way they see the world changes from the way others see it. But having said this, I also believe that a cult merely shows the extremes of

287

normal behaviour. A society is affected by similar alternative behaviours. The religionist often seems to live in a different world to the scientist, for instance; and the same data can be seen in radically different ways. Could it be that the communal psyche that outs itself in the poltergeist is actually there all the time in society, defining how we think as groups and building alternative consensus? Such an idea could answer so much in terms of human knowledge, disagreement and conflict. And if so, maybe none of us really know the world, just the hallucinated view decreed by the particular consensus to which we belong".

Who Is Anthony North?

Anthony states, and I quote. I have spent over thirty years writing on and researching the paranormal. Note, I said paranormal and not supernatural. I highlight the difference because I do not think other worldly forces are involved. Rather, it seems to me that we are dealing with a wider and rational psychology not yet fully understood by science. Many believers may not like my use of words such as hallucination. However, new knowledge must take existing intellectual baggage with it, taking small steps into the unknown rather than great leaps of faith. I hope to show in my studies that all reality is part illusion, which is little different from hallucination. A major stumbling block to understanding is the preponderance of labels attached to the subject. We speak of ghosts, of reincarnation, telepathy, the poltergeist and a whole lot more. To me, these are not causes, but effects of the forces at work in paranormal phenomena. I'm convinced that an understanding of the paranormal can add greatly to human experience and not understanding it leads to many problems we seem to be unable to overcome.

CINDY DOLOWY. 'Several Types of Poltergeists'!

Cindy Dolowy comes from Chehalis WA, America and herself has experienced many paranormal happenings. She stated.

Hi Malcolm,

"I'd be happy to tell you what I think poltergeists are. I think there are actually several types of poltergeists. The common thread is they all have a highly emotional trait. These entities may be super-sensitive, super-reactive, highly intelligent, strong-willed, highly perseverant, very strong personalities etc or a combination of all these things. This is how they were in life which undoubtedly carries over in death. These are the ones that have the energy to reach through the veil far more than the average individual. But poltergeists can be split into many distinct categories. Some were/are just really mean people. Maybe a narcissistic that is spitting mad that other people are inhabiting 'HER HOUSE'! Or maybe the neighbourhood grinch who knows nothing other than always being mad at everything. Some were/are violent in nature the ones that tortured and killed other living things and still have that murderous craving after death. This type of poltergeist has learned to use their great negative energy to create havoc. Some are people who are simply furious that they died and are just too stubborn to accept it, probably due to an unjust death such as a freak accident or unexpected murder. Or maybe the guy who was always the class clown or life of the party, the really outgoing types who are just naturally high energy. Others I think were the empaths and sensitive's when alive. They were far greater in tune with the universe in life and far more able to understand and navigate the afterlife. They are able to continue being sensitive's and can focus their energy to achieve communication with the living. The empaths have enormous emotional energy which does not change upon death. These are the ones who are around their families or former homes. I think this is the category I will be in. I don't want to leave my children to fend for themselves. I told them all long ago I will do my best to contact them after death and continually haunt them if possible. Others are just highly intelligent, inquisitive, possibly scientifically or scholarly minded. They were constantly learning, questioning, educating themselves in life and continued into the afterlife. They are just

289

still learning and experimenting in this new existence as they did in life. (You easily fall into this category) So that's what I think. People who naturally had unusually strong energies in life or at time of death carry that energy over to the next plane".

Who Is Cindy Dolowy?

Cindy lives in the United States in a town called Chehalis, WA. Which, she tells me, is an awesome location just a short drive East to the Cascade Mountains or West to the Pacific Ocean. She can see Mount St. Helen's from her house and Mount Rainier just a few hundred feet down the road. She is extremely interested in all things weird and wonderful, more so the numerous 'Bigfoot' sightings to which she has studied.

NICK KYLE 'Multi-Dimensional Realities?

"In brief, poltergeist phenomena are often thought of as ghostly phenomena, childish or mischievous in its behaviour, and not fully formed in how its words or personality expresses itself. There are cases to support this view, but phenomena is often around adolescents who have unresolved stressful issues and/or puberty involved, which brings in a psychological perspective without the need to invoke spirits. The more cases that I investigate, the more I find that upset minds, and emotions, are triggering and sustaining factors. If chairs are found inexplicably piled up, that suggests intelligence, or at least dexterity, as does mysterious writing that can appear, but not always to be regarded as negative or threatening. One case involved raining sweets on witnesses; another involved corroborated sexual assault. My observation is that 'poltergeist' might be too narrow and vague a label for a wide range of paranormal phenomena that have causes beyond our imagination, multi-dimensional realities?"

Who is Nick Kyle?

Nick is a retired Deputy Head teacher, now working part time as a Teaching Specialist in the university sector. Nick has been psychically aware since early childhood. Trying to understand his 'spirit' communications, he began to explore religion, including shamanism and spiritualism, as a young man. Impressed by the late Professor Archie Roy, Nick expanded his interests to include psychical research, and for over ten years he was President of the *Scottish Society for Psychical Research*. He has investigated ostensible cases of paranormality over three decades, counselling people who are upset by their anomalous experiences, confidentially free of charge and without publicity studying mediums, experiencing hauntings and developing a special interest in physical mediumship. Nick was the co-organiser of the Scottish Paranormal Conference held in Stirling in 2014. Nick blends an open-minded scepticism with mediumistic sensitivities to investigate where the evidence leads him, including:

- Materialisations in England and Scotland
- Hauntings and poltergeists in Scotland
- Ghosts in Italy
- Hauntings in the USA and Canada
- An Ayahuasca ceremony in Peru
- Spiritual healing in Brazil

Nick is a leading paranormal investigator in Scotland:
- He is a knowledgeable, experienced, and engaging speaker on paranormal topics.
- He has trained paranormal investigators.
- He is a writer and editor, having co-written a novel on his paranormal adventures, currently finishing a biography of a Scottish medium. And proofreading books on mediumship, time travel and paranormality.
- He is a teacher of meditation, delivering transformative workshops, and exploring how to use altered states for healing.

TRICIA ROBERTSON. 'Deep Set Negative Emotions'

"Defining the poltergeist effect is not straight forward. The word poltergeist itself implies that a 'ghost' is involved. Not necessarily so. Whatever is behind movement of objects etc requires some kind of energy. It is a fact that nothing can move without an energy source. From experience this energy source can appear to come from a person who is experiencing very negative emotions which, in some way unknown to us, externalise themelves by moving objects, causing noises etc. In cases where a deceased person may be involved the impetus and energy source is supplied by them. There may also be a case in saying that because of a person's deep set negative emotions that sometimes a deceased person could latch on to these and create further activity"

Who is Tricia Robertson?

Tricia J Robertson is the author of 'Things You Can Do When You're Dead' and 'More Things You Can Do When You're Dead' (White Crow Books) Tricia is a renowned Psychical Researcher who has examined many paranormal topics over many years and whose two published books have been well received, earning five star reviews on Amazon. Originally a maths and physics teacher, she then became a tutor for the Department of Adult and Continuing Education (DACE) at the University of Glasgow. Her passion is in gathering quality evidence showing survival of consciousness after death. In addition to 30 years of experience, carrying out her own research and in investigating spontaneous cases, Tricia has appeared on various TV programmes, usually documentaries and on radio programmes including America's Coast to Coast, twice, UK's Radio City, USA Darkness Radio, Celtic Radio, Beyond 3D, Hayhouse radio, Past Lives Podcast, Talk Radio and The unexplainedtv.com and has been invited, over many of years, to speak to varied organisations throughout the United Kingdom and abroad. She also has had three published papers regarding mediumship in a peer reviewed journal. Check her out on www.tricarobertson.weebly.com

JENNY RANDLES 'Physical and a Psychological Components'

Hi Malcolm

"It's not something that I would consider that I have any expertise in. So, these are personal views based on many types of phenomenon. I think that there is a physical and a psychological component to most such events, and that in the right circumstances, the two can interact and create changes in the physical world that are detectable to anyone present. I suspect there are parallels between poltergeist cases, UAP (Unidentified Aerial Phenomenon) and abductions, where an energy exists latently and how it manifests externally, depends on several factors. The person at the focus who is sensitive and their perception of what they believe to be occurring is one. And their ability to mould or modify that energy so that it expresses externally what they feel they are communicating with rightly or wrongly. I am sure there is much more to it than that. But at heart I feel this builds bridges between seemingly diverse phenomena. Not much help I know and just my feelings".

Best wishes, Jenny.

Who is Jenny Randles?

Jenny Randles is a prolific author and Investigator of most things weird and wonderful. She is the former director of investigations with the British UFO Research Association (BUFORA), serving in that role from 1982 through to 1994 and has written and co authored over 50 books on UFOs and the Paranormal selling 1.5 million copies worldwide. She has appeared on many U.K. and worldwide television programmes and coined the term, 'Oz Factor', a term which aptly describes witnesses describing the odd state of consciousness that they have found themselves in whilst either observing a UFO or in a paranormal setting. Their whole perception of time and space seems to alter and change. Jenny Randles was instrumental in myself (Malcolm Robinson) getting into these subjects. And at the start of my UFO and Paranormal career, I avidly read all her books and attended many of her lectures.

PHILIP KINSELLA 'Trapped soul eager to cause havoc'?

"Some years ago, I had been asked to see if I could help a family involving what is commonly referred to as a Poltergeist. The mother of the son concerned no longer lived with him, as their small flat was being wrecked by an unknown force, seemingly connected to her adolescent boy. The lad, whom I shall refer to as 'J' moved in with his grandparents in a large, detached Victorian property in Stevenage. I, along with a few other mediums, (one of whom has appeared a few times on national television) went to investigate the property to see if we could shed any light on what was going on. To begin with, we had met the mother in a café in 'Marks and Spencer's,' along with her son where she discussed the history of this poltergeist, and that we had to prepare ourselves before entering her parent's house. We were to carry nothing in our pockets, because the thing they called 'IT' had a habit of taking then from you. Initially, I had been sceptical of the whole thing. Being a medium myself, I had always been dubious about poltergeists and the reports of what they were capable of doing. I didn't realise that I was in for the biggest shock of my life. The events which had transpired forced me to reconcile my negative thoughts regarding such entities. On entering the beautiful property, I was amazed to find that most of the windows to the house downstairs had been smashed. It looked like a warzone. Boards had been used to cover the damage. There had been a large table in the hall, settee and chair in the lounge, and that was about it with regards to furniture. All their possessions had been stored within an outer building

294

down the large garden out back, as 'IT' tended to manifest objects from one room to another. Looking around, I noticed large chunks taken out of the walls where the poltergeist had literally thrown objects. The fireplace had been completely boarded up. This was no way for an old couple to live. They were making no money from their claims, and I had also been aware that the police and other people had been witness to 'IT's' destructive powers. Now, with their belongings stored safely away, 'IT' had a hard time of manifesting things and smashing them. At least, that's what we all thought. The old lady and gentleman invited us warmly into their shell of a house. We had a look round and nothing much happened within the course of the early afternoon. The young lad had a radio playing in the lounge to try and lift the spirits a bit and proceeded to show me on his cracked mobile phone, footage he'd taken of him and his grandparents seemingly talking with the entity. 'IT' had used a chair as a means of communication. They'd been asking 'IT' questions, and the chair would move left or right in reply through a simple 'YES' or 'NO.' I couldn't see the base of the chair, so it was hard to tell if someone had been moving the furniture other than this said poltergeist. I'd noticed a large mound out back, and this was where 'IT' had told them money had been buried. The family had dug up the garden, only to find they'd been lied to. It was generally believed that the 'Spirit' was that of the young lad's unborn twin brother who'd died at birth. Things got even stranger when the old couple made us a sandwich. We ate from paper plates, drank from paper cups and had been informed that on many occasions, 'IT' would produce items they had hidden in the outer building from thin air especially knives. The grandmother told us that the poltergeist would wave a knife in her direction in a threatening manner, and it had been decided that all dangerous implements had to be banished out back. The grandson, along with his grandparents slept together on a mat in the living room. If they tried to leave the house, then 'IT' would become nasty and bite them. We did ascertain that this thing was somehow linked with the boy. He seemed to enjoy the attention 'IT' had created, but we felt and saw nothing, until around 4 pm when we decided to call it a day. As soon as we

295

were about to leave, the radio in the lounge started playing songs like 'I want to break free' and 'Please release me, let me go.' The atmosphere became charged and all of us stood rooted in the large sitting room, expectant that something was about to kick off. I sensed as though something was 'sniffing me' out. To my mind, it reminded me of a Great White Shark coming up to its prey. Did 'IT' put this thought in my head? I have always feared this situation, however remote its chances".

"A small bottle of fizzy drink which 'J' had left on the fireplace, shot up in the air, struck the high ceiling and came down with a thump. Everyone froze. There came a bright flash of light from the boarded windows to the living room, followed by a loud 'crack.' Something had apported through the ceiling. This had been a half packet of polo mints. On picking it up, we each discovered that its silver wrapping was red hot. None of us had brought these into the house and wondered how 'IT' had got hold of them. It was during this point when I wanted to get the hell out of there. Moving across the hall to the front door, the large, wooden table sitting there was lifted all by itself and sent crashing into the lounge. I turned around and saw the grandmother had raised both her arms up around her head in order to protect herself as something else shot past her from the closed bathroom toilet downstairs. I shall never forget the look on her face. After examining what had been thrown, we discovered that the loo-roll holder from the toilet's closed door had somehow been ejected through solid matter. This defied the laws of physics. I got back in the car and did not enter the house again. I feared that 'IT' had connected itself to me, and I couldn't wait to get home and have a shower because I felt dirty, or, contaminated in some way. Needless to say, and because of ego, the other medium wanted exclusive rights to the case, and so we had been shown the door. All we had wanted to do was help that poor family, and yet it had been exploited for monetary gain. I never knew what became of the case or the sweet folks along with their grandson, or if 'IT' is still about. I have all the names of those concerned and can prove that this had been a legitimate case, but I would prefer not to get involved in other people's egos or personal agendas".

"I still, to this day, could not tell you what a poltergeist is. My initial thoughts, like others, are that the entity appears to be a trapped soul eager to wreak havoc, fear and mischief upon its unfortunate victims. It was interesting to see how 'IT' was able to apport objects through the ether. Indeed, UFOs may also use this method, because their crafts come in and out of our airspace within the blink of an eye. Perhaps the entity in question did not fully cross over to what we call the Other Side. It had also used the boy as its conduit, yet I fail to understand what purpose the poltergeist would have in creating chaos. I leave that for the reader to speculate, but there is one thing I can confirm, poltergeists are true and are NOT to be meddled with. You'll pay the price for this, like the poor family we tried to help".

Who is Philip Kinsella?

Philip Kinsella is a good friend of mine and has been involved with the weird and wonderful all his life. Not only is he a gifted clairvoyant who has sell out audiences eating out of his hand, he is also a UFO abductee who has had some strange and bizarre UFO encounters. Philip won the British Mediumship Award in Portsmouth in 2008 and is the author of a number of books on subjects relating to UFOs and Paranormal.

JOHN FRASER. 'An Energy Inside Us'?

Hi Malcolm,

"The first thing about Poltergeists, is that put 6 experts in a room, and you would likely get 7 theories. About the only thing you can say about Poltergeists is that they are very much under researched, which is why I very much wish Malcolm every success with his latest book which, in addition to mine(*), may well help lead the re-activation of a subject not fully explored for 39 years (since Colin Wilson's book 'Poltergeist!' 'A Study in Destructive Haunting' New English Library 1981). If pressed to

commit to a theory, I would tend to believe that Poltergeists come from an energy inside us, rather than the afterlife. The reasoning behind this is multi layered, but a simple way of putting it would be to say that, "There are few if any Poltergeists' you would want to have a pint in the pub with"!

"The Andover poltergeist did nothing better than badly predicting upcoming football results, the Black Monk of Pontefract made famous by Wilson, spent about a year creating havoc without communicating anything of interest at all. If you count the talking Mongoose of Cashen's gap as a Poltergeist case, his claims to being 'The eighth wonder of the world' would have got a little dull listening to after the first half pint. This may sound a little flippant, but it does make the point that the average Poltergeist does little of any intelligence. They throw things around make banging noises, create confusion and havoc but say or do little of interest that would make someone think of it as a spirit of a deceased loved one who has an important message. One of the few exceptions is the Enfield poltergeist , but as 'his' communications came through the vocal chords of a young girl, this makes it a very unusual case, certainly worthy of further research but not worthy in itself of bucking this trend. Poltergeists never the less remain the key to discovering the paranormal as their activities have no psychological explanation. They cannot be down to hallucinations or seeing things through the corner of the eye. They can only likely be (paranormal) fact or fraud of some kind, which can be tested under the right conditions. This is why after possibly 39 years we need more of this kind of work".

Who is John Fraser?

John Fraser is a Council Member of the Society for Psychical Research (SPR) and has also written a book about Poltergeists entitled, 'Poltergeist! A New Investigation into Destructive Haunting, Including the Cage St Osyth' (6th books, Winchester Washington July 2020). He is also a member of the prestigious 'Ghost Club' and is the author of 'Ghost Hunting A

298

Survivor's Guide' (History Press 2010) John lives in Croydon, United Kingdom.

VIVIAN POWELL. 'Energy of 'Living' Human Beings'!

Hi Malcolm,

Here are my thoughts on what I believe a Poltergeist to be. I hope this is ok for you.

"What do I think a Poltergeist to be? Well, I do not believe it to be a noisy Ghost that is for sure. This is where my years of research and investigation and the years of helping people in real trouble has led me this far. I have been investigating strange phenomena for let's just say over 20 years now, both on a spiritual level and as a Paranormal investigator. I have been called out and approached by many people for what I call private cases, from all over the country and found in my research that 'Poltergeist Activity' had some defining characteristics. For example,"

* Some form of life changing event within the household.
* Someone within the household who could not express themselves.
* Changes so big that there was no control over it.
* Not understanding what was happening/or going to happen and how that would affect the rest of their life.
* Depression.

"At this stage I cannot confirm that a child going through Puberty or the sex of the child going through Puberty is a factor, but depending on the household, any strict or religious upbringing and or if the subject was strictly taboo, this could be a factor, but I have not come across this as of yet. So, what do I think it is"?

"I believe that Poltergeist activity is centred around energy, that we as living humans manifest. In all cases that I have encountered, the individuals are not aware that they are doing

299

this. For example, a case that I had worked on in the past, there was Poltergeist activity reported within a home that was terrifying a woman and her 5 year old son. Voices were heard coming through the TV's external speakers when everything was switched off and unplugged. Coats were being thrown from the coat hook by the front door down the hallway and hitting the wall with enough force to alert the household that this had just happened. In the middle of the night in the kitchen, crockery could be heard smashing and when the mother gathered enough strength to go see what was happening, she would find smashed plates across the kitchen with all the cupboard doors and drawers open and no explanation how that could happen. After going to meet the mother and spending time with her son and gaining trust, it was made apparent that the father had left some months ago for another younger woman. He was found out to be having an affair and left quite abruptly with not much in the way of belongings. The man was seeking access to his son and wanting the rest of his belongings. There was a lot of quarrelling and crying after one of his visits, and the boy hurried into his room upstairs while this went on. Now the young boy was not sure why this was happening. His whole life seemed to change overnight. A mum who just cried all the time, a father he was not allowed to see, fighting and arguing when he was around, being hurried out of the way all the time and being rather frightened".

"Who did he go to for comfort? A 5 year old does not understand grown up things or does he? How does he express how he is feeling? Who does he talk to? Remember not all children are chatterboxes, not all children cry when they are scared. It was only when spending a lot of time with the mother and child and recording activity and keeping logs, that I realised that activity followed a pattern after the father had visited. The mother and father, after a lot of persuading and with the help of a trained councillor at the time, explained to the child that they were parting but it was not his fault, that they both loved him very much and he would be able to visit his father and spend time with him as well. It was a long process but weeks after the boy was allowed to go and see his dad, all

300

activity in the house ceased just as quickly as at started. To my knowledge it never came back".

"In conclusion to this particular case, it was the boy that manifested this Poltergeist activity in frustration, sadness and sheer fright of all the screaming and shouting. All that pent up energy building had to go somewhere. Just like a balloon filled with air, when this fills too much, it explodes and the air inside is released, just like this poor little boy's energy. He is not aware that the coats are flying or the plates are smashing or the voices and music coming through speakers after they are unplugged, it just happened. I want to make one thing very clear, with Poltergeist activity, the individual is not aware that their energy is making things happen, but with Telekinesis the individual is willing for things to happen and is completely aware. This is what I believe although the research continues".

Who Is Vivian Powell?

Vivien has been immersed in the strange world of the paranormal all her life. She is one of the organisers of Paraforce U.K. which brings together a number of British and Overseas speakers to present their findings to the public. (Myself being one) In Ashley Knibb's web site www.ashleyknibb.com he provides the following information about Vivien and her psychic experiences.

"I had my first experiences as a very young child, seeing a strange man in my house. I lived in a very haunted house for the first 7 years of my life. Very frightening indeed and not understanding what I was seeing. It made my very young childhood years, very miserable indeed. I grew up seeing more and more, and not just in my house, and it was in my teens I found that I could hear disembodied voices too! It all reached a peak in my early twenties, where I was taken to a spiritualist church in Ashford Middlesex and I joined a closed circle. With the help of a great Medium called John Reese in Uxbridge, these gifts were explained and I was guided and it

301

was not very long before I was serving the churches in and around Greater London giving demonstrations of mediumship".

RON HALLIDAY 'An inexplicable force with an intelligence behind it'!

"The subject of poltergeist manifestation has been discussed intensively over a long period of time with no definite conclusion reached about what exactly is taking place There's always an explanation from sceptics of course: it's all in the imagination, or it's people doing it themselves for various reasons such as attention seeking, mental disturbance and so on. Does that explain the phenomenon? I would have to give an emphatic 'no'. There have been too many cases of documented 'poltergeist' phenomena to simply dismiss it as non-existent or not worthy of examination. Cases of stone throwing from an invisible source have occurred on numerous occasions and have been recorded to at least the 1670s in Scotland with the famous 'Rerrick Poltergeist' case in Dumfriesshire. What may cause scepticism, is the triviality of much that goes on when a poltergeist manifests. From witnesses, I've heard of a range of minor and, it might be added pointless, activities from vases and coins being moved, to a line of green peas being laid out on a carpet floor. Certainly, the description of 'noisy spirit' which is what 'poltergeist' means seems less apt in these cases more like 'senseless spirit'! There seems a sort of playfulness behind it, all on the level of childish games. But, unfortunately, as some terrifying encounters will testify, that is not always the case. Objects being thrown at people, televisions exploding, and deliberately smashed crockery, are also experienced, which suggests a malevolent intention rather than mere trickery. But can it all be explained by physical anomalies? Or even by forces not currently known to science but explicable by science? Could micro-changes to the gravitational field, sudden alteration of magnetic forces or just plain minor tremors or a land slippage be the rational answer"?

"One can hardly deny that an element of the above could be responsible in some cases, except that quite often it appears

that an intelligent force is behind the poltergeist activity. Witnesses through the centuries have reported writing appearing on walls with messages that appear to be directed towards them, often of a threatening nature. Voices occasionally make themselves heard again often with communication directed towards whoever inhabits the place where activity is taking place. This suggests that there is 'something' behind the poltergeist with an ability to think and carry out independent actions however strange and irrelevant those actions might appear to us. I think this is the problem when assessing the poltergeist phenomenon. It strikes us as pointless unless the aim is to frighten people one area where it does frequently succeed but for what purpose? and why this person or property and not that one? There seems no rhyme or reason to it. And if it is simply random, your bad luck in other words, that doesn't bring us any nearer to an answer. So, to sum up, I'm convinced that we are dealing with an inexplicable force which probably has an intelligence behind it, but what it is or where it comes from, is for the moment, one of the unsolved problems of our amazingly mysterious universe".

Who is Ron Halliday?

Ron Halliday is another good friend of mine and is a well-known investigator and prolific writer on the paranormal. I've worked with Ron for many years on UFO and Ghost cases and found him to be a great source of knowledge and inspiration. He currently runs Scottish Earth Mystery Research and lives in Bridge of Allan near Stirling Central Scotland.

BRIAN ALLAN

I asked fellow Scottish researcher Brian Allan what he thought a poltergeist might be and he replied with his thoughts on the Sauchie case. He stated.

"I am pretty sure, based on my lengthy conversation with Dr. Logan and what he witnessed, that something was going on

303

there and it was not any conventional phenomena either. Was it a polt? Probably not, I think it was produced by the girl"

Who is Brian Allan?

Brian is the editor of the popular British internet magazine, Phenomena. He is a prolific author of a number of paranormal and esoteric books and is an accomplished public speaker. Brian lives in Kincardine near Alloa, Central Scotland.

STEVE MERA

"In accordance to our research, the Phenomena are split into three separate types and difficult to differentiate initially on preliminary investigations. The first is clearly a form of PK in association often with adolescent individuals and strangely enough females more than males. The parapsychology departments would have us believe such PK abilities produced by those we call the (Agents, Catalysts, Focus) are often suffering from vexation caused through family problems, financial difficulties, poor living conditions, illnesses. However, this is only theoretical at best as there are incidents that such poltergeist infestations can demonstrate occurrences when the (Agent, Catalyst or Focus) is not present at the location. The second: there seems in some cases a fine line between Interactive Intelligent Hauntings (where objects are seen to be manipulated, moved, arranged etc) and poltergeist type disturbances. This can cause confusion when it comes to identifying such profound paranormal incidents. And three: in a number of small cases, the poltergeist type disturbances manifest around elderly couples and not adolescent individuals. The rulebook certainly needs a clearer definition and thorough understanding before rigid conclusions are met, sometimes prematurely".

"These three types of occurrences could be referenced":

1. Poltergeist Infestation - An Intelligent Interactive Entity of Unknown Origin.
2. An Intelligent Interactive Type Haunting that is associated with Object Manipulations.
3. Poltergeist Looking Disturbances - Psychokinetic Occurrences in proximity to the Agent, Catalyst or Focus.

"When closely analysing the mechanics of poltergeist actions, one could argue that in accordance to the results of the double slit experiment that witnesses often report things being thrown such as objects, once they take their eye off them. The electrons would react differently when looking at these objects and become locked in non-motion and once we take our eyes off them, the electrons act differently and scatter into wave forms possibly allowing unrestricted movement. This would fall in line with many reports. Those that have seen an object move from point A to B may be observing the affects of an intelligent interactive haunting or PK from an individual in that location. Again, much more research is required in this particular field of para-physics. On numerous occasions those cases considered to be real poltergeist disturbances may have objects that have moved, measuring the distance in a straight line from their starting location to the point where they have been seen to arrive can be a repeatable number. Thus this (displacement) has a mechanics behind it, somewhat of a paranormal blueprint. One common faculty when analysing true poltergeist occurrences is that the phenomena seem to follow a progressive pattern" ...

A. Audible Disturbances.
B. Object Manipulations.
C. Physical Interactions.
D. Apparitional, Amouphous Shapes etc.
E. Psychological Affects.

Who Is Steve Mera?

Stephen is an investigative researcher in both the subjects of aerial phenomena as well as the paranormal. He has been an active researcher for over 30 years and is the chairman of MAPIT (Manchester's Aerial Phenomena Investigation Team, established 1973) and the founder of SEP (The Scientific Establishment of Parapsychology, Established 1996).

He is the owner of Phenomena Magazine (www.phenomenamagazine.co.uk) a free monthly E-zine with over 1.2 million subscribers over 12 countries and 4 languages. Stephen is the CEO of Awakenings Expo in Manchester, UK Europe's largest conference of its kind, and the CEO of Zohar Global Group. Stephen was also the co-founder of Onstellar social media platform. He is an author of 6 books and is an international lecturer. Stephen is the official spokesman for a number of TV series, documentaries and subject related movies and has appeared in many TV shows.

ADVANCES IN SCIENCE CHANGE PERCEPTIONS!

Whilst the following is not so much a quote about what or what not a poltergeist could be, it's certainly food for thought. One of my Facebook friends, Michelle Brooks, sent me her thoughts about the strange world of the paranormal, and how to one generation, one thing seems impossible and unrecognisable, yet to a future generation through further research and advancements in science, it's seems quite the norm. Here is what she sent me. I had asked the question, 'what is the proof behind paranormal phenomenon, what will the public accept'?

"Because we need to learn so much more about this, of what is beside us, and around us, infringing into our reality and our senses. Once we know more, then it will not seem so frightening and scary. Then we can all be able to deal with it with much more thoughtful understanding and less fear. With more logical reasoning, we will become less superstitious and more scientifically able to make sense of these unusual things that occur that seem so strange to us. Therefore, it will not be as supernatural to us but to many more people, it will become naturally acceptable as just other layers of subtle vibrational and dimensional spaces and spirits interacting with our world

306

and vice versa. It is like in the old times exploring new lands that was once thought to not really exist, until they were actually seen, proven and understood by a mass mind rather than a few that would have been called crazy for their beliefs. It became acceptable as a local truth, once it was accepted by more than just a few, the mass societies who thought it was superstitious nonsense of lands exiting beyond their site, and of other types of beings or people existing. To their minds and time, it just couldn't be possible, if it wasn't for the few explorers believing in the unknown to make it become known. The gap of understanding is our bridge into new unknown waters, and people who investigate the unknown are the bridge builders, exploring these unknown waters or territories to make it known. They are the paranormal scientist, the explorers of the unseen, to make it seen, so yes on the scale, it's a 10 for me for social importance for all humans to understand these, other senses around us, parallel to us. The people who are investigating these things are making a difference bit by bit over time it is changing the way we all perceive the supernatural, to a more sensible consideration, rather than the fearful ignorant manner of our past medieval times. Paranormal science is so very necessary for our spiritual evolution".

THE GHOST ON THE BALCONY?

Now admittedly the following report has nothing to do with a poltergeist, but I felt that I just had to report it here. I give many lectures on UFOs and the Paranormal throughout the United Kingdom and Europe talking about the weird and the wonderful, but never in my wildest dreams did I ever think that I would suddenly be propelled into that world whilst sitting in a chair! Let me explain.

I am assistant editor of the online Magazine, 'Outer Limits' expertly compiled by seasoned researcher Chris Evers, and in 2019 I gave a talk on the famous Dechmont Woods UFO Encounter. The venue was the Pontefract Town Hall in Yorkshire, England, and the last thing in the world that I expected to see and experience, was, wait for it, a bloody ghost!

307

Yes, you read correctly, a ghost! Whilst conference organiser Chris Evers was doing his introduction at the start of the conference, I casually looked up onto the balcony area of this old and lovely town hall. Now let me stress 100% that no one was up on the balcony at this point as the large audience were all seated downstairs in the main auditorium. As I casually gazed up, I saw a ghostly grey human shaped figure, move from right to left along the balcony; I nearly had to change my trousers! I looked away then looked back, and this ghostly figure was still moving very slowly along the balcony. The ghostly shape that I saw was difficult to ascertain as either male or female, as it was just the contours of the human body. One thing which I will say that I found equally strange, was the fact that this ghostly shape wasn't side on as one would expect as a person would be as it walked along the balcony, it was 'front on' moving along the balcony as if it was side stepping! As if this wasn't strange enough, just then, a strange illuminated wee thing, God knows what it was, flew from a big light situated on the ceiling, into the wall and never came out! I stared at this space waiting for this light 'thing' to come out, it didn't. It wasn't a circular orb, that I can say for sure, it looked like to all intents and purposes, a very large white insect, (dare I say fairy!, no that would be stretching things a bit far!) Just then, as I am still staring at the wall where this white light 'thing' flew into, a thin streak of white light flew across the upper ceiling of the Town Hall from left to right. Now listen up dear reader, I was sitting there taking in Chris Evers introduction and suddenly here I was being subjected to some paranormal event. Never in a million years was I expecting this, what the bloody hell was going on. I punched my friend Bill Rooke (aka Alien Bill) hard on the arm that was sitting next to me alongside his wife Victoria and proceeded to tell him what I had just seen. Bill of course started taking photographs of the area, and, as you will see from the photographs in the photographic section, he managed to get a ball of light in the very same area where I saw this light 'thing'. As I say, I never saw an orb as is depicted in Bill's photograph, what I saw, clearly had extended appendages on a white body. It may well have been an insect, I accept that, but it was very big, way bigger than a moth or other flying insect, I'm talking about the size of my hand! Of course being a researcher I sat there trying to explain this, maybe it was a trick of the light, or some external shadows being cast in at the side of the shutters that were keeping the light out of the Town Hall so people could see the screen properly. None of these I accept as the answer. I did a small post on my Facebook page about this and I got a few replies, one of the more interesting ones came from Jason Gleaves who also saw something in that area, he stated.

"I was sat behind you during the talk at the back of the hall just after I noticed the anomaly. I saw you and Bill looking up in the same location where I saw it too. I saw a bright illuminated orb shaped object in this area briefly as I listening to one of the speakers".

Another comment left on my Facebook page regarding this sighting, came from Annette Williamson, who said,

"Hiya Malcolm.

What is time? As many dimensions are happening in the now. I sometimes see glimpses of other dimensions. There is no death only change of energy/form. Keep grounded enjoy and carry on. We are all connected, quantum in nature"

Another comment on my Facebook page came from Henry Philip Vigé, who stated.

"Yes, Malcolm, when you least expect it these types of phenomena do occur, and they can be very vivid"!

Henry further stated.

"I remember once in Nashville, Tennessee, I was on my cell phone talking in the kitchen of a friend's home. This was a relatively new construction, probably 8 to 10 years old. It stood on property that was once a large farm in the late 1700s. A barn or some other type of building stood where this house was

recently constructed. I was leaning on the island countertop in the middle of the kitchen and could see the bottom part of the doorway going into the dining room from that vantage point (I was wearing a baseball cap so the brim of the hat was blocking part of my vision"). "All of a sudden when I looked again in the direction of the bottom half of the doorway into the dining room, there in that doorway was the lower part of a woman standing in the doorway! I am assuming her fashion of dress was from the 1800s time period with button-up shoes. I could see this as clear as day, 3-D no flimsy see-through image it was as if a real alive woman was standing there! I could see the folds of the dress moving too! Of course, I couldn't believe my eyes. When I stood up and looked at the doorway there was nothing there. She had vanished! I always felt like I was being watched in that house. And there was always a tinkling of a bell in the large great room. This was a huge house and was fairly new construction as I mentioned before. I asked my friend about the sound of a bell tinkling. I told her that I didn't see a mantle clock anywhere so where was the sound coming from. She smiled and said, "Oh so you've heard my ghost!" That is an experience I will never forget!"

Another Facebook post regarding my sighting came from Margaret Tollan who on observing the photograph that I placed alongside my report stated.

"It just looks like the place is pretty cold and desolate. I think it would give me a wee shiver down the spine type of place, maybe it's the colouration, if it was painted pink and blue and lilacs I could find it a more warming a place, but it looks cold and intimidating. Don't know why I thought of acoustics! Then your chance meeting, maybe all this is a sign to something? The conversation or topic of conversation with the person was way mind blowing. My gut feeling is he was finding comfort in you, he was unloading all this grief onto a wonderful person who listened, and he told you that a problem shared is a problem halved. He was doing that I'm sure, just knowing you cared enough to take it on board, he had found a friend in his very empty world."

Margaret went on to state.

"I wonder how he died, maybe fell from the balcony or was pushed. I think you need to find out. Maybe this was a sign for you to investigate, did this 'body' walk to you out of thin air and disappear as quickly as he came?"

I stated to Margaret that as far as I could recollect, the shape was initially just standing there, I looked away for a few brief seconds, looked back, and the 'shape' was gliding along the balcony area from right to left then disappeared.

Vincent Palmer, a friend of mine on Facebook, asked me why I didn't take a photograph of the ghost, I replied (which was true), that I was struck dumb, jaw on the floor, and before I knew it, it had disappeared! I should point out to the reader, that although the balcony area was open to the public for this conference, only a few people were up there, and that was to take photographs. (But none were there at the time I was looking up, none at all) I only ever saw two people up there the whole day; one was Juliette Gregson from the LAPIS UFO group, and a video photographer, who only filmed for part of the day. There might have been others, but I certainly never saw them.

Jackie Wren stated.

"Wow how wonderful. There would have been so much energy from the people attending. Thanks for sharing the experience".

Denise O'Neil also commentated.

"Thank you for sharing amazing. It reminded me of St Mary in the Castle in Hastings East Sussex. I used to attend church there and saw figures in the balcony area, the minister told me he used to see them while giving the service. No pretty lights though just ghostly figures".

311

Mark Anthony Wyatt gave quite an interesting comment when he stated.

"So cool to actually see one during a paranormal conference. I suspect that they are drawn out by the fascinating speakers talking about them. We have an unseen guest here in our home, I hear her talking to the dogs sometimes, if we discuss her, she'll sometimes make little knocks of recognition, or make the lights flash".

Martino Catalano stated.

"I was sat two seats from you Malcolm Robinson, and I noticed the man next to me randomly taking photos of the upper areas. I just thought he was admiring the architecture. If only I'd known lol".

Philip Kinsella stated.

"Amazing Malcolm lovely to see you, and keep doing the good work, ghosts and all, lol".

Joan Duddle Bradbury stated.

"Oh my goodness Malcolm, what a fantastic experience (I think lol)"

One always gets some funny replies on Facebook to certain posts and Neil Geddes Neil Geddes Ward replied, *"Bloody ghost got in for free"!*

Now a week or so before this, I had been in communication with a gentleman by the name of Joe Peters who sadly was getting some terrible ghostly manifestations in his family home, some quite demonic. Anyway, I said to Joe, *"I wish the buggers would come and visit me"* to which he replied, *"I'll see what I can do"!* And here I was a week later seeing a ghost! Indeed, Joe came onto that thread about my ghost sighting at Pontefract Town Hall and he stated,

312

"Well you did ask me to send them to you! I asked that spirit should show themselves to you, as you wasn't scared of them. Do you remember saying that to me! There is more to come! I have done more communication and keep asking them to visit you, keep us posted if you get any more strange encounters".

Well I most certainly will Joe!

Needless to say, I decided to do a check on the internet to find out if Pontefract Town Hall was haunted and I came across the web site www.haunted-yorkshire.co.uk/pontefractsightings.htm (which incidentally Dave Philips also found and sent me the link) What I found was short and brief and read thus,

"A phantom woman has been spotted on the staircase and is reputed to be a bride who was killed in the hall many years ago".

So, short and sweet, that is all it said. This ghost was spotted on the staircase and not the balcony where I saw it. I couldn't find any other ghostly sightings from this old building, but if anyone 'out there' knows of any, do let me know. So, a strange start to the Outer Limits Conference for Malcolm Robinson, and one I'll sure not forget in a hurry.

FINAL THOUGHTS

Well we have come to the end of this book. I have shared a few of what I hope are some puzzling and startling poltergeist cases of which I hope to have opened up your eyes. Let us be very clear here, the poltergeist phenomenon has been with us throughout the centuries and, I dare say, will continue to be so as the decades pass. We've heard from my fellow paranormal researchers each of whom have, to some degree, a different take as to what a poltergeist is. Do you agree with any of them? Is the poltergeist phenomenon so cut and dried as to have a conclusive answer, or is the poltergeist a combination of a number of puzzling factors? So many if's and butt's, but I guess that is why I love this subject so much. Will we ever get to the bottom of what a poltergeist is? For those who say that they have the definitive answer I would say, *"Really"!* Life is an adventure; the poltergeist makes life even more interesting.

And what of the main stay of this book, the Sauchie Poltergeist? I've looked at this puzzling case three times in my life now, 1987, 1994, and 2020, each research provided mixed results. Come what may, we should recognise that this case stands head and shoulders above any other case of its kind in Scotland, simply because of the veracity of the evidence. We have a number of church minsters, three local doctors, all who testified to the bizarre events in the Campbell home. And what about the audio tape of the actual sounds of the Sauchie Poltergeist? For me, this was incredible, what a wonderful time capsule of paranormal events this is, recorded by men of integrity, pillars of the community, solid reliable witnesses. Let's be honest, the simple truth needs no assistance to make it more impressive. The problem of course with any poltergeist case, is of course the sheer futility of it all! Its pointless attacks on people and houses, and one may ask the question, why this person and not another person?

I hope that you have enjoyed this book, and I also hope that as an interested individual of the paranormal, you extend your journey into the realms of the strange and bizarre. Remember, mankind does 'not' know it all, there are so many wonders left to explore. Please continue your own personal search, but please do so with an open mind, for sometimes, things are not always what they seem! God bless you all.

"There is a tendency in 21st century science, to forget that there will be a 22nd century science, and indeed a 30th century science, from which vantage points our knowledge of the universe may appear quite different".

(Dr J. Allen Hynek)

THE END

Amanda Holden, Sean Ryder, Malcolm Robinson, and
Philip Schofield. Television Studios London, July 2015

Karen Robinson. Following in her father's footsteps.

Malcolm Robinson and his love of the Ghost Train. 1963

Author Malcolm Robinson presenting his findings to an
audience on the U.K. Lecture Circuit
(c) Juliette W. Gregson

Pontefract Town Hall 2019 (c) Malcolm Robinson

The balcony where the ghost walked along. Pontefract
Town Hall 2019 (c) Malcolm Robinson

318

Bill Rooke & Malcolm Robinson

Where the author (white shirt) was sitting prior to seeing ghost on the balcony. Pontefract Town Hall
(c) Jason Gleaves

REFERENCES

CHAPTER ONE
(A Brief History of Poltergeists)

Wikipedia.

The Oxford Interactive Encyclopedia.

Ghosts and Hauntings. Dennis Bardens: Fontana Books 1967.
ISBN 10: 1859-585-585183

Poltergeist Over Scotland. Geoff Holder, The History Press
2013. ISBN: 978-0-7524-8283-5

Poltergeist. A Study in Destructive Haunting, New English
Library 1981. Colin Wilson. ISBN: 978-0450048807

Poltergeists. (A History of Violent Ghostly Phenomenon) P. G.
Maxwell-Stuart. Amberley Publishing 2011. ISBN: 978-1-
84868-987-9

The Poltergeist Phenomenon. Headline Books, 1996. John and
Anne Spencer. ISBN: 0-7472-1801-3

The Poltergeist. (A Star book published by Wyndham
Publications) William G. Roll. ISBN: 13: 978-1931044691

Helvetica's Indie Horror Stories.

The Rochdale Poltergeist. http://www.soul-
guidance.com/houseofthesun/showerswater.html
Photographs, complimentary (MAPIT Administration and
Investigations with assistance from NARO - Northern
Anomalies Research Organisation) Steve Mera.

The Pontefract Poltergeist: Sun Newspaper report 31st October 2017. Chloe Kerr & Holly Christtodoulou.

The Pontefract Poltergeist:
https://www.hauntedrooms.co.uk/30-east-drive-pontefract-poltergeist-house

Enfield Poltergeist: Wikipedia.
The Sun Newspaper. 'House of Horror'. 12TH April 2018

South Shields Poltergeist.
https://monkeywah.typepad.com/paranormalia/2008/04/the-south-shiel.html Robert McLuhan

Amazon

The Pitmilly Poltergeist Book Review by Tom Ruffles.
https://www.spr.ac.uk/book-review/pitmilly-house-poltergeist-manor-lorn-macintyre

The Rochdale Poltergeist: http://www.mapit.kk5.org/rochdale-poltergeist/4535286696

The Rochdale Poltergeist: http://www.soul-guidance.com/houseofthesun/showerswater.html

CHAPTER TWO
(Other Famous Scottish Poltergeist and Ghost Cases)

http://www.scottishbrewing.com/breweries/forthvalley/forthvalley.php

http://www.bbc.co.uk/scotland/education/as/sixties/standard/city/industry.shtml

Wikipedia

CHAPTER THREE
(Clackmannanshire and Sauchie, a Brief History)

Sauchie and Alloa - A People's History, John Adamson 1988

Clackmannanshire: Wikipedia.

Sauchie: Wikipedia

New Sauchie.
https://www.genuki.org.uk/big/sct/CLK/Towns/NewSauchie

https://www.alloaadvertiser.com/news/17760397.walk-past-history-alloa-glassworks/

CHAPTER FOUR
(The Sauchie Poltergeist)

The World of James M. Deem.
https://jamesmdeem.com/stories.ghost9.html

Poltergeist Phenomenon. An in-depth Investigation into floating beds by Michael Clarkson. Paperback: 288 pages. Publisher: Career Press/New Page Books (20 Jan. 2011) ISBN-10: 1601631472

Sauchie Poltergeist. https://psi-encyclopedia.spr.ac.uk/articles/sauchie-poltergeist

The Legacy of the Sauchie Poltergeist. An SPI Case File, By Brian Allan (2000)

CHAPTER FIVE
(So, What Is A Poltergeist?)

Wikipedia

Light Force Network:
https://www.lightforcenetwork.com/olivia/sauchie-poltergeist-case

NHS. Hallucinations and hearing voices.
https://www.nhs.uk/conditions/hallucinations/

Gas Safe Register Website:
https://www.gassaferegister.co.uk/help-and-advice/carbon-monoxide-poisoning/?gclid=CjwKCAiAsIDxBRAsEiwAV76N88F7Wqkg
KLkNhz7pA0RUEi2J3tGpiD_vrw9H3Vs0HgALQTwJr64X5x
oCJkUQAvD_BwE

Rethinking Mental Illness: https://www.rethink.org/advice-and-information/about-mental-illness/learn-more-about-conditions/schizophrenia/?gclid=Cj0KCQiA04XxBRD5ARIsA
GFygj8Ym7GwOgjhmNOXsUR1vyzrA0vcOVo3BylgWizB3D
273AEfoUoyyKIaAlgjEALw_wcB

Wikipedia. Histrionic personality disorder:
https://en.wikipedia.org/wiki/Histrionic_personality_disorder

Infra Sound. Diana Brown. 'How Things Work.'
https://science.howstuffworks.com/science-vs-myth/extrasensory-perceptions/infrasound-paranormal-activity.htm

Richard Wiseman: The Ghost in the Brain.
https://richardwiseman.wordpress.com/2009/01/06/the-ghost-in-the-brain/

The Scotsman. A spirited experiment: the science of ghosts. 09 March 2009

https://www.scotsman.com/lifestyle-2-15039/a-spirited-experiment-the-science-of-ghosts-1-1028384

Anthony North:
https://anthonynorth.com/essays/paranormal/
Anthony North:
https://www.smashwords.com/books/view/994829

Occult World Web Site: https://occult-world.com/poltergeist-cases/sauchie-poltergeist/

www.ashleyknibb.com

https://www.urigeller.com/section-two-connections-past-present/

The Hutchinson Effect. Nikola Telsa inspires a bizarre discovery. Tasha Shayne. January 1st 2020. Gaia web site. https://www.gaia.com/article/the-hutchison-effect-nikola-tesla-inspires-a-bizarre-discovery

Pontefract Town Hall: www.haunted-yorkshire.co.uk/pontefractsightings.htm

FURTHER READING

Archives of the Society for Psychical Research. Poltergeist file. P4, 1940/1967.

A Fenland Poltergeist. A.D. Cornell & Alan Gauld. Journal. SPR 40:705 September 1960 343-358.

Are Poltergeists Living or Are They Dead? Ian Stevenson. Journal of the American Society for Psychical Research (SPR) 66, no. 3 (1972): 233–52.

Encyclopedia of Ghosts and Spirits. John and Anne Spencer. Headline Book Publishing of 338 Euston Road, London, England NW1 3BH, ISBN: 0 7472 7169 0.

Borley Postscript. Peter Underwood. White House Publications, P.O. Box 65, Haslemere, GU27 1XT, England ISBN: 0-9537721-1-X

Contagion. Darren W. Ritson & Michael J. Hallowell. The Limbury Press; First edition July 2014. ISBN: 9780956522894

Can We Explain the Poltergeist? A.R.G. Owen (1964). (New York: Garrett)

Case File P55, premises in Brighton. 1948 SPR Archive, Cambridge University Library.

Enfield Revisited: The Evaporation of Positive Evidence. Playfair, Guy Lyon and Grosse, Maurice (1988) JSPR 1988-89 Vol 55 No 813 208-219

Edinburgh After Dark. Ron Halliday. 2013. www.blackandwhitepublishing.com

Fife's Fiery Ghost. Psychic News, 16 December 1967.

Famous Scots and the Paranormal. Ron Halliday. 2012
www.blackandwhitepublishing.com

Ghost Taverns of the North East. Darren W. Ritson &
Michael J. Hallowell. Amberley Publishing. March 2012.
ISBN: 9781445607535

Ghosts at Christmas. Darren W. Ritson. The History Press.
November 2010. ISBN: 9780752457673

Ghosts Over Britain. Peter Moss. Elm Tree Books 1977.
ISBN: 10: 024-1897-432

Ghosts and Hauntings. Dennis Bardens: Fontana Books 1967.
ISBN 10: 1859-585-585183

Haunted Glasgow. Ron Halliday. 2008.
www.blackandwhitepublishing.com

Haunted Gardens. Peter Underwood. Amberley Publishing,
Cirencester Road Chalford, Stroud, Gloucestershire, GL6 8PE.
ISBN: 978-184868-261-0

Haunted Wales. Peter Underwood. Amberley Publishing,
Cirencester Road Chalford, Stroud, Gloucestershire, GL6 8PE.
ISBN: 978-184868-2634

Haunted Pubs And Inns of Derbyshire. Jill Armitage.
Amberley Publishing, Amberley Publishing, Cirencester Road
Chalford, Stroud, Gloucestershire, GL6 8PE ISBN: 978-1-
4456-0464-0

Haunted Newcastle. Darren W. Ritson. The History Press.
January 2009. ISBN: 9780752448800

Haunted Durham. Darren W. Ritson. The History Press Ltd.
UK. April 2010 ISBN: 9780752454108

Haunted Northumberland. Darren W. Ritson. The History Press Ltd. UK. August. 2011. ISBN: 9780752458618

Haunted Carlisle. Darren Ritson. The History Press. August 2012. ISBN: 9780752460871

Haunted Berwick. Darren W. Ritson. The History Press. November 2010. ISBN: 9780752455488

Haunted Wearside. Darren W. Ritson. The History Press. 1 September 2013. ISBN: 9780752460888

Haunted Tyneside. Darren Ritson. The History Press Ltd. November 2011. ISBN: 978075245824

Human Personality and Its Survival of Bodily Death. Myers, Frederic W. H. Vols. I & II. New York: Longmans, Green & Co., 1954. First published 1903.

In Search of Ghosts. Darren W. Ritson. Amberley Publishing. November. 2008. ISBN: 978184681217

Investigating the Paranormal. Tony Cornell. New York Press 2002.

More Anglesey Ghosts. Bunty Austin. Amberley Publishing, The Hill, Stroud, England, UK, ISBN: 978-1-4456-0332-2

On the trail of the Poltergeist. Nanor Fodor. New York, The Citadel Press, 1958.

On the Track of the Poltergeist. D Scott Rogo, Englewood Cliffs, N.J.: Prentice-Hall, 1986.

Paranormal Hertfordshire. Damien O Dell. Amberley Publishing, ISBN-13: 978-1848681187

More Things You Can Do When You Are Dead. (What can you truly believe?) Tricia Robertson. White Crow Books 2015. ISBN: 978-1-91012144-3

New Developments in Poltergeist Research in Proceedings of the Parapsychological Association. Hans Bender (1969) 81-102.

Paranormal Bath. Michael Cady. Amberley Publishing, Cirencester Road Chalford, Stroud, Gloucestershire, GL6 8PE ISBN: 1848681763

Paranormal Dorset. Roger Gutteridge. Amberley Publishing, Cirencester Road Chalford, Stroud, Gloucestershire, GL6 8PE ISBN: 978-1-84868-118-7

Paranormal Leicester. Stephen Butt. Amberley Publishing, Cirencester Road Chalford, Stroud, Gloucestershire, GL6 8PE ISBN: 978-1-84868-462-1

Paranormal Lancashire. Daniel Codd. Amberley Publishing, Cirencester Road Chalford, Stroud, Gloucestershire, GL6 8PE ISBN: 978-4456-0658-3

Paranormal North East. Darren W. Ritson. Amberley Publishing, Cirencester Road Chalford, Stroud, Gloucestershire, GL6 8PE   ISBN: 978-1-84868-196-5

Paranormal South Tyneside. Michael J Hallowell. Amberley Publishing, Cirencester Road Chalford, Stroud, Gloucestershire, GL6 8PE. ISBN: 978-1-84868-730-1

Paranormal Surrey. Marq English. Amberley Publishing, Cirencester Road Chalford, Stroud, Gloucestershire, GL6 8PE. ISBN: 978-1-84868-896-4

Paranormal Sussex. David Scanlan. Amberley Publishing, Cirencester Road Chalford, Stroud, Gloucestershire, GL6 8PE. ISBN: 978-1-84868-462-1

Paranormal Case Files of Great Britain (Volume 1)
Malcolm Robinson. Publish Nation. www.publishnation.co.uk
2010-2017. ISBN: 978-1907126-06-2

Paranormal Case Files of Great Britain (Volume 2)
Malcolm Robinson. Publish Nation. www.publishnation.co.uk
2016. ISBN: 9781-3268-74-22-3

Paranormal Case Files of Great Britain (Volume 3)
Malcolm Robinson. Publish Nation. www.publishnation.co.uk
2018. ISBN: 978-0244-11172-4

Psychic Quest. Natalie Osbourne Thomason. Claireview
Books, Hillside House, The Square, Forest Row, East Sussex,
RH18 5ES, ISBN: 1-902-636-341

Poltergeist Over Scotland. Geoff Holder. The History Press
2013. ISBN: 978-0-7524-8283-5

Poltergeist. A Study In Destructive Haunting, Colin Wilson.
New English Library 1981) ISBN: 978-0450048807

Poltergeists. (A History of Violent Ghostly Phenomenon) P. G.
Maxwell-Stuart. Amberley Publishing 2011. ISBN: 978-1-
84868-987-9

Poltergeists, London: Alan Gauld, and A. D. Cornell.
Routledge and Kegan Paul, 1979.

Poltergeists: An annotated bibliography of Works in
English, circa 1880-1975. Michael Goss. (1979)
Scarecrow Press, New York.

Poltergeist in a Scottish Mansion House. J.W. Herries.
Psychic Science. Vol. 21, No. 3, October 1942, pp.88-92.

Poltergeist Over England. Three Centuries of Mischievous
Ghosts, Harry Price. London: Country Life, 1945.

329

'**Poltergeist**'! A New Investigation into Destructive Haunting. Including the Cage St Osyth' (6th books, Winchester / Washington July 2020). John Fraser.

Pitmilly House. Lorn Macintyre. Priormuir Press, October 2011. ISBN-13: 978-0956768124

Paranormal County Durham. Darren W. Ritson. Amberley Publishing. June. 2012 ISBN: 9781445606507

Report on psychokinetic activity surrounding a seven-year-old boy. Maurice Gross and M. Barrington in Journal SPR (2001) Vol 65 207-217.

Seeing Ghosts. Hilary Evans. John Murray 50 Albemarle Street London England W1S 4BD. ISBN: 0 7195-5492-6.

Scottish Haunts and Poltergeists II. JSPR Vol. 42, March 1964, pp.223-7. Lambert, G W.

Supernatural North. Darren W. Ritson. Amberley Publishing November. 2013. ISBN: 9781848682771

This House Is Haunted: The True Story of a Poltergeist (1980) Guy Lyon Playfair. White Crow Books. ISBN: 978-1907661785

The Poltergeist Phenomenon. Headline Books, 1996. John and Anne Spencer. ISBN: 0-7472-1801-3

The Encyclopedia of Ghosts and Spirits. (Volume 2) John and Anne Spencer. 2001 Headline Publishing. ISBN: 0-7472-7169-0

The South Shields Poltergeist. Darren W. Ritson & Michael J Hallowell. The History Press. October 2009. ISBN-13: 978-0752452746

The Haunting of Willington Mill. Darren W. Ritson & Michael J. Hallowell. The History Press. ISBN: 9780752458786

The Rochdale Poltergeist. (A True Story) Jenny Ashford and Steve Mera. Bleed Red Books 2015. ISBN-13: 978-15177-56123

Things You Can Do When You Are Dead. (True Accounts of After Death Communication) Tricia Robertson. White Crow Books 2013. ISBN: 978-1-908733-60-3 Cirencester Road Chalford, Stroud, Gloucestershire, GL6 8PE ISBN 978-1-84868-394-5.

This House is Haunted: (The True Story of the Enfield Poltergeist). Guy Lyon Playfair. Publisher: White Crow Books. 5 May 2011. ISBN-10: 1907661786

The Andover Case. (A responsive rapping poltergeist). Barrie Colvin Journal of the SPR. 2008. Vol 72, 1-20.

The Poltergeist. William Roll. (1972) Paraview Special Editions; Special edition. March. 2004. ISBN-10: 1931044694

Yorkshire Stories of the Supernatural. Andy Owen. Countryside Books, 3 Catherine Road, Newbury Berkshire, England, U.K. ISBN: 1-85306-594-3

SOME BRITISH PARANORMAL SOCIETIES

ASSAP. (The Association for the Study of Anomalous Phenomena) Tel: 020 8798 3981 assap@assap.org http://www.assap.ac.uk/index.html

SPI Scotland. (Strange Phenomena Investigations) Alyson Dunlop https://spiscotland.wordpress.com/ spiscotland@gmail.com

SPI Anglia Region. (Strange Phenomena Investigations) David Young. https://www.facebook.com/groups/358025484712267/

SPI Inverness. (Strange Phenomena Investigations). https://www.facebook.com/Strange-Phenomena-Investigations-SPI-Inverness-383337621775153/

SPI Dundee. (Strange Phenomena Investigations). https://www.facebook.com/spi2015dundee/

SPI Edinburgh. (Strange Phenomena Investigations) Sandra Fraser. https://www.facebook.com/groups/667586660009029/

SSPR. (The Scottish Society for Psychical Research). 020 7937 8984 Innes Smith. https://www.spr.ac.uk/link/scottish-society-psychical-research

SEMR. (Scottish Earth Mysteries Research) Ron Halliday. https://www.facebook.com/ron.halliday.18

GHOST OFFICE. (Hastings, U.K.) (Darren Garcia) www.ghostoffice.co.uk

FORTEAN PICTURE LIBRARY. The Image Works. http://theimageworks.com/collections-Fortean.php

SPI HASTINGS UFO & PARANORMAL MEETINGS.
(Malcolm Robinson)
https://www.facebook.com/groups/malckyspi/

THE GHOST CLUB. (The World's oldest organisation associated with psychical research). Established, circa 1862. Flat 48, Woodside House, Woodside, London, SW19 7QN
https://www.ghostclub.org.uk/index.html

TO CONTACT THE AUTHOR

Research group Strange Phenomena Investigations (SPI) are always interested to hear from anyone who believe that they may have had a UFO or paranormal experience, or indeed may have a photograph or piece of film footage which may appear to show something paranormal. If so, please contact the author at the address below. (All submissions will be treated in confidence)

Malcolm Robinson,
Flat 5, Unicorn House,
Croft Road, Hastings,
East Sussex, England,
United Kingdom,
TN34 3HE.

www.facebook.com/malcolm.robinson2
You can e-mail the author direct at malckyspi@yahoo.com
Facebook: www.facebook.com/malcolm.robinson2

"The eye sees only what the mind is prepared to comprehend."
Robertson Davies, Tempest Tost

Printed in Great Britain
by Amazon